A MUSEUM GUIDE TO COPYRIGHT AND TRADEMARK

AMERICAN ASSOCIATION OF MUSEUMS
WASHINGTON, D.C.
1999

A Museum Guide to Copyright and Trademark

Copyright © 1999, American Association of Museums, 1575 Eye St. N.W., Suite 400, Washington, DC 20005. All rights reserved. This book may not be reproduced in whole or in part, in any form, except brief passages by reviewers, without written permission from the publisher.

The individuals and entities involved in the publication of this work are not rendering legal advice with this publication. The reader should refer specific questions to his or her attorney.

Project Manager: Diane M. Zorich
Editor: Ellen Hirzy
Designer: Susan v. Levine

Library of Congress Cataloguing-in-Publication Data

A museum guide to copyright and trademark / by the American Association of Museums; co-authors
  Michael S. Shapiro, Brett I. Miller ; edited and introduced by Christine Steiner.
        p. cm.
    Includes bibliographical references and index.
    ISBN 0-931201-63-2
  KF 2996.S53 1999
  346.7304'82—dc21   99-043466
                                                                  CIP

A MUSEUM GUIDE TO COPYRIGHT AND TRADEMARK
by the American Association of Museums

Coauthors

Michael S. Shapiro

Brett I. Miller, Morgan, Lewis & Bockius LLP

Edited and introduced by Christine Steiner

AMERICAN ASSOCIATION OF MUSEUMS
WASHINGTON, D.C.
1999

Table of Contents

PREFACE

A Museum Guide to Copyright and Trademark is designed to help museums develop a clearer understanding of the importance of intellectual property—the intellectual property owned by museums and the intellectual property of others that museums hold in trust. It is intended to guide informed, careful decisions about how to manage intellectual property and how to establish best practices for developing institutional policy and procedural statements.

Mindful of the growing number and complexity of issues surrounding museums' intellectual capital, the American Association of Museums began to increase its involvement in the intellectual property area in 1994, the year the Conference on Fair Use was established. We realized that everyone on a museum's professional staff involved with management of the collections, as well as trustees and other volunteers responsible for the museum's financial and legal health, should understand the basics of both copyright and trademark. Moreover, we heard from museum professionals that they needed a much deeper understanding of these topics as they face the complex choices that result as technology advances.

We developed *A Museum Guide to Copyright and Trademark* in response to this need for in-depth information. Although the book in no way constitutes formal legal advice, it can help museum administrators identify what issues are at play and decide when they need to seek professional counsel. In addition, AAM will make technical resources available on our Web site (www.aam-us.org) and provide links to other sites with more detailed information than was appropriate for this book. AAM will continue to advocate for museums on issues of intellectual property, provide professional development seminars, and publish articles in our bimonthly magazine *Museum News*. We will also continue our collaboration with other national groups, particularly the National Initiative for a Networked Cultural Heritage (NINCH), a coalition of museums, libraries, and universities committed to helping "shape a digital environment through the intensive, collaborative, and thoughtful action of its constituent members."

We would like to express our deep appreciation to all who contributed to this important project. We are especially grateful to the lawyers who helped us to produce this guide—Michael S. Shapiro, Brett I. Miller, and Christine Steiner. *A Museum Guide to Copyright and Trademark* could not have been published without their assistance. We are also grateful to the other project team members for their efforts: Diane M. Zorich, project manager; Jane Sledge, project manager, Getty Information Institute; Barry Szczesny, government affairs counsel, AAM; and Ellen Hirzy, editor. We acknowledge with gratitude the contributions of several of the attorneys in the Intellectual Property Practice Group of Morgan, Lewis & Bockius LLP, including but not limited to James R. Sims III, partner, and Barbara A. Friedman, of counsel, both of the Washington office, and Kerry A. Kryznowek, associate, of the New York office. The project also benefited from the guidance of Jerold Kappel, AAM's director of development.

We want to thank the project's advisory committees, whose names are listed in appendix F. Members of the Legal Advisory Committee, who are attorneys with extensive knowledge and expertise in museum law, provided a careful review of the manuscript and offered detailed and thoughtful comments. The Museum Advisory Committee, composed of museum professionals with a deep interest and practical expertise in intellectual property matters, reviewed the manuscript and provided guidance on the project. Thanks are also due to the many museum staff members who participated in focus groups and gave us a grounding in the real-world issues that they face on a daily basis.

Access to excellent resources is the key to a successful project. This project would not have succeeded without the generous support of the Pew Charitable Trusts and the expertise provided by the J. Paul Getty Trust. Pew's interest in this project stems from its dedicated involvement with the museum community over many years. The very generous Pew grant enabled us to employ the best talent and provide one free copy of the guide to each museum in the United States. The Getty has undertaken many excellent projects and publications on information and image management. We are deeply appreciative.

Patricia E. Williams
Vice President, Policy and Programs
American Association of Museums

"As keepers of our national treasures, museums are stewards of our collective heritage. The Pew Charitable Trusts are very pleased to be able to work with the American Association of Museums and The J. Paul Getty Trust to produce this guide. Providing museums with this timely and important advice will help them balance the rights of the intellectual property owner and the public's access to these cultural riches."

Rebecca W. Rimel
President & Chief Executive Officer
The Pew Charitable Trusts

This publication is made possible by a major grant from The Pew Charitable Trusts, with additional support from The J. Paul Getty Trust.

Introduction
INTELLECTUAL PROPERTY IN MUSEUMS

A visitor encounters a museum's intellectual property from the moment she sees its name and logo on banners outside the building, over the entrance, or in the newspaper announcements that prompted her visit. Once inside, she picks up a self-guiding brochure at the information desk and notices the banners and posters highlighting current exhibitions and programs. She walks into the latest special exhibition, stopping first to read the introductory wall text. As she immerses herself in the exhibition, she is enjoying the creative work of many museum professionals, whether she is viewing a display of dazzling archeological discoveries, paintings by a contemporary artist or a Renaissance master, an introduction to the solar system, or a history of jazz in America. She watches the educational video accompanying the exhibition and takes an illustrated brochure as she leaves. The visitor stops in the museum shop, and enters the commercial realm. Available for purchase is a variety of merchandise with the museum name and logo, objects designed for the special exhibition she visited, and reproductions of objects from the collection that incorporate the museum name. She buys the illustrated exhibition catalogue, postcards showing the museum building, gifts inspired by similar objects in the collections. At home, she encourages her family to visit the museum's Web site, which presents a rich array of text and images from the collection and prominently displays the museum name.

To address the complex intellectual property issues embedded in every aspect of museum practice, *A Museum Guide to Copyright and Trademark* introduces copyright and trademark principles for the museum community. Its five chapters will serve equally for those who want a general understanding of copyright and trademark in a museum-specific context and for those who need an answer to a specific question or issue. Chapter 1 addresses copyright law—what it is (and is not), its requirements, duration, and limitations. Chapter 2 deals with trademark law—what it is, why it matters, how to use it. In chapters 3 and 4, two increasingly significant issues for museums—the World Wide Web and licensing—are treated in depth. Chapter 5 highlights international protection matters, critical today because museums no longer operate in a comfortable world of relative isolation.

This guide does not address patents, trade secrets, or design issues. Nor does it cover certain other intangible interests in the cultural communities, including moral rights and neighboring rights (the European protection for "rights nearing copyright," including performance rights and certain other rights relating to copyright not recognized in the United States), or cultural patrimony (the growing call for protection of cultural property through display norms for objects of cultural significance). In a manner similar to copyright, the latter presents two distinct property concepts: the ownership of the physical object as distinct from issues related to the representation of that object. These interests and certain others in the field (such as donor relations, artists' rights, rights of publicity, and privacy rights) often touch on the copyright and trademark issues at hand; when relevant, they are addressed in the text. Because museum practice is governed as strongly by ethical considerations as it is by purely legal considerations, this guide seeks to introduce ethical principles throughout.

The basic information provided in this guide is intended as practice-oriented advice for the museum professional. The book sets out the legal framework for understanding copyright and trademark principles and applies that framework through examples, both actual and hypothetical.

Different disciplines may be guided by different norms. For example, anthropology museums may have ethical decisions about the possible uses of field information, or history museums may require guidelines governing the display of photographs or appropriate uses of oral histories. For these needs, the journals and ethical codes of the fields and disciplines may provide insight and best practices, and colleagues in other museums and research institutions should be consulted.

Readers should know that this book is not intended as a substitute for legal advice. The attorney authors and editor are not furnishing legal advice; the guide is designed to provide information to assist museum professionals in the performance of their duties. Specific intellectual property issues may require more in-depth treatment, and some may require the assistance of counsel. In extreme circumstances, proper resolution might be accomplished only through litigation. When contemplating litigation, whether as a plaintiff or as a defendant, a museum must balance the possible favorable outcome against the administrative time, the potential negative publicity, the likely expense, and the possible adverse outcome.

The efforts to provide education on the important subject of intellectual property do not end here. The resource list contains additional sources of information. Worth special note are Marie Malaro's *A Legal Primer on Managing Museum Collections*—the pioneering work in our field—and the Web site for the American Law Institute-American Bar Association (ALI-ABA). The annual course of study, cosponsored by the Smithsonian Institution and the American Association of Museums, provides informative updates on intellectual property issues for museums.

Much of the work in developing this guide was informed by focus groups of museum professionals convened in a spirit of sharing. In the con-

stantly changing field of intellectual property, especially as copyright and trademark law evolve to mesh with the needs of a digital age, the sharing of information and experiences will be of immeasurable benefit to the museum community. The framework provided by *A Museum Guide to Copyright and Trademark* is a sound and useful starting point.

What is Intellectual Property?

What specific properties are *museum* intellectual property? Why are intellectual property issues especially significant for museums today?

Intellectual property rights—particularly copyright and trademark—have always been relevant for museums in their multiple roles, as they build and preserve collections, conduct research and interpret the collections for the public, organize exhibitions, and provide educational programs and services. Museums use works created by others, and at the same time they create original works, own collections in trust for the public (images, objects, specimens, documents, databases), sell products, and license their names for reproductions of objects and images. As educational institutions, museums are also entitled to fair use of the copyrighted work of others. A working knowledge of the basic principles of intellectual property is essential if museums are to respect and maintain the legal relationships that define and govern these various roles.

The rapid advance of communication technologies and the resulting demand for content have focused even greater attention on intellectual property issues. Changing norms of operating in the new digital environment, which involve new ways of using and protecting museum resources, raise challenging questions for museum professionals. They recognize that their commitment to presenting and protecting the tangible assets in museum collections must extend equally to intellectual property. Displaying, lending, and borrowing may be as significant for representations of objects as for the objects themselves.

Commonly grouped under the rubric of "intellectual property," separate and distinct protection regimes govern the traditional categories—copyrights, trademarks, patents, and trade secrets. The brief definitions developed by the U.S. International Trade Commission are helpful in distinguishing these terms of art:

- A *copyright* is a form of protection provided by a national government to authors of original works of authorship including literary, dramatic, musical, artistic, and certain other intellectual works.

- A *trademark* is any word, name, symbol, or device, or any combination thereof, adopted and used by a manufacturer or merchant to identify his goods and distinguish them from those manufactured or sold by others.

- A *patent* is a grant issued by a national government conferring the right to exclude others from making, using, or selling the invention within the national territory.

- A *trade secret* is information, including a formula, pattern, compilation, program, device, method, technique, or process, that derives independent economic value, actual or potential, from not being generally known, and not being readily ascertained by proper means, by other persons who can obtain economic value from its disclosure or use, and is the subject of efforts that are reasonable under the circumstances to maintain its secrecy.[1]

This book focuses on copyright and trademark, the primary protection schemes of concern to museums. Copyright and trademark are legal control mechanisms enacted by Congress and enforced by the courts. The two subjects lend themselves to joint treatment. Both have registration schemes that offer distinct advantages, both have established fair use principles, both are increasingly important in the international context, and both are widely misunderstood.

While museums are concerned about protecting ownership rights, they are at the same time concerned about protecting and preserving fair use and use of works in the public domain. Essential for creativity are protecting originality and free use of unprotected material; creativity thrives in a vibrant and massive public domain. As this guide goes to press, the *Bridgeman Art Library v. Corel* case has just been decided, and its import is not yet known. In *Bridgeman*, the trial court in New York held that faithfully reproduced images of two-dimensional works of art (including paintings and drawings but not sculptures or other objects) in the public domain are not eligible for copyright because they are not sufficiently original. This decision might require a major policy shift in some museums, while it will have little effect on the operations of others; it may simply mark a growing emphasis on contract and trademark protection, because the image without the museum's name and the value-added features of scholarship and research has less worth in the marketplace.

Copyright and Trademark: A Comparison

Copyright and trademark are different concepts, protecting different types of property through different enforcement mechanisms. Copyright is described as a "bundle of property rights," and it is indeed akin to physical property. Copyright can be owned, sold, leased, and borrowed and, like real property, it has owners, licensees, and trespassers. The Copyright Law of the United States, incorporated in Title 17 of the United States Code, is a slim volume that has generated shelves (and disks) of case law. The law states that copyright protection subsists "in original works of authorship fixed in any tangible medium of expression, now known or later developed, from which they can be perceived, reproduced, or otherwise communicated." It grants exclusive rights to copyright owners and curbs those exclusive rights with certain limitations that further the public interest.

A trademark is the exclusive right to use the objective symbol signifying the goods and services offered in commerce by the owner. Congress enacted the first trademark laws in the mid-19th century, and in 1946 passed the current comprehensive trademark legislation, known as the Lanham Act. The Lanham Act provides the structure for registering and enforcing trademarks at the federal level. It does not supplant common-law rights. This national system is different from (and more advantageous than) common-law trademark rights under state law. Trademark raises certain procedural issues—distinctiveness, relevant market, likelihood of confusion, types of marks, prior use—that are peculiar to the commercial arena.

Copyright and trademark have some notable differences. Copyright is a constitutional grant of right protecting an author's creative expression. Trademark, in contrast, originated later, and it is an identification right that attaches to products and services directly related to commercial activity. Trademark and copyright also differ with respect to the requirement of use. Copyright subsists from the moment of creation until expiration of the statutory duration, regardless of whether the property lies dormant or is so popular that it is used, adapted, and reproduced on a daily basis. Trademark, in contrast, is acquired by commercial usage or by showing, before use, a "bona fide intention to use the mark in commerce." In trademark, the rule is "use it or lose it." To maintain a trademark, the owner must use the mark on the products or services and must prevent competitors from using it for their own purposes. This concept has two different meanings. First, a trademark is in force as long as it is used in commerce

(subject to several requirements outlined in chapter 1) rather than for a statutorily fixed duration. Second, the failure to vigorously enforce the exclusive trademark identifier may result in abandonment of the mark. Copyright law does not have the principle of abandonment; a copyright owner can selectively enforce its rights without risking loss of those rights. For this reason, museums must zealously prevent others, even its friends, from using the museum name or logo in a way that ties it to the products or services of others. An unauthorized use should trigger a protest, either gentle or aggressive depending on the nature of the use. The concept of fair use applies to trademark as well as copyright. Certain uses in trademark are fair uses and, as is the case in copyright, fair use is an exception to the rule of exclusive property; it allows use of the exclusive property of another for defined, noncommercial purposes that further the public interest.

The Digital Environment

In the burgeoning global realm of the Internet, museums are legitimately concerned about the ease and quality with which images can be reproduced, the broad and unchecked scope of access, and the ability to change or modify an image. These issues are not new. Images from museum collections have been susceptible to alteration or exploitation for some time, but issues raised in the digital environmental are different in degree and scope. Uncertainty over how emerging technologies will be used, nationally and across borders, raises potential liabilities that museum professionals could not have imagined even a decade ago. This development heightens sensitivity for all owners and users of intellectual property. In the past few years, protection of U.S. intellectual property abroad has become the cornerstone of U.S. trade policy, and domestic intellectual property litigation has increased exponentially.

Museums rightly assume that any Web-based materials—including the museum's name and content resources—are subject to unauthorized manipulation, cropping, color changing, and alteration of context. Borrowing the analogy of protecting physical property, museums can protect electronic resources by posting the signs, stationing the guards, and setting the alarms. The elements of infringement described in chapters 1 and 2 will apply equally in the electronic and print environments.

Museum professionals understandably seek certainty in this constantly changing area, but it is unlikely that they will find it for some time. Consider the issues surrounding the introduction of photocopy technology. For decades, photocopy machines have been indispensable in increasing business productivity, furthering research, and spreading knowledge, but they also have made possible fast and cheap infringement. Generations of users were confounded by uncertainty about the appropriate use of photocopy machines, but the courts required years to articulate the bright line separating infringement from fair use. Many cases grew out of photocopying issues, including lawsuits against copy shops, universities, corporations, law firms, and other entities. There were many national conferences, educational campaigns, and suggested guidelines for classroom copying, organizational statements, and best practices. Over the years, the boundaries of appropriate use have been sketched incrementally and gradually; photocopy cases continue to be litigated. Similarly, we cannot expect to know the contours of the law of cyberspace at this early stage. Best practices, rooted in a firm understanding of copyright and trademark, are being developed within the museum community in publications, seminars, conferences, and the like.

Fair Use

Fair use—an equitable doctrine that balances the rights of a copyright owner with those of society—speaks to specific uses of copyrighted works that are considered fair under the Copyright Act. Museums are both users and creators of works, and they may find themselves taking potentially competing positions on fair use issues.

The tension between an owner's financial and security interests and society's legitimate access to intellectual property led Congress to incorporate and codify a growing body of case law when it revised the Copyright Act in 1976. Fair use strives to ensure that an author's exclusive bundle of property rights will not hinder the very creativity the law was designed to foster. The doctrine recognizes that new works draw inspiration from older works and that productive use of older works promotes the progress of science, arts, and literature. Fair use permits certain good-faith uses that, in other contexts, would be infringement. These uses include criticism, comment, news reporting, teaching, scholarship, and research.

Fair use is a case-by-case determination. An activity may qualify in one instance as fair use, while it would be an infringing activity in another context. The fact that a work is intended for an educational purpose does not automatically make it eligible for the fair use exception. For example, educational publishing is a large segment of the publishing market and, while its audience is educational users, it is a commercial activity that relies on obtaining permission to use the copyrighted materials of others. Museum rights departments fulfill many textbook requests, at commercial rates, and would never consider these uses to be fair uses. Similarly, a number of museum activities are not eligible for the fair use exception although they are designed for educational purposes.

The U.S. Copyright Office's informational circular on fair use acknowledges that the distinction between fair use and infringement is unclear and not easily defined. It provides examples of activities that courts have regarded as fair use: "quotation of excerpts in a review or criticism for purposes of illustration or comment; quotation of short passages in a scholarly or technical work, for illustration or clarification of the author's observations; use in a parody of some of the content of the work parodied; summary of an address or article, with brief quotations, in a news report; reproduction by a library of a portion of a work to replace part of a damaged copy; reproduction by a teacher or student of a small part of a work to illustrate a lesson; reproduction of a work in legislative or judicial proceedings or reports; incidental and fortuitous reproduction, in a newsreel or broadcast, of a work located in the scene of an event being reported." [2]

Fair use in the context of objects and images is even more uncertain. Not only must one determine and apply the fair use test, with all its nuances and inconsistencies, but one must do so without a settled body of fine art–specific case law and in light of new challenges presented by electronic media. The growth of the Internet has been accompanied by a liberal interpretation of both freedom of speech and the fair use exception. The ease and speed of downloading and manipulating images, and the mass of unrestricted images on the Internet, lull many users into assuming implied licenses to copy, print, and distribute Internet materials. Some liken transmitting copyrighted materials via e-mail to sharing the newspaper or showing a picture to a friend. Computer networks and bulletin boards compound infringement because distribution is quick, easy, and inexpensive.

Uploading an image implicates the rights of reproduction and distribution; downloading and printing an image represent two acts of reproduction; and modifying an image implicates the rights of reproduction, distribution, and adaptation. If the use is a fair use, these activities will not infringe the copyright owner's exclusive rights. But if these uses are deemed not to be fair, then each separate act is a separate (presumably compensable) infringement. Other issues raised by the transition to an online environment include whether a digital image differs enough from an original image to garner its own copyright; whether a reproduction of a work in the public domain is eligible for copyright when it is digitized (the question addressed in *Bridgeman*, noted earlier, and answered "no" in a recent case in New York); how to deconstruct the separate copyright components of a multimedia project; and who is liable for third-party infringement.

Policy Issues for Museums

The ability to attract "virtual visitors" to "virtual display cases" allows museums to offer previously inaccessible images and to increase exposure in electronic formats through a cost-effective means of providing education, publications, information, and promotional materials. The irresistible allure of the medium is, of course, its potential to throw open the doors free of charge and at all hours. However, increasing virtual display decreases virtual security. Museums balance the goals of increasing and simplifying access to images with the need to protect the integrity and economic interest in the copyrighted images. Museums must do so not only to protect their own interests, but also to safeguard the property of others where a party other than the museum owns the copyright interest.

Moreover, fair use grows more complicated because electronic media encourage joint works and compilations. When the museum uses the works of others in a multimedia presentation, building on various copyrighted components to create a new work, it must be rigorous in obtaining permission to use the many creative components if the multilayered new work does not fall within the fair use doctrine.

An understanding of the law governing copyright and trademark issues is not an end in itself. It is the necessary predicate knowledge upon which museum professionals can set institutional policy and make informed judgments about specific issues. Important steps toward a comprehensive approach include an overarching copyright statement for staff and volunteers that addresses such issues as work for hire and appropriate use of museum materials; a rights and reproductions policy for outside users that articulates appropriate uses and applicable fees; and a trademark policy that identifies properties eligible for trademark protection and squarely addresses enforcement responsibility.

Museums make policy decisions in every department: Who has access to the collections? Who has permission to reproduce items from the collections? May sponsors use the museum name and images, and, if so, how? Should the donor be consulted if the museum plans to make a commercial use of a donated object? Should the museum require transfer of copyright when acquiring a work in its copyright term, or is a nonexclusive license more appropriate? When and how should a museum negotiate with artists' rights societies? Who "clears" rights that the museum does not own, the museum or the third-party user? When a museum has conducted an adequate but unsuccessful search for the copyright owner, what next? When is it appropriate to institute litigation against infringers, and how aggressive should the museum be?

Museums adhere to shared rights and responsibilities in ethical codes that vary in practice from museum to museum (for example, all professionals owe a duty of loyalty to the museum, but some museums permit outside employment while others do not). Similarly, it will reasonably be

expected that museums will approach management of intellectual property differently depending on the nature of the institution, its mission, structure, size, location, print and electronic outreach activities, product development, and a host of other factors. State and local museums may be governed by state laws that specify access to museum records under freedom of information laws, open meeting laws, and regulations governing rental of facilities, fee arrangements, procurement, and revenue generation.

The law reflects a balance of competing interests, but professional ethics may articulate a duty above the minimum threshold of the law. Museums have the right to decide how, when, and by whom collections information is used, and they have the responsibility to exercise that right in an even-handed manner. Museums also have the responsibility to respect the intellectual property of others. Activities undertaken without permission, such as systematic photocopying of copyrighted works, duplicating videotapes, copying single-user licensed software, and other undetected and unreported infringement—without a favorable case-by-case fair use analysis—have no place in museum practice. Museums must establish policies to vigorously monitor copyright and trademark issues in-house. The principles developed in the following chapters will provide the necessary guidance.

What Lies Ahead

Intellectual property questions touch every department in a museum: The registrar receives a request to reproduce a work in the collection. A curator writes an exhibition catalogue and wants to quote liberally from a recent book on the subject. The director learns that a local business has appropriated the museum's name. A press packet prepared by the public affairs staff includes a photograph of children taken during an educational program. The museum shop sells a line of merchandise incorporating the museum name. The development office relies on a database of visitor statistics for fund raising. The restaurant's menu "honors" popular contemporary artists by naming entrees after them. The education staff creates a curriculum guide, in print and online, with images and text. A volunteer researches source material for an upcoming exhibition. "Visitors" from every nation in the world browse the image-rich Web site.

These scenarios illustrate the breadth of the day-to-day intellectual property challenges facing museums at the beginning of the new century. Museum experience in publishing, licensing reproductions from collections, and educational film and video projects provides the necessary conceptual framework for analyzing uses and rights in the new technologies. As museums evaluate rights and uses in the digital and electronic media and explore outreach activities, it is important to work from prior practice. Many museums have procedures for deciding how collections should be used, for controlling physical access, for registering valuable properties, and for the spectrum of intellectual activities governed by the laws described in the following chapters. Continued and frequent sharing of policies and best practices is essential; it answers the question one museum professional raised in a focus group during the research phase for this guide: "What do you do when you don't know what to do?" The answer: Ask, study, share. Museums can prepare for the future by building on what has been successful in the past.

Christine Steiner

Chapter 1

COPYRIGHT

American copyright law is unique because its *purpose* is expressly set forth in the preamble to the copyright clause of the U.S. Constitution: "To promote the Progress of Science and useful Arts by securing for limited Times to Authors and Inventors the exclusive Right to their respective Writings and Discoveries."[1] Unlike some foreign systems of copyright, copyright in the United States is not granted in recognition of any "natural right" of the author in a creative work. Instead, U.S. copyright law provides economic incentives for individual creativity to promote the public welfare. The Supreme Court put it this way:

> Creative work is to be encouraged and rewarded, but private motivation must ultimately serve the cause of promoting broad public availability of literature, music, and the other arts. The immediate effect of our copyright law is to secure a fair return for an "author's" creative labor. But the ultimate aim is, by this incentive, to stimulate artistic creativity for the general public good.[2]

To secure the ultimate benefit of creativity for the public welfare, copyright law attempts to reach a balance between the conflicting interests of owners and users of creative works. This balancing of interests is woven throughout U.S. copyright law and the court decisions that interpret that law. The law expressly enumerates the rights of owners, but they are made subject to a number of statutory limitations. Artists, authors, and scholars are economically rewarded for their efforts, but other creators may build on their accomplishments through the fair use of protected works. Expression is protected, but ideas, facts, and procedures are excluded from protection. As owners, users, and producers of protected works—and sharing a similar vision of the public good—museums reflect the inherent balance in copyright law and policy in the United States.

Congress enacted the first U.S. copyright legislation in 1790. Since then, there have been four general revisions and many amendments of the copyright law. For much of the 20th century, the Copyright Act of 1909 provided the basic structure for protecting creative expression in the United States. Congress overhauled the copyright law when it enacted the Copyright Act of 1976, which took effect on January 1, 1978. However, the 1909 act rules continued to apply generally to works that were published or registered before January 1, 1978. For museums, which are custodians of works produced under both laws, a working knowledge of the principles and rules of both the 1909 and 1976 acts is important. Finally, since 1976, there have been several significant amendments to the copyright law, including the Digital Millennium Copyright Act of 1998.

Subject Matter of Copyright

Criteria for Protection

Under the 1976 Copyright Act, copyright protection is available for "original works of authorship fixed in any tangible medium of expression, now known or later developed, from which they can be perceived, reproduced, or otherwise communicated, either directly or with the aid of a machine or device."[3] This sentence is viewed as the cornerstone of U.S. copyright law, for it sets forth three fundamental copyright principles: authorship, originality, and fixation.

Authorship

Although the Constitution refers to "authors," nowhere in the copyright law is the term defined. "As a general rule," according to the Supreme Court, "the author is the party who actually creates the work, that is, the person who translates an idea into a fixed, tangible expression entitled to copyright protection."[4] If the authorship concept conjures up images of poets like Wordsworth and Coleridge, there is good reason, for copyright law grew up in England alongside romantic literary theory. This romantic conception of the author also is reflected throughout the U.S. case law. Justice Oliver Wendell Holmes once characterized the creative act of authorship as follows: "The copy is the personal reaction of an individual upon nature. Personality always contains something unique. It expresses its singularity even in handwriting, and a very modest grade of art has in it something irreducible, which is one man's alone."[5]

Over the years the authorship notion has expanded to encompass a range of creative people, including architects, artists, choreographers, composers, computer programmers, novelists, playwrights, and filmmakers. In the museum setting, issues of authorship cut across the many roles and functions of museums. The director working on a speech, the curator drafting an exhibition script, and the designer preparing a scale model for an exhibition are all authors. Fortunately, the vast majority of such creative efforts do not give rise to copyright questions. Occasionally, however, an issue of ownership may arise, a topic covered later in this chapter. In their role as custodians of intellectual property, museums also encounter a wide range of authorship issues. Who is the author of the unpublished Civil War diary recently donated to the museum? Who is the author of the Works Progress Administration mural in the museum? Determining authorship for copyright purposes can become complex. However, the same files used by curators to document an original work often contain the answers to copyright authorship questions.

Originality

The second criterion for copyright protection is originality. While the framers of the Constitution were interested in promoting new knowledge,

they did not have in mind the originality standard that doctoral candidates must satisfy to earn their advanced degrees. In fact, copyright's test for originality is not very hard to meet. The Supreme Court recently explained: "To qualify for copyright protection, a work must be original to the author. . . . Original, as the term is used in copyright, means only that the work was independently created by the author (as opposed to copied from other works), and that it possesses at least some minimal degree of creativity."[6] To meet this standard, a work need not be "novel," "ingenious," or even have "aesthetic" merit. In the words of the Supreme Court, there must simply be a "creative spark."

Art museum curators, who routinely make judgments about the aesthetic quality of objects, are often surprised to learn that copyright law has no "aesthetic merit" requirement. All original works of authorship are eligible for protection. Indeed, Justice Holmes warned against the danger of turning judges into art critics: "It would be a dangerous undertaking for persons trained only in the law to constitute themselves final judges of the worth of pictorial illustrations, outside of the narrowest and most obvious limits."[7] According to Justice Holmes, on questions of aesthetic merit, it is only the "taste of any public" that counts, at least for copyright purposes.[8]

In a 1999 case closely watched by museums, the U.S. District Court for the Southern District of New York considered the question of whether color transparencies of paintings that are in the public domain satisfy copyright's originality standard. The case is *The Bridgeman Art Library, Ltd. v. Corel Corporation*,[9] which involved a dispute between a British company engaged in the business of licensing reproduction rights in works of art and a Canadian software producer. Bridgeman, which obtains the reproduction rights from the owners of the underlying works (including museums) and from freelance photographers, maintains a library of reproductions in the form of large-format color transparencies and digital files. In its complaint, Bridgeman alleged that Corel infringed its exclusive rights in 120 transparencies and digital image files when it produced a CD-ROM product that contained 700 digital images of paintings by European masters. Corel defended by arguing, among other things, that the Bridgeman transparencies and digital files were not sufficiently original to be protected under copyright law.

In two separate opinions, Judge Lewis A. Kaplan agreed with Corel. In his first opinion, Judge Kaplan explained that "one need not deny the creativity inherent in the art of photography to recognize that a photograph which is no more than a copy of the work of another as exact as science and technology permit lacks originality. That is not to say such a feat is trivial, simply not original."[10] Without undertaking a detailed discussion of the creative choices in photographic art reproduction, Judge Kaplan compared making transparencies of works of art to photocopying documents. In this case, he found that "there has been no independent creation, no distinguishable variation, . . . nothing recognizably the author's own contribution."[11] Therefore, Judge Kaplan concluded that "Bridgeman's images lack sufficient originality to be copyrightable" under British copyright law.[12]

After reargument and reconsideration, Judge Kaplan issued a second opinion, this time also analyzing the copyrightability of the images under the originality standard in U.S. copyright law. He noted that the "overwhelming majority" of photographs reflect the modest amount of originality for copyright protection, but he declined to extend protection to "slavish copies" of public-domain works of art.[13] Judge Kaplan stated: "While it may be assumed that this required both skill and effort, there was no spark of originality—indeed, the point of the exercise was to reproduce the underlying works with absolute fidelity. Copyright is not available in these circumstances."[14]

Fixation

The third basic condition of copyright protection is that a work must be "fixed in a tangible medium of expression."[15] A work becomes "fixed" when it is "embodied" in a physical object. The manner and medium of fixation are virtually unlimited. The sculptor uses a chisel to capture creative expression in stone, the author a word processor. Creative expression may be captured in "words, numbers, notes, sounds, pictures, or any other graphic or symbolic indicia."[16] The physical object embodying that expression may be "written, printed, photographic, sculptural, punched, magnetic, or any other stable form."[17] Producing a work eligible for copyright requires the merger of an original work and a physical object. A creative work, moreover, may be captured in multiple fixations, such as a sketch for a sculpture (a pictorial work), the sculpture itself (a sculptural work), and a photograph of the sculpture (a photographic work).

Suppose that at the opening of a major, much-publicized exhibition at the American Gallery of Art, director Richard Hills gave a brilliant extemporaneous speech on the life and times of the artist whose work was exhibited. Though Hills' remarks were creative, they were not fixed in a tangible medium of expression. The speech is not eligible for copyright protection. Suppose further that without Hills' knowledge, a reporter for a local newspaper tape-recorded his comments, which appeared in the next morning's edition. Copyright law does not reward the reporter for his behavior, because by definition, a fixation occurs only if the copy is made "by or under the authority of the author."[18]

Congress anticipated that the technology used to capture creative expression would continue to change. Accordingly, the copyright law states that a fixation may be in any tangible medium "now known or later developed, from which [the work] can be perceived, reproduced, or otherwise communicated, either directly or with the aid of a machine or device."[19] This does not mean that every electronic trace of human creativity is eligible for copyright. Copyright law requires that the medium of fixation be "sufficiently permanent or stable" to be perceived for a "period of more than transitory duration."[20] Thus, truly ephemeral digital art, no matter how original, may not be eligible for copyright protection. Such digital art would exist in permanent form, for instance, if it were captured on a CD-ROM.

Consider these two examples: A famous anthropologist working for the Hanover Museum of Anthropology has just returned from the Paradise Islands, where she conducted extensive fieldwork. She used a tape recorder to capture her observations. The tape recordings are eligible for copyright protection because the material is original and "fixed" in a tangible medium of expression. Suppose that the anthropologist later scans typescripts of her field notes into the random-access memory of her computer. These "digital field notebooks" are also probably eligible for copyright protection because they are original and exist in a tangible medium for more than a brief moment.[21]

Types of Works Protected

Over the years, Congress and the courts have extended copyright protection to a wide range of creative works. The current copyright law includes this long list of categories: literary works; musical works; architectural works; dramatic works; pantomimes and choreographic works; pictorial, graphic, and sculptural works; motion pictures and other audiovisual works; sound recordings; and vessel hull designs. While this guide focuses on the categories that are most important for museums, a museum should carefully review all the overlapping categories of protection. Classifying a work can make a big difference, because under the Copyright Act certain rights are not available to copyright owners of certain categories of works.

Literary Works

Each year museums produce a wide range of literary works, from exhibit scripts to scholarly articles. Under the copyright law, a "literary work" is a work (other than an audiovisual work) that is expressed in words, numbers, or other verbal or numerical symbols or indicia, regardless of its physical form.[22] Literary works include histories, biographies, scientific and technical reports, books, periodicals, computer programs, and encyclopedias and other reference materials.[23] Computer programs (including both source code and object code) are protected as literary works. The programs may be recorded in any storage medium, including encoding on a computer chip. Congress made clear that the term literary works "does not connote any criterion of literary merit or qualitative value."[24] All are candidates for copyright protection.

Pictorial, Graphic, and Sculptural Works

Of special importance to museums is the category of "pictorial, graphic, and sculptural works," which includes two- and three-dimensional works. Designed to cover a variety of visual expression, this category includes works of fine, graphic, and applied art, photographs, prints and art reproductions, maps, globes, charts, diagrams, models, and technical drawings, including architectural plans.[25] However, common geometric shapes are unlikely to meet copyright's originality standard.

The artistic features of useful articles, such as the decorative base of a lamp, have always presented a dilemma for copyright purists. The purely utilitarian aspect of the design (physical support for the lamp) clearly is not eligible for protection under copyright law, for that is the province of patent law. However, the decorative aspect of the lamp base is eligible for copyright protection because the artistic element of any useful article may be copyrighted if the artistic element can stand by itself as a work of art.[26] More precisely, copyright protection is available for the design element only if it "can be identified separately from, and [is] . . . capable of existing independently of, the utilitarian aspects of the article."[27] The artistic element may be "physically separable" (such as a decorative finial on a lamp) or "conceptually separable" (such as a cookie jar in the shape of an elephant). As you might imagine, notwithstanding Justice Holmes' warning to avoid making aesthetic judgments, deciding when a design element is "conceptually separable" can be a daunting task for a judge.

Consider the example of Joe Crystal, an exhibit designer for the Riverside Natural History Museum, who developed an original display case for the reinstallation of a world-renowned emerald, one of the great treasures of the museum. The display case, which was shaped like a box, contained a rotating free-form sculpture used to support the gemstone. The display case itself is not eligible for protection because it is a "useful article." The sculpture (no matter how beautiful) is not eligible for protection because it is neither "physically" nor "conceptually" separable from the display case. Moreover, the Copyright Act states that "[a]n article that is normally a part of a useful article is considered a 'useful article.'"[28]

Photographs

Museum work is hardly imaginable without photographic images. From an original Mathew Brady glass negative in the collections to a thumbnail image in the collection records, photographs play a central role. As early as 1865, photographs were eligible for copyright protection. In a landmark 1884 decision, the Supreme Court made it clear that photographs can be original works of authorship.[29] Subsequent decisions have held that photographic images may embody an array of creative choices made by the photographer, including lighting, shading, timing, color balance, and the positioning of the subject.[30] In 1976, Congress listed photographs as examples of pictorial, graphic, or sculptural works.

A typical example is the case of a photographer working for a museum who takes several photographs of the museum building for use in promotional brochures. The photographs are eligible for copyright protection. Copyright's originality requirement is satisfied by the range of creative choices the photographer made, including decisions related to timing, composition, lighting, shading, and positioning. However, although photography is inherently creative, not every photograph will be eligible for copyright protection. In the recent *Bridgeman* case, a federal district court recently ruled that a photograph that is "a copy of the work of another as exact as science and technology permit" is not copyrightable.[31] Over the next few years, museum attorneys will be closely monitoring copyright cases to see if courts in other parts of the country follow the *Bridgeman* decision or if it remains an isolated opinion.

Audiovisual Works

Perhaps of equal importance to museums are works such as motion pictures, television programs, and videos. Museums use interactive audiovisual works in their galleries and classrooms and on their Web sites to showcase their collections, enhance interpretation and education, and reach wider audiences. Under copyright law, most of these materials would be categorized as "audiovisual works," which are defined as "works that consist of a series of related images which are intrinsically intended to be shown by the use of machines or devices such as projectors, viewers, or electronic equipment."[32] Such works include the accompanying sounds. "Motion pictures," which are defined as "series of related images which, when shown in succession, impart an impression of motion, together with accompanying sounds, if any," are also audiovisual works.[33]

A local historical society and museum, for example, recently created an audiovisual program in connection with the celebration of the town's

200th anniversary. As the producer, the historical society may claim a copyright in the work, but it should be sure that it owns or has permission to use all the protected works (that is, in copyright) in the audiovisual program, including any literary, musical, and pictorial or graphic works. If the historical society uses photographs with people and unpublished correspondence from family albums, it should evaluate whether the use would intrude on the donors' privacy. The law of privacy is discussed in appendix E.

Music and Sound

From the gentle tinkling of a harpsichord in a historic house museum to the roar of a dinosaur in a natural history museum, music and sound have become integral parts of the museum experience. Under copyright law, protection is extended to music in two important categories: musical works and sound recordings. A musical work consists of the musical notes and lyrics (if any) in a musical composition, which may be fixed in sheet music, audiotape, a compact disc, or almost any other medium. Copyright law makes an important distinction between an underlying musical composition and a sound recording, which is eligible for a separate copyright. A sound recording is a work that results from the fixation of a series of musical, spoken, or other sounds. Copyright in a musical work protects the composer; copyright in a sound recording protects the record company.

Take the case of the Plainville Zoological Society, which used the copyrighted sound recording *Stomping through the Jungle* in a multimedia work for sale in the museum shop after obtaining permission from the composer of the song. The composer's permission will be of little comfort to the Plainville Zoo if it is sued for copyright infringement by the Triangle Music Company, which owns the copyright in the sound recording. The important differences in licensing these categories of copyright protection for music are discussed more fully in chapter 4.

Architectural Works

A museum building can be an integral part of the museum's identity. Try to imagine, for example, the Guggenheim Museum without Frank Lloyd Wright's splendid structure. Museum buildings also serve the functional needs of museums, housing the collections and defining the public spaces. Museum buildings are eligible for copyright protection, but there are a number of exceptions and limitations. In general, architectural works created on or after December 1, 1990, and any architectural works that were unconstructed and embodied in unpublished plans and drawings on that date, are eligible.

Copyright law defines "architectural work" as "the design of a building as embodied in any tangible medium of expression, including a building, architectural plans, or drawings."[34] The term includes the "overall form as well as the arrangement and composition of spaces and elements" in the design of a building.[35] Under this definition, the exterior design of the Guggenheim Museum would be part of its overall form. The broad definition of architectural works makes it clear that, in addition to protecting architectural plans and drawings, copyright law protects the artistic elements in a building itself. Not all parts of a museum building are eligible for copyright protection. For example, standard features, such as common windows, doors, and other building components, would not be protected.

More broadly, copyright protection is not available for functional parts of a protected architectural work, no matter how original the overall conception. Does this mean that courts must make judgments, as in the case of useful articles, about the physical and conceptual separability of design elements in museum buildings? Not exactly. In determining whether a design embodied in a museum building is protected, a court would begin by analyzing the overall exterior shape and interior spaces of the building to determine whether original design elements are present. If so, the court then would evaluate which elements were functionally required. To the extent that design elements are not functionally required, the work may be protected without reference to the physical or conceptual separability test. Copyright protection for a design embodied in a building is subject to another important limitation. It "does not include the right to prevent [others from] . . . making, distributing, or public[ly] display[ing] . . . pictures, paintings, photographs, or other pictorial representations of the work, if the building in which the work is embodied is located in or ordinarily visible from a public place."[36]

The following example illustrates the relationship of copyright to museum buildings. The American Football Hall of Fame is housed in a building in the form of a huge football, designed by one of the country's leading postmodernist architectural firms and built in 1996. Although the Hall of Fame owns the copyright in the protected design elements embodied in the distinctive building, it cannot stop visitors from photographing the exterior. Recently, however, the Sports Emporium, a retail chain, began to market a poster based on a photograph of the Hall of Fame taken without the museum's permission. An almost identical poster is sold in the museum shop. The museum cannot do anything to stop the Sports Emporium, because the original design elements embodied in the building may be protected under copyright, taking a photograph of the building is perfectly lawful, but using the museum name and "trading on" the image for private commercial gain is not lawful.[37] (See chapter 2, "Format and Subject Matter of Trademarks," for a discussion of a similar case involving the protectability of a distinctive museum building as a trademark.)

Derivative Works and Compilations

Museums own and produce creative works from preexisting materials, some of which already may be copyrighted. Exhibition catalogues, posters, and merchandise sold in museum shops are just a few examples. Such "second-generation" works are also eligible for copyright protection. Copyright law recognizes two types of works that employ preexisting materials: derivative works and compilations. Derivative works turn up in many museum activities, from collecting (a lithograph based on a painting) to merchandising (an engagement calendar based on the lithograph). Compilations, which are also important to museum work, range from scientific databases to the proceedings of a scholarly symposium.

A derivative work is "based upon one or more preexisting works" in which the underlying work is "recast, transformed, or adapted."[38] When a photograph of an original work of art is transformed into a poster, for example, a separate derivative work is created. A compilation is a work "formed by the collection and assembling of preexisting materials or of data that are selected, coordinated, or arranged so that the resulting work as a whole constitutes an original work of authorship."[39] When a museum collects and assembles materials for an exhibition catalogue, a separate compilation is created. A compilation may be composed of unprotected facts, such as a database,[40] or materials that are themselves protected, such as articles in an encyclopedia.[41]

Before taking a closer look at the nature of derivative works and compilations, there are two special rules to keep in mind. First, copyright in the new work extends only to the original material added by the later author. It does not in any way affect the copyright or public domain status of the preexisting or underlying material.[42] Copyright protection is limited to the compilation author's original expression. Second, copyright does not extend to "any part of the work in which such material has been used unlawfully."[43]

Illustrating this point is the case of the Riverside Natural History Museum, which, in conjunction with a symposium on volcanoes, compiled an anthology of papers by some leading experts. The

Riverside's copyright extends to its selection, coordination, and arrangement of the papers (and any separate contributions by the museum) but does not give the museum copyright in the contributions of the participating scholars. When organizing the next symposium, museum staff may want to ask the participating scholars to "assign" their copyrights to the museum, a topic discussed later in this chapter.

A derivative work may be two-dimensional (such as a poster) or three-dimensional (such as a scale reduction of a sculptural work). Although the issue is not free from doubt, to qualify for a derivative work copyright, the "recasting, adaptation, or transformation" of the underlying work must involve something more than a change from one medium to another (such as making a plastic mold sculpture of a 19th-century toy in the museum's collection). The underlying work may be copyrighted or in the public domain. However, a derivative work copyright will not restore protection in the underlying public domain material. If the original work is protected, and if the museum does not own the copyright, it must obtain the owner's permission before creating the derivative work.

To be copyrightable, a derivative work must be an original work of authorship. But just how different from the underlying work must an authorized derivative work be to qualify for a separate copyright? This question has proven particularly troublesome for reproductions of works of art. Does the same low threshold of creativity that applies to original copyrightable subject matter also apply to derivative works? Indeed, many courts ask only that the adapter of the original work bring a "modicum of creativity" to the task. But most courts impose a higher standard of originality, "some substantial variation, not merely a trivial variation" from the original work on which the derivative work is based.[44]

Somewhat surprisingly, the courts are still wrestling with the basic meaning of the words "recast, transformed, or adapted." In a recent case before a federal appeals court, the court held that mounting notecards of copyrighted drawings onto ceramic tiles did not produce infringing derivative works.[45] The court noted that mounting a work on tile is no more of a "transformation" than changing the frame of a painting. "No one believes that a museum violates [the derivative work right] . . . every time it changes the frame of a painting that is still under copyright," wrote the court.[46] However, in disputes with similar facts, another federal appeals court reached the opposite conclusion.[47] Another court in the same jurisdiction held that the defendant infringed the copyright in a book of art prints by cutting out the prints, mounting each on a canvas, and placing them in frames.[48]

Compilations and collective works are also integral aspects of museum life. Museums expend considerable effort and resources on "collecting and assembling" preexisting materials, facts, or data and then "selecting, coordinating, or arranging" them into a new whole. When the selection, coordination, and arrangement are done in a way that constitutes an "original work of authorship," the resulting work is eligible for a separate compilation copyright.

The courts continue to struggle with the level of originality required for a compilation copyright. The leading case is *Feist Publications, Inc. v. Rural Telephone Service Co.*, which involved a white pages telephone directory.[49] In *Feist*, the Supreme Court held that compilations of facts, unlike facts themselves, are eligible for copyright protection, but only when the selection and arrangement of data meet the originality requirement of the U.S. Constitution. The court recognized that the originality requirement was quite low—"even a slight amount will suffice." Still, it ruled that a garden-variety white pages telephone book did not meet this test. Nor did it matter, the court held, that the telephone company had made a substantial investment of time and resources in compiling the database.[50]

A museum example might be the New World Natural History Museum's published list of terms used for identifying certain animal groups of North America, with artwork and explanatory text. The terms, which were identified through extensive archival research, were selected and arranged according to historical animal habitats. The museum's compilation is eligible for copyright protection because of the originality involved in selecting and arranging the terms according to animal habitat, not because of the extensive archival research conducted.[51]

Exclusions from Protection

Certain works, no matter how original, are not eligible for copyright protection. As we learned from the *Feist* case, facts alone are not copyrightable. Protection is also not available for "any idea, procedure, process, system, method of operation, concept, principle, or discovery, regardless of the form in which it is described, explained, illustrated, or embodied in such work."[52] What about the name of a museum, the title of an exhibition, or a snappy slogan on a T-shirt or coffee mug sold in the museum shop? Words and short phrases, such as names, titles, and slogans, also generally are not eligible for copyright protection.[53] The public policy behind this rule makes sense. As part of the common language, such phrases generally remain free for all to use. However, when a title, name, short phrase, or slogan serves as a source identifier for museum goods and services, trademark protection may be available.

The hypothetical American Heritage Village, an outdoor history museum well known for its historic restaurants and taverns, published a cookbook, *The Old Tavern Sampler*, containing recipes for some of the most popular dishes at the village. The cookbook consisted of simple lists of ingredients and prosaic instructions. The recipes contained no expressive elaboration. Recently, a commercial publisher began marketing a book, *Colonial Fare*, which features several recipes that

are functionally equivalent to those in *The Old Tavern Sampler*. Does American Heritage Village have any copyrightable subject matter to protect? The recipes probably are ineligible for copyright protection because the lists of ingredients are mere statements of fact lacking the requisite element of originality. The cooking instructions are excluded from protection as a "procedure, process, [or] system."[54] This is not to say that all recipes are ineligible for copyright protection. As one federal appeals court recently stated: "There are cookbooks in which the authors lace their directions for producing dishes with musings about the spiritual nature of cooking or reminiscences they associate with the wafting odors of certain dishes in various stages of preparation."[55] Moreover, the selection, coordination, and arrangement of the recipes may be protected under a compilation copyright (see "Derivative Works and Compilations," earlier in this chapter). In this example, the protectable elements include the text, the arrangement, the images, and, of course, the village name, but not the historical recipes themselves.

Historical facts present special legal and policy problems under copyright law. Suppose that the Old Commonwealth Historical Museum included the following sentence in an exhibit label: "Confederate General Robert E. Lee surrendered his army to Union General Ulysses S. Grant on April 9, 1865, marking the end of the Civil War." Should such a sentence qualify for copyright protection? The courts have struggled with where to draw the line between unprotected historical facts and protected historical narratives. The meeting of Grant and Lee at the Appomattox Courthouse, Virginia, is one of the most dramatic moments in American history. Owing its origin to no author, the courts have reasoned, it should be freely available to everyone.

But what if the curators of Old Commonwealth developed a detailed historical account of the events leading up to Lee's surrender, carefully weaving historical facts into a narrative that included a setting, plot, characters, and interpretations of fact? Such a nonfiction narrative undoubtedly would be eligible for copyright protection. One federal court noted that copyright law would protect the "manner of expression, the author's analysis or interpretation of events, the way he structures his material and marshals facts, his choice of words, and the emphasis he gives to particular developments."[56]

A fundamental principle of copyright law is that only the expression of an idea and not the idea itself is protectable. There is a corollary principle, sometimes called the "merger doctrine" or the "idea-expression dichotomy." Under the merger doctrine, even expression is not protected when there are so few ways of expressing an idea that protection of the expression would effectively accord protection to the idea itself.[57] In such cases, the idea and its expression are said to merge, and protection will be denied.[58] Declining to apply the merger doctrine, one federal appeals court recently held that fish mannequin forms (used to display fish skins) are copyrightable sculptural works fashioned to display their own appearance.[59] The court stated: "[We] cannot say that all realistic fish are necessarily so similar to each other that to copyright any of them would be tantamount to copyrighting an idea rather than an artistic manifestation."[60]

Finally, certain works are categorically excluded from copyright protection from the moment of their creation. One would hardly expect to find, for example, a notice of copyright on the U.S. Constitution or, to take a more recent example, the U.S. copyright code itself. Public policy, of course, demands that such works be freely and widely circulated. Thus, copyright protection does not extend to "any work of the United States Government."[61] This rule applies to works prepared by federal government employees as part of their official duties but not to most works created by state government employees.[62] Employees of

state museums should consult applicable state and local laws. The Copyright Act does not prohibit the U.S. government from receiving or holding copyrights transferred to it by assignment, bequest, or otherwise.[63] The copyright in research conducted under a federal grant or contract generally belongs to the author.[64] However, a federal agency may need to balance the need to have the resulting work made freely available to the public against the need of a private author to secure a copyright.[65]

Securing Copyright

One of the most misunderstood aspects of copyright is the way protection is secured. Unlike establishing patent or trademark rights, securing copyright requires no application or examination. Since 1978, copyright protection begins automatically from the moment that a work is fixed in a tangible form. But obtaining copyright protection in the United States has not always been that easy. Until quite recently, certain copyright requirements imposed by the government on authors were a distinctive feature of U.S. copyright law. Museums still need to have a basic understanding of these older, formal requirements, which may hold the key to the copyright status of works in their collections.

Notice

Before January 1, 1978, works published in the United States were required to have a proper notice of copyright as a condition of protection.[66] The failure to include such a notice usually meant that the work entered the public domain, available for all to use without obtaining permission or paying a fee. In fact, prior to 1978, the works of many American artists and foreign authors, unfamiliar with these "formalities," entered the public domain precisely for this reason. In 1976, Congress tried to mitigate this harsh result by providing ways to "cure" omitted or defective notices within five years of publication of the work.

In 1989, Congress eliminated the notice requirement as a condition for obtaining copyright protection.[67] Thus, for works first published on or after March 1, 1989, the use of copyright notice became optional. While no longer mandatory, copyright notice continues to serve several useful purposes. First, it identifies the copyright owner (at the time of the notice) and provides information on the date of publication. Second, it provides a warning to unauthorized users. Third, it deprives an alleged infringer of the so-called "innocent infringement" defense, under which a judge may reduce monetary compensation when the alleged infringer was unaware that the work was protected. Under current law, proper copyright notice includes: an appropriate copyright symbol (such as the symbol ©, the word "Copyright," or the abbreviation "Copr."); the year of first publication of the work; and the name of the copyright owner.[68]

Publication

Before 1978, the concept of publication was extremely important in U.S. copyright law. The actual date of publication marked the dividing line between state protection and federal copyright protection. On one side of the line, state common law offered the author perpetual protection if the work remained unpublished. On the other side, the author was given a fixed period of protection under federal copyright law upon publication of the work (or registration with the Copyright Office for unpublished works). However, the author might find herself with no protection at all because failure to strictly comply with the technical notice requirements of federal copyright law usually meant that the work fell into the public domain.

What constitutes publication? Nowhere in the 1909 act is there a definition of this critically important term, although the "date of publication" was defined as the "earliest date when copies of the first authorized edition were placed on sale, sold, or publicly distributed"[69] by the owner. The 1976 Copyright Act filled this gap by codifying the definition of publication long used by judges. For copyright purposes, publication means: "the distribution of copies or phonorecords of a work to the public by sale or other transfer of ownership, or by rental, lease, or lending. The offering to distribute copies or phonorecords to a group of persons for purposes of further distribution, public performance, or public display, constitutes publication. A public performance or public display of a work does not of itself constitute publication."[70] It makes no difference if the transfer of ownership is by sale, rental, lease, or lending. For example, a sound recording may be distributed through the sale of a compact disc, an audiovisual work through the rental of a video-cassette.

Works of visual art have always presented especially difficult publication issues. Part of the explanation is that the very notion of publication, developed for the distribution of books, never fit comfortably with the distribution of works of visual art, which are sold as unique works or in limited editions. The publication of a photograph of a work of art by a commercial gallery would seem to be an offer to distribute the work. But what if a commercial gallery simply displayed the work? Does displaying a work of art in a commercial space constitute a publication? Would it make any difference if the gallery restricted photography of the work? Unfortunately, the answers to these questions are far from clear in the old cases interpreting the 1909 copyright law.

Even under the formality-ridden 1909 act, not every disclosure of a work was a publication. In part to avoid forfeitures of copyright, judges sometimes ruled that a "limited" or "restricted" disclosure of a work did not constitute a "general publication," but rather a "limited publication," which would not divest the owner of copyright protection if the owner failed to comply with copyright formalities. To qualify as a limited publication, a work generally had to be communicated only to a select group, for a limited purpose, with no further right of distribution. The application of the test for limited publication, developed by the courts largely for public speeches, presented especially nettlesome problems when used in connection with transfers of works of art, photographs, and prints.

Suppose that the Downtown Museum of Art owns a painting by Jorge Cortes, a longtime professor at the Art Students League. Cortes displayed the painting in his 1939 basic studio course, which had about 20 students enrolled. The publication was limited because the artist displayed the work to a select group (his students) for a limited purpose (instruction) with no intent of further distribution. From these facts, the museum should draw no inference regarding possible loss of copyright because of publication without notice.

Under what circumstances would the public display of a work of art, whether in a museum or a commercial gallery, constitute a "general publication," possibly divesting the owner of copyright protection if the owner failed to include a proper copyright notice on the work? Unfortunately, the older cases do not shed much light on this question. The rule under the 1909 act seems to be that when a work of art was publicly displayed or distributed in a way that made it readily available to the public, a general publication occurred. Under the old law, the critical factor appears to be whether the publication was "to a limited group for a limited purpose" or to the public at large. For purposes of determining publication, the sale, offering for sale, or distribution of the original work was regarded as a distribution of a copy.

The Uptown Museum of Art, for example, owns the acclaimed *Mechanical Man*, a futurist sculpture first publicly displayed in the Spanish Pavilion at the 1939 New York World's Fair. Millions of visitors to the fair snapped photo-

graphs of the pioneering work, and many of the photographs were distributed without copyright notice. The public display of *Mechanical Man* probably constituted a "general publication," divesting the artist of copyright in the work because he failed to comply with the notice requirements of U.S. law. Without such clear evidence of unrestricted and widespread public copying, however, the museum should not draw any conclusions regarding the loss of copyright through public display. Of course, there are other ways that a protected work may enter the public domain because of a publication without notice, including the public sale or offering for sale of a work without copyright notice and the publication of reproductions of the work without notice.

Although publication no longer plays such a central role in copyright law, its significance continues in a number of provisions of current law.[71] Since 1978, the deposit of copies of registered works with the Library of Congress is mandatory only for works published in the United States. The term of protection for works made for hire (discussed more fully in "Ownership," later in this chapter) is 95 years from the date of first publication or 100 years from creation, whichever comes first. While all unpublished works are protected regardless of the author's nationality or residence, there are special conditions for the protection of published works by foreign authors. Finally, certain remedies are available for published works only if registration preceded infringement or if the work was registered within three months after publication.

Registration

Registration of a work with the U.S. Copyright Office is voluntary, but there are a number of significant benefits in doing so. Registration is generally required before an author of a work that originated in the United States can bring an infringement action in court.[72] The registration certificate from the Copyright Office makes it easier to prove certain facts in a copyright lawsuit (see "Evaluating the Merits of a Claim," later in this chapter).[73] Additional remedies, including statutory damages and attorneys' fees, may be available in successful infringement suits if the copyright owner registers with the Copyright Office in a timely manner.[74] The basic copyright registration procedure is not difficult, requiring the registrant to submit the appropriate registration form, filing fee, and deposit copies.[75]

Deposit

To enhance the collections of the Library of Congress, the Copyright Act requires the deposit of two copies of each work published in the United States for which copyright is claimed within three months after publication.[76] This requirement is mandated by statute, but failure to comply may result in a fine rather than the invalidation of the owner's copyright. The copyright law also requires a deposit in connection with registration, which serves to fulfill the mandatory deposit requirement. Failure to comply with this requirement will result in refusal by the Copyright Office to register the work.

Exclusive Rights and Their Limitations

Copyright law gives copyright owners the exclusive right to reproduce, adapt, distribute, publicly perform, and publicly display their works.[77] To this list, Congress recently added the right to perform a sound recording by "digital audio transmission."[78] A copyright owner may use, or authorize others to use, any or all of these exclusive rights. For example, the owner of a copyright in a photograph may authorize its publication or decide to leave it unpublished. Later, the owner may adapt the photograph into a poster or deny permission for its use on a coffee mug. The owner may publicly exhibit the photograph or authorize its television broadcast. Each of these exclusive

rights is subject to a number of specific statutory limitations.[79] Copyright's "bundle" of exclusive rights can be a powerful tool for museums in using and controlling the use of their collections.

Reproduction Right

The right to reproduce a work is the right to make copies of the work in almost any tangible medium. The Copyright Act defines "copies" as "material objects, other than phonorecords, in which a work is fixed by any method now known or later developed, and from which the work can be perceived, reproduced, or otherwise communicated, either directly or with the aid of a machine or device. The term 'copies' includes the material object, other than a phonorecord, in which the work is first fixed."[80] To violate the reproduction right, a copy need not be identical, just "substantially similar," a concept discussed more fully later in this chapter. Printing, photocopying, and photographing a protected work are all examples of the exercise of the reproduction right.

Right to Prepare Derivative Works

The right to prepare a derivative work is the right to create a new work "based on" a preexisting copyrighted work by "recasting, transforming, or adapting" the original work.[81] This right is sometimes called the right to adapt a work, and the resulting works are called "new versions," such as translations, musical arrangements, dramatizations, and art reproductions. Derivative works may be found in a museum's permanent collection or in the museum shop's inventory. Consider the range of works that may qualify as a derivative work: a lithograph based on a painting, a poster based on a photograph, and a necktie based on a drawing. In many cases, the derivative work right overlaps the reproduction and distribution rights. As museum merchandising continues to expand, derivative work rights will be of increasing importance to museums.

Consider the case of the Cosmopolitan Museum of Art, which is planning a sales program in connection with a major exhibition of the works of a contemporary artist. Although the artist retained copyright in her work, she later granted permission to the museum to create prints, posters, notecards, and dessert plates using the most popular images. All these products are derivative works, eligible for separate protection if they meet the appropriate originality standard. As the owner of a derivative work copyright, the museum may sue Denaro Duplicates, Inc., for infringement of its derivative work, reproduction, and distribution rights if it begins to distribute a substantially similar line of merchandise.

Right to Distribute the Work

The distribution right gives the copyright owner the right to control the initial public distribution of copies of the work by sale, rental, lease, or loan.[82] When a museum enters into an arrangement with a commercial publisher for an exhibition catalogue, it is exercising both its reproduction and distribution rights. The distribution right is separate from the reproduction right. If a museum signs a licensing agreement with a manufacturer to produce reproductions of a teapot in its collections, and the manufacturer sells a production overrun to the public, the manufacturer has infringed the museum's distribution right (in addition to violating the terms of the license), unless otherwise provided in the contract.[83]

The distribution right is subject to an important limitation. The Copyright Act provides that "the owner of a particular copy or phonorecord lawfully made under this title, or any person authorized by such owner, is entitled, without the authority of the copyright owner, to sell or otherwise dispose of the possession of the copy or the phonorecord."[84] This rule is known as the first sale doctrine. For example, after a customer purchases an exhibition catalogue from a museum shop, the buyer is perfectly free to give it to the local library, lend it to

neighbor, or resell it at a secondhand bookstore. None of these actions would violate the museum's distribution right. What the new owner may not do is make multiple copies of the catalogue for further distribution.

Purchasers of computer software and sound recordings, on the other hand, are generally not permitted to rent their "particular, lawful" copies of these products. Congress provided two exceptions to the first sale doctrine for such works because it felt they were simply too easy to copy. The general rule is that no one may rent, lease, or lend computer software or sound recordings without the permission of the appropriate copyright owner, subject to certain exceptions for nonprofit educational institutions and libraries.

Consistent with the basic policy of the first sale doctrine, artists in the United States (except in California) generally are not entitled to share in the profits of future sales of their works. The law in a number of European countries, most notably France, is quite different. Under resale royalty right (*droit de suite*) laws in those countries, artists may share in the profits of later sales of their works. The converse is not true; artists are not required to compensate buyers for decreases in the value of their works. California is the only state to enact a resale royalty law,[85] and in that state there is a divergence of opinion as to the law's effectiveness and level of adherence.

Right to Publicly Perform the Work

One usually thinks of theaters and concert halls as places where works are publicly performed. But a museum's public spaces—its galleries, auditoriums, theaters, and gardens—are also settings for the public performance of all kinds of copyrighted works. Delivering a lecture (a literary work), singing a song or performing an instrumental work in a quartet (musical works), reciting lines of a play (a dramatic work), dancing a ballet (a choreographic work), showing a film or playing a videocassette (audiovisual works)—all may be public performances. Even the use of prerecorded music in museum shops and restaurants, while designed to make shopping and dining more pleasurable, may constitute public performances of copyrighted works. Museums will need to consider the public performance right when videotaping or otherwise recording programs at the museum.

What is a public performance? Under the copyright law, "perform" means to "recite, render, play, dance, or act" a work in a public place or to transmit it to the public.[86] In the case of a motion picture and other audiovisual works, showing the work's images in sequence is a performance. Under the Copyright Act, three types of public performances can be distinguished: (1) a performance at a place open to the public; (2) a performance by transmission to a place open to the public; and (3) a performance to an audience that may be separated in time, place, or both.[87] A "public place" is "any place where a substantial number of persons outside of a normal circle of a family and its social acquaintances is gathered."[88] To "transmit" a performance means "to communicate it by any device or process whereby images or sounds are received beyond the place from which they are sent."[89]

Under these definitions, many activities undertaken in the public spaces of museums probably are public performances requiring the owner's permission when copyrighted works are involved. The law does not provide much guidance on the meaning of a "substantial number of persons," but it probably would exclude performances at most routine business meetings in museums. On the other hand, a performance at a large reception at a museum (perhaps following an exhibition opening) probably would come within the meaning of "substantial number of persons," even if not open to the general public. Museum exhibitions, in the traditional sense, probably are not public performances because physical objects

are generally "publicly displayed" (explained later in this chapter) and not "publicly performed." However, as noted above, the concept of public performance goes well beyond live performances in physical settings. Thus, an exhibition transmitted, in whole or in part, for viewing by persons in geographically dispersed locations or at different times could constitute a public performance.

Who has the right to perform a work in public? In general, the public performance right initially belongs to the creator of the work. The composer or playwright, not the singer or actor, controls the right to perform his or her works. Although the public performance right is extremely valuable, it is often impossible for the individual creator to monitor multiple performances across the country or to enter into numerous individual licenses. Individual owners of music copyrights solve this problem by collectively licensing their public performance rights through groups like the American Society of Composers, Authors, and Publishers (ASCAP), Broadcast Music, Inc. (BMI), or the Society of European Stage Authors and Composers (SESAC). The purpose of these performing rights organizations, which are described more fully in chapter 4, is to issue blanket licenses (usually covering all the music in the association's repertoire), monitor their public performance, and collect and remit royalty payments to members. Under such licenses, every time a musical work is broadcast over radio, television, or, for that matter, performed in a museum shop or restaurant, the copyright owner of the public performance right in the music is entitled to compensation.

The owner of a copyright in a musical composition also may license the right to make sound recordings of the work (granting a so-called "mechanical license") through the Harry Fox Agency, another collective rights organization. Under such circumstances, the record company may become the owner of a separate copyright in the sound recording, sometimes called a "phonorecord." Unlike the owner of a copyright in the underlying musical work, the owner of a copyright in a sound recording generally receives no compensation for the public performance of the sound recording. Instead, until quite recently, record companies have been compensated solely through the sales of physical objects like tapes, compact discs, and laser discs. However, in 1995, Congress amended the copyright law to provide a limited right for the public performance of sound recordings made "by means of a digital audio transmission."[90] The new performance right covers only transmissions by "music subscription services" (such as a cable service) and "interactive services" (such as a "celestial jukebox" service). The new right does not extend to free over-the-air radio and television broadcasts to the public, analog transmissions, or digital transmissions of audiovisual works.

Somewhat different rules apply to videotapes, as the case of the Hampton Botanical Garden illustrates. The botanical garden videotaped lectures by recipients of its annual award for distinguished contributions to botanical science. The Hampton's archive contains copies of the videotapes, but the botanical garden is not sure how it can use these materials without the speakers' permission. The institution is right to be concerned, but it need not be overly concerned. Though the award winners own the copyrights in their speeches, the botanical garden owns the copyright in the videotapes, which includes the right to publicly perform the tapes. Nonetheless, it would be advisable for the Hampton's administrators to obtain the speakers' permission in writing before publicly airing the tapes, since other rights (such as the rights of privacy and publicity) may be involved—not to mention good old-fashioned courtesy. The botanical garden may not publish the text of the lectures without first getting the permission of the speakers.

Does this mean that the botanical garden also may publicly show videotapes of the Vivace Quartet, a local group of musicians that recently performed

there? Before doing so, the botanical garden first needs to clear any rights in the underlying musical works that were performed. Moreover, the botanical garden must double-check its contract with the performers to ensure that the members of the ensemble have granted permission to show their performance of the music.

The public performance right is subject to other limitations, which are discussed more fully at the end of this chapter (see "Other Statutory Limitations"). For now, it is enough to note that, in addition to the general doctrine of fair use, there are other specific statutory limitations on this right, including exemptions for face-to-face instruction, educational broadcasting, and certain charitable benefit performances.

Right to Publicly Display the Work

While many people would agree that exhibition is a central function of museums, few may be aware of the legal meaning of "public display." For copyright purposes, to display a work means "to show a copy of it, either directly or by means of a film, slide, television image, or any other device or process or, in the case of a motion picture or other audiovisual work, to show individual images nonsequentially."[91] The right of public display applies with equal force to the exhibition of original works of art and to their reproductions, because a "copy" includes any material object in which the work is fixed. The word "public" has the same meaning as discussed in connection with the public performance right. Also, many of the exemptions to the public performance right for educational activities noted in passing above also apply to the public display right, including the face-to-face teaching and instructional broadcast exemptions.[92]

Suppose that a museum acquires an original oil painting from an artist but fails to obtain the copyright. Could the artist require the museum to request permission every time it exhibits the work? Under the normal rules governing the transfer of copyrights, the artist could do so because the museum only acquired the physical painting, not the right to publicly display it. However, the copyright law avoids this unhappy result by providing for special treatment of the public display of protected works. Specifically, as the owner of a particular copy lawfully made under the copyright law, or with the authorization of the owner of the work, a museum may "display that copy publicly, either directly or by the projection of no more than one image at a time, to viewers present at the place where the copy is located."[93] This public display right extends only to the immediate physical surroundings of the work. Without express authorization, the museum would not be permitted to project images of the work into other galleries or to multiple computer workstations over a local area network, or, much less, transmit the copy of the work over computer networks for viewing at multiple locations—unless that use is a fair use, discussed later in this chapter.

Moral Rights

In 1990, the Visual Artists Rights Act (VARA) established for the first time in U.S. federal law a limited grant of moral rights to authors of works of visual art. Specifically, the new law recognized the author's right of attribution, right of integrity, and right to prevent the destruction of copies of certain works of art.[94] VARA became effective on June 1, 1991, and applies to works created on or after that date and to works created before that date if title has not yet been transferred by the artist. The artist's rights under VARA are in addition to the exclusive federal rights discussed earlier and "preempt" (displace) "equivalent rights," if any, under state law.[95] VARA rights may not be transferred but may be waived if the artist expressly agrees to such a waiver in a written instrument signed by the artist. VARA rights generally last for the artist's lifetime. However, when the artist retains title to a work created before June 1, 1991, the work is protected for the full

copyright term (currently, the life of the artist plus 70 years). Significantly, for reasons discussed more fully later in this chapter, the scope of protection for artists is much more limited under VARA than under foreign moral rights laws.

VARA applies to a very limited range of works that fall within the act's definition of a work of visual art. In general, this means original paintings; drawings; single copies or limited editions of prints; sculptures; and still photographs intended for exhibition purposes.[96] Perhaps just as important is VARA's long list of excluded works. For example, even if a work falls within a protected category, it will be excluded from coverage under VARA if issued in limited editions of more than 200 copies or in editions of fewer than 200 copies that fail to comply with certain numbering and marking requirements. For obvious reasons, disputes are likely to arise regarding what constitutes a work of visual art under VARA. Congress anticipated such disputes and directed the courts to "use common sense and generally accepted standards of the artistic community" in determining whether a particular work falls within the scope of the definition.[97]

Consider another example from the Downtown Museum of Art, which lawfully acquired a limited-edition print and the copyright in the work from Peter Printer, who did not waive his VARA rights. The Downtown Museum subsequently used a photograph of the print to produce a museum tote bag and umbrella that it offered as a premium in its annual fund-raising campaign. Deeply offended by what he considered a trivialization of his work, Printer sued the Downtown Museum under VARA. The museum is on solid legal ground because it owned the right to make derivative works based on the original, and the artist's rights of attribution and integrity under VARA extend only to the prints in the original limited edition. (However, in certain states, the artist may have a claim against the museum under applicable state law to the extent not preempted by federal law.)

VARA's exclusive rights are also narrowly defined. Under the attribution right, an artist may claim authorship of her work; prevent the use of her name as the author of any work she did not create; and prevent the use of her name as the author of any work that has been distorted, mutilated, or otherwise modified in a way that would be prejudicial to her honor or reputation.[98] Under the right of integrity, an artist may prevent any intentional distortion, mutilation, or other modification of his work that would be prejudicial to his honor or reputation and prevent the destruction of a work of "recognized stature" through intentional or grossly negligent acts.[99]

Two exceptions to liability under the right of integrity are important to museums. First, a museum would not be liable if the destruction, distortion, mutilation, or objectionable modification resulted from the passage of time or the inherent nature of the materials. Second, a museum would not be liable if the objectionable modification resulted from conservation treatment or public exhibition, including lighting and placement, unless caused by gross negligence.[100]

VARA also sets forth special rules for works of visual art that are incorporated into buildings, including detailed procedures for their removal. An artist may waive these rights by signing an agreement (either before or after the installation of the work), consenting to the possible destruction or damage of installed works of art during removal. Absent such a waiver, the owner of the building is required to notify the artist of the planned removal. If the artist responds to the owner's notice, the artist has 90 days to remove the work or pay for its removal. If the artist fails to respond or cannot be found, the artist's rights are deemed to be waived, and the owner may remove the installed work.

Duration

How long should copyright last? The debate over copyright duration is as old as copyright law itself and probably will continue as long as copyright exists. It is an important question because copyright term establishes not only the amount of protection accorded an author but also the boundary between individual property rights and the public domain. As both owners and users of copyrights, and as custodians of works in the public domain, museums have a vital interest in this policy debate. The U.S. Constitution does not provide an answer; it merely authorizes Congress to grant copyright for "limited Times." Congress need not grant copyright at all, but if it does, it must be limited in duration.

Over the years, Congress has used this authority five times, each time trying to balance the interests of authors, owners, and the public. Most recently, in October 1998, Congress adjusted the balance again, adding 20 years to the previous duration of copyright.[101] Current copyright duration rules discussed in this section are summarized in figure 1.

Works Created On or After January 1, 1978

Under the 1998 Term Extension Act, for works created on or after January 1, 1978, copyright protection begins with the creation of the work and lasts for the life of the author plus 70 years (previously 50 years).[102] A work is "created" when it is "fixed" in a tangible medium. In general, protection lasts until the end of the calendar year 70 years after the author's death.

Suppose that in 1980, the pop artist Hendricks sketched his whimsical *Subway Mickey* and five years later donated the original signed drawing along with its copyright to the Downtown Museum of Art. Hendricks died in December 1990 at the age of 42. *Subway Mickey* is an indi-

Figure 1: COPYRIGHT TERM

	PRE-1999	NEW
Subsisting (pre-1978) copyrights	28 years, + 47-year renewal term = 75 years	28 years, + 67-year renewal term = 95 years
Works created on or after January 1, 1978	Life of the author plus 50 years	Life of the author plus 70 years
Joint works	Same as above, measured from life of last surviving author	Same as above, measured from life of last surviving author
Anonymous and pseudonymous works and works made for hire	75 years from publication or 100 years from creation, whichever expires first	95 years from publication or 120 years from creation, whichever expires first
Works created but not published before 1978	Same as post-January 1978 works, but term expires no earlier than December 31, 2002 If work is published before December 31, 2002, term shall not expire until December 31, 2027	Same as post-January 1978 works, but term expires no earlier than December 31, 2002 (no change from previous law) If work is published before December 31, 2002, term shall not expire until December 31, 2047
Presumption as to author's death	After 75 years from publication or 100 years from creation, whichever expires first; the author is presumed to have been dead for 50 years if Copyright Office records do not indicate that the author is still living or died within the past 50 years	After 95 years from publication or 120 years from creation, whichever expires first; the author is presumed to have been dead for 70 years if Copyright Office records do not indicate that the author is still living or died within the past 70 years
Termination	Pre-1978 grants may be terminated during 5-year period commencing 56 years from date copyright was first secured	If previous termination right has already expired and was not exercised, copyright owner has a new termination right during 5-year period commencing 75 years from date copyright was first secured

Source: David Carson, General Counsel, U.S. Copyright Office

vidual work created after January 1, 1978, so the museum's copyright in the drawing will last until December 31, 2060 (70 years after the artist's death).

Copyrights in works of joint authorship (other than works made for hire) last until the end of the year of the 70th anniversary of the last surviving author's death.[103] Anonymous or pseudonymous works (if the name of the author is not revealed) and works made for hire are protected for 95 years (previously 75 years) from the date of first publication, or 120 years (previously 100 years) from the date of creation, whichever is shorter.[104] Nothing in the 1998 term extension law restores copyright protection for any work that fell into the public domain prior to October 27, 1998, the effective date of the legislation.

Continuing the example of *Subway Mickey*, the Downtown Museum exhibits the drawing in a 1995 Hendricks retrospective, for which the museum staff prepares an exhibition catalogue. The catalogue is a work made for hire created after January 1, 1978. The museum's copyright in the catalogue will expire on December 31, 2090 (95 years from first publication). However, if the museum does not publish the catalogue until after 2020 (or never publishes it), its copyright in the catalogue will expire on December 31, 2115 (120 years from creation).

Unpublished Works Created Before January 1, 1978

Museums are also the custodians of a vast body of unpublished works such as diaries, letters, and manuscripts, many of which date to the 18th or 19th century. Many museum professionals (and lawyers alike) are surprised to learn that these works also are still protected under federal copyright law.

For works created before January 1, 1978, but never published or registered as unpublished works with the Copyright Office before that date,

the same duration rules discussed above apply, with two important differences.[105] First, the earliest date that copyright can expire for works in this category is December 31, 2002 (if the work remains unpublished). Second, to encourage publication, the copyright term for such works is extended through December 31, 2047 (if the work is published before December 31, 2002).

To illustrate these rules, take the example of the Museum of American Heritage, which owns a collection and the copyright in the images of World War I vintage photographs taken by Thomas Vincent, a local war hero and amateur photographer who died in 1965. The Vincent photographs were never sold, exhibited, reproduced, or distributed to the public. They are unpublished works created before January 1, 1978. Copyright in the photographs in the Vincent collection will expire on December 31, 2035 (70 years after the photographer's death).

Suppose that the museum publishes the Vincent collection before December 31, 2002. In that case, copyright in the photographs will be extended through December 31, 2047. The museum has a choice. It can do nothing and enrich the public domain, or it can disseminate the works through publication and gain an extension in its copyright. For archives and museums, repositories of rich holdings of unpublished oral histories, genealogies, letters, and manuscripts, the Copyright Act's duration rules on unpublished materials present planning opportunities.

Works Created and Published Before January 1, 1978

The rules for determining copyright term for works created and published before January 1, 1978, are much different, and, regrettably, much more complex. Still, for many years to come, museums will need to be familiar with the old rules, which remain applicable to many works in museum collections. The general rule for works created under the 1909 Copyright Act was that copyright protection began on the actual date of publication (or the date of registration for unpublished works) and lasted for 28 years, subject to a renewal term of 28 years, for a total potential term of 56 years.

To apply these rules for works created or published before January 1, 1978, a museum should always bear in mind three fundamental differences between the old and current copyright laws. First, under the 1909 act, copyright term was measured from the publication or registration of the work and not from the creation of the work. Second, copyright lasted for a definite number of years rather than the indefinite period measured by the life of the author and a fixed number of years. Third, copyright term included a mandatory renewal feature. Failure to comply with any of the formalities of publication associated with notice or renewal could have harsh results, placing the work in the public domain.

Suppose that the acclaimed American photographer Alfred Steiner bequeathed to the American Maritime Museum his famous work, a photograph entitled *American Schooner*, along with his copyright in the work at the time of his death in 1959. A review of Steiner's will and other documents suggested that he owned the copyright in *American Schooner*. The museum then carefully examined the photograph, which included the familiar copyright symbol © and the initials "AS." The museum learned that under the 1909 act the initials or symbol of an artist or a photographer in conjunction with a proper copyright symbol satisfied the notice requirement at the time. Next the museum researched the publication history of *American Schooner* and learned that the photograph was published in *Scribners* magazine with proper copyright notice on September 5, 1925. The museum correctly concluded that the initial copyright term on *American Schooner* began on September 5, 1925, the actual date of publication with appropriate notice.

Renewal of Works Created and Published Before January 1, 1978

In theory, the renewal feature of the old copyright law was a mechanism to give authors and artists a chance to regain their copyrights after 28 years. In practice, renewal often operated as a trap for unwary copyright owners. To maintain copyright protection during the second, or renewal, term, the copyright owner had to file a renewal application with the Copyright Office during the 28th year of the initial term. Failure to comply in a timely manner with these strict requirements meant that the work fell into the public domain.

In the 1976 revision of the statute, Congress abolished the two-term system. However, it retained the renewal feature for works copyrighted before 1978 and still in their initial terms before January 1, 1978. If the owner complied in a timely manner with the renewal requirements, there were substantial benefits. The copyright owner could get a renewal term of 47 years (bringing to 75 years the total possible period of protection for renewed copyrights). But if the copyright owner was unaware of or failed to comply with the renewal requirements, copyright in the work would be lost forever.

In 1992, in part to prevent such forfeitures of copyright, Congress eliminated the mandatory renewal registration requirement, automatically extending the second term for works copyrighted between January 1, 1964, and December 31, 1977.[106] The renewal term for works in this category was automatically extended to 47 years.[107] In 1998, Congress added another 20 years of protection to works in the 47-year renewal term, bringing the total possible term of protection for works in their renewal term to 95 years from the date copyright protection was originally secured (either through publication or registration).[108] Let's see how these changes in the law would have affected the American Maritime Museum.

From a thorough search of Copyright Office records, the museum found out that an application for renewal of the copyright in *American Schooner* was filed before the end of 1953 (the 28th year after the term of statutory copyright protection began upon publication of the photograph in 1925). Under the 1909 Copyright Act's renewal provision, the museum correctly concluded, the photograph entered its second 28-year period of protection upon renewal, with copyright lasting through 1981. On January 1, 1978, the museum benefited from Congress's automatic extension (from 28 to 47 years) of works in their renewal term, bringing the period of protection to 2000. Finally, in 1998, the museum again benefited from Congress's decision to add another 20 years of protection to any work still in its renewal term. As a result, copyright in the Steiner photograph will expire on December 31, 2020, 95 years from the date copyright protection was originally secured.

In its 1992 renewal legislation, Congress provided a number of important incentives to encourage the voluntary filing of renewal applications. First, a renewal registration is a prerequisite to bringing an infringement action and obtaining monetary damages. Second, a certificate of renewal registration from the Copyright Office makes it easier to prove the validity of a renewed copyright in court. Third, by voluntarily filing a renewal application, any person who was granted the right to make a derivative work based on the original work during the first term of the copyright must obtain a new license to continue to use the work after the first term.

Suppose that the American Maritime Museum owns all copyright interests in *Boston Harbour*, a photograph by William Walden created in 1964. Shortly before its term of protection was about to expire in 1992, the museum decided to voluntarily file a renewal application in 1992 with the Copyright Office rather than simply relying on the automatic renewal provision. The following scenario illustrates the benefit to the museum of the voluntary filing.

Sometime later, the American Maritime Museum discovered that the Old Mariner's Home, a charitable organization, was using *Boston Harbour* on the cover of its engagement calendar, which it gave away as a premium in its annual fund-raising drive. The museum wrote to the director of the Mariner's Home informing him that the museum owned the copyright in the photograph and that its use on the calendar may be infringing the museum's reproduction and distribution rights. The director wrote back, enclosing a copy of a license dated 1970 and signed by the photographer granting permission to the Mariner's Home to use the image for charitable purposes. Who is right? Prior to 1992, the Mariner's Home, as a licensee during the first term of the work's protection, would have been permitted to continue to distribute the calendar without obtaining the permission of the American Maritime Museum, the subsequent owner of the renewal term. However, since the museum took advantage of the incentives of the 1992 renewal law by voluntarily filing a renewal application, the museum may require a new license for the continued use of *Boston Harbour*. The museum did just that but waived any licensing fees on a year-to-year basis in light of the charitable nature of the use, thus retaining its rightful control over the use of the work.

The Public Domain

Copyright term marks the boundary between individual property rights and the public's ultimate benefit. To put the matter another way, copyright term is the dividing line between the author's limited monopoly grant and the public's welfare. The interests of museums fall on both sides of that line. As owners and producers of protected works, museums generally favor longer periods of protection. As users and custodians of public domain materials, museums prefer shorter periods of protection to enrich the public domain.

Although it is not possible to resolve the inherent tensions in copyright law, museums should be aware of the competing visions of the public domain. In their book *The Nature of Copyright*, Ray Patterson and Stanley Lindberg give this lyrical account of the public domain: "The public domain is not a territory, but a concept: there are certain materials—the air we breathe, sunlight, rain, ideas, words, numbers—not subject to private ownership. The materials that compose our cultural heritage must be free for all to use no less than matter necessary for biological survival."[109] For other copyright theorists, there is no such metaphorical territory. Instead, the public domain is simply what's left over when copyright expires (as a rule of thumb, works published or unregistered in unpublished form more than 75 years ago) or lapses (for example, because of the failure of the author or owner to comply with such copyright formalities as publication with notice or filing a renewal application). In addition, the public domain consists of works initially excluded from copyright protection for public policy reasons, such as federal government works,[110] and facts, ideas, and processes.[111] Figure 2 summarizes the principal reasons a work enters the public domain.

Consider another example involving the Cosmopolitan Museum of Art. In 1955, the museum acquired an important drawing by the Italian modernist artist Monte Mantissa, *Carnival Figures*, but did not acquire copyright in the work. The drawing, which was signed by the artist and dated 1935, contained no notice of U.S. copyright. A thorough search of Copyright Office records turned up no registration or transfer records. Moreover, the Cosmopolitan uncovered a copy of the April 20, 1935, issue of *American Art World* in which *Carnival Figures* appeared prominently without copyright notice. In 1992, the Cosmopolitan wanted to use *Carnival Figures* in an exhibition, *Mantissa's Figures*, and an accompanying catalogue and a poster. To be on the safe side, the museum consulted its attorney, who con-

firmed that *Carnival Figures* entered the public domain in the United States on April 20, 1935, when it was published without copyright notice (which was required by the 1909 act) and, therefore, could be used without fee or permission. Two years later, the attorney's advice may have been quite different.

Copyright Restoration

In 1994, Congress enacted the Uruguay Round Agreements Act (URAA), which implemented the General Agreement on Tariffs and Trade (GATT) and the World Trade Organization (WTO) Agreement, international trade treaties signed by the United States that for the first time covered certain intellectual property matters. Under the URAA, copyright was restored in certain foreign works that had previously entered the public domain in the United States for failure to comply with certain formalities under U.S. copyright law.

The new law had a significant potential impact on museums. For example, on August 30, 1996, the U.S. Copyright Office published in the *Federal Register* a notice of intent to enforce (NIE) restored copyrights in more than 200 works by Pablo Picasso. The NIE further provided that the owner of a restored copyright may immediately enforce the copyright against individuals who infringe his or her rights after the date of restoration, although enforcement was delayed against "reliance parties." (A reliance party is a person who in good faith used a now-restored work before January 1, 1996, and continued to do so after that date.) But such notices were only the tip of the iceberg. The vast majority of restored foreign works required no notice at all; restoration was automatic upon enactment of the URAA. With little or no warning, a substantial number of such foreign works— many previously used by museums in good-faith reliance on their public domain status—were again protected by copyright.

Figure 2: WHEN WORKS PASS INTO PUBLIC DOMAIN
Includes material from new Term Extension Act, PL 105-298

DATE OF WORK	PROTECTED FROM	TERM
Created January 1, 1978, or after	When work is fixed in tangible medium of expression	Life + 70 years[1] (or if work of corporate authorship, the shorter of 95 years from publication, or 120 years from creation[2]
Published before 1923	In public domain	None
Published from 1923 to 1963	When published with notice[3]	28 years; could be renewed for 47 years; now extended by 20 years for a total renewal of 67 years
Published from 1964 to 1977	When published without notice	28 years for first term; now automatic extension of 67 years for second term
Created before January 1, 1978, but not published	January 1, 1978, the effective date of the 1976 act, which eliminated common-law copyright	Life + 70 years or December 31, 2002, whichever is greater
Created before January 1, 1978, but published between then and December 31, 2002	January 1, 1978, the effective date of the 1976 act, which eliminated common-law copyright	Life + 70 years or December 31, 2047, whichever is greater

1. Term of joint works is measured by life of the longest-lived author.

2. Works for hire, anonymous and pseudonymous works also have this term. 17 U.S.C. § 302(c).

3. Under the 1909 act, works published without notice went into the public domain upon publication. Works published without notice between January 1, 1978, and March 1, 1989, effective date of the Berne Convention Implementation Act, retained copyright only if, e.g., registration was made within five years. 17 U.S.C. § 405.

Notes courtesy of Professor Tom Field, Franklin Pierce Law Center.

Source: Laura N. Gasaway, director of the law library and professor of law, University of North Carolina-Chapel Hill. Periodic updates are available at www.unc.edu/~unclng/public-d.htm

For most American museums, the very notion of copyright restoration was deeply unsettling. "Recapturing" works from the public domain seemed to be at odds with everything American museums knew about copyright law. Could there really be copyright life after death? Was it true that the new law treated foreign artists more favorably than American artists? Could museums be liable for selling publications containing images now under newly restored copyrights? Such questions, unimaginable a few short years ago, became commonplace as museums adjusted to the new world of copyright restoration. The URAA copyright restoration rules are quite complex, usually requiring a museum to consult with an attorney. Still, museums should be familiar with the basic framework governing the eligibility of foreign works for copyright restoration in the United States and the rights and remedies for infringement of restored copyrights, including the special rules for reliance parties.

To decide whether a foreign work is eligible for copyright restoration in the United States, it is first necessary to determine the source country of the foreign work. The source country is the place where the work was first published or, if unpublished, the country in which the author is a national or permanent resident. To qualify for restoration, the work must originate in an eligible source country, that is, a country (other than the United States) that is a member of the Berne Convention or the WTO, treaties discussed in greater detail in chapter 5. This definition makes it clear that American works are not eligible for copyright restoration. Moreover, given the large number of nations that are members of either the Berne Convention or the WTO, works published in the last 70 years almost anywhere in the world may now qualify for copyright restoration in the United States.

Continuing the example of the Cosmopolitan Museum of Art, the museum will pursue the following steps: (1) Determine whether the work

originated in an eligible source country. (2) Determine the copyright status of the work under foreign law. (3) Determine the period of protection for the restored work. (4) Determine the identity and rights of the owners of the restored copyright. (5) Determine whether the museum qualifies as a reliance party. At the end of the analysis, the Cosmopolitan will learn that the restored copyright will last until December 31, 2030, and that the museum probably qualifies as a reliance party because it in good faith used a now-restored work before January 1, 1996, and continued to do so after that date.

Based on careful art historical research, the museum first learned that Monte Mantissa was a permanent resident of France in 1935 when he drew *Carnival Figures*. Because France was a member of the Berne Convention in 1935, *Carnival Figures* originated in an eligible source country. The next step is to determine the copyright status of the foreign work. To qualify for restoration in the United States, the foreign work must still be under copyright in its source country and in the public domain in the United States for one of three reasons: (1) failure to comply with formalities (such as notice or renewal requirements) imposed at any time by U.S. copyright law; (2) a lack of national eligibility (for works originating in a country with which the United States did not have copyright relations); or (3) a lack of subject matter jurisdiction (for example, for pre-1972 sound recordings that were not protected by the United States). In addition, at least one author of the foreign work must have been a national or permanent resident of an eligible country at the time that the work was created. Finally, if published, the work must have been published in an eligible country and must not have been published in the United States within 30 days of that publication.

Working with counsel, the Cosmopolitan found out that *Carnival Figures* was still under copyright in France, although it fell into the public domain in the United States when it was published without copyright notice in the April 20, 1935, edition of *American Art World*. Mantissa also was a permanent resident of France, an eligible source country, at the time that *Carnival Figures* was created. Finally, although *Carnival Figures* also was published in, *Arts Français*, the publication did not occur within 30 days of the U.S. publication.

The third step is to determine the period of protection for restored copyrights. When does such copyright protection begin? For qualifying foreign works, copyright restoration is automatic, with protection beginning on January 1, 1996, the effective date of the URAA. How long does such copyright protection last? Once restored, copyright protection runs for the remainder of the term that the work would have otherwise enjoyed had it never entered the public domain in the United States. Thus, the general duration rules discussed above apply with equal force to restored copyrights in foreign works.

If *Carnival Figures* had been published in *American Art World* with proper notice in 1935 and renewed before the end of 1963, Mantissa would have been entitled to a term lasting through December 31, 1991. Although in 1978 Congress automatically extended the duration of works in their renewal terms from 28 years to 47 years, Mantissa did not benefit from this extension because *Carnival Figures* had already fallen into the U.S. public domain. However, as of January 1, 1996, under the URAA, Mantissa's estate could recapture the lost copyright in *Carnival Figures*, with the remaining term treated as if it had been published with proper notice and renewed. Thus, as of January 1, 1978, the restored copyright of *Carnival Figures* would expire on December 31, 2010 (75 years after U.S. copyright in *Carnival Figures* would have come into existence). There is one more twist. As of October 27, 1998, Congress added another 20 years of protection to works in their renewal terms. Thus, as a result of copyright

restoration and term extension legislation, the restored copyright in *Carnival Figures* will last until December 31, 2030.

The next step is to determine the identity and rights of owners of restored copyrights. The general rule is that the restored copyright belongs to the author or the initial rights holder of the work as determined by the law of the source country of the work. With one exception, described below, the owner of a restored copyright has the same enforcement rights and remedies that are available to any other copyright owner. The owner of a restored copyright may sue for infringements occurring after January 1, 1998, and, if successful, may obtain damages and injunctions.

Again working through counsel, the Cosmopolitan learned that upon the artist's death all of the copyright interests were transferred to the Monte Mantissa estate. On January 1, 1996, the restored copyright in *Carnival Figures* automatically vested in the estate. Thus, in most cases, the estate would be entitled to begin immediately to enforce the restored copyright against infringing uses of *Carnival Figures*.

The important exception to the foregoing relates to reliance parties, persons who in good faith used a now-restored work before January 1, 1996, and continue to do so after that date. In the usual case, a reliance party is a person who was already using the work before December 8, 1994, the date URAA was enacted. Special enforcement rules apply with reliance parties. To enforce a restored copyright against a reliance party, the owner of the restored copyright was required to file a notice of intent to enforce with the U.S. Copyright Office between January 1, 1996, and December 31, 1997, or directly serve the particular reliance party anytime after January 1, 1996. Museums should check the series of NIE lists, which the Copyright Office published in the *Federal Register* every four months for two years beginning in May 1996. These NIE lists are also posted on the Copyright Office's Web site.[112]

Unlike notices served on particular reliance parties, which are effective only against the party served or persons with actual knowledge of the notice, the Copyright Office NIE publications are effective against all reliance parties. Whether the notice is filed or received, a reliance party is only responsible for infringing acts commenced more than one year after the notice was published in the *Federal Register* or received by the reliance party. During this one-year grace period, a reliance party may distribute, publicly perform, or publicly display previously made copies of a newly restored work but may not reproduce or make derivative works based on the restored work. In reviewing the NIE lists, museums should take care to check listings under both the artist's (or estate's) name and the names of agents for the artist or the estate, including artists' collective rights organizations such as the Artists Rights Society (ARS) and the Visual Artists and Galleries Association (VAGA).

The Cosmopolitan Museum of Art probably qualifies as a reliance party because it was using *Carnival Figures* in its exhibition catalogue before the enactment of the URAA, in good-faith reliance on the public domain status of the work, and continues to do so after that date. Even if the Cosmopolitan's use of the restored work is not fair use, as a reliance party, the museum would be permitted to continue to sell existing copies of the Mantissa exhibition catalogue for a one-year grace period. However, during this period, the Cosmopolitan would be prohibited from using *Carnival Figures* to create new compilations or derivative works without permission. Further, unless the Cosmopolitan and the Mantissa estate reach an agreement permitting continued use of the restored copyright in the exhibition catalogue, the museum must discontinue all unauthorized uses of the work at the end of the grace period.

There are also detailed rules for derivative works created by a reliance party based on an underlying foreign work in which copyright has been restored. For such existing derivative works created before December 8, 1994, the law permits the reliance party to continue to exploit the work, not just for the one-year grace period, but for the duration of the restored copyright, if the user pays "reasonable compensation" to the owner of the restored copyright.

Under the special rule for restored copyrights in existing derivative works, the Cosmopolitan would be permitted to continue selling its *Carnival Figures* catalogue if it can agree on reasonable compensation with the Mantissa estate. Artists and their estates regularly grant royalty-free licenses to museums, but if the parties cannot agree on compensation, the matter may have to be resolved in an action in federal district court or before a mediator.

Ownership

Who owns the copyright? This question should come up every time a museum accepts a gift, purchases an object for the collections, hires a designer or photographer, produces a multimedia program, or engages in countless other routine activities. Everyone who works in a museum should be familiar with basic copyright ownership rules. Unfamiliarity increases the risk that the museum's intellectual property rights will not be adequately protected. Perhaps worse yet, the museum may be placed at legal risk of infringing the rights of others.

Untangling even the most complex copyright ownership problem should begin with one simple proposition: copyright initially belongs to the creator or author, the person who conceives the work and fixes it in a tangible medium.[113] From the moment of fixation, it is the novelist, playwright, composer, painter, or photographer who owns the copyright. But what if two authors decide to collaborate on a work or agree to merge their creative efforts? Consider the case of Gilbert and Sullivan.

John Gilbert, an artist living in New York City, and Laura Sullivan, a writer living in San Francisco, have decided to create a home page on a Web site for contemporary artists. Gilbert will contribute the graphics and Sullivan the text. But who owns the copyright? What are the rights of each party? Under copyright's joint authorship rules, Gilbert and Sullivan are the coauthors of a joint work, which means "a work prepared by two or more authors with the intention that their contributions be merged into inseparable or interdependent parts of a unitary whole."[114] As joint authors, both Gilbert and Sullivan own an undivided share in the copyrighted work.[115] The home page qualifies as joint work. Either joint author is free to exercise any of the exclusive rights of copyright even without consulting the other party.[116] However, neither Gilbert nor Sullivan may grant an exclusive license without the consent of the other or do anything that destroys the value of their joint work. Gilbert and Sullivan also must share equally any royalties resulting from the use of their joint work.

In a museum, creative activity is more likely to occur through the efforts of employees working together or with contractors. How do copyright ownership rules apply under such circumstances? For example, who owns the copyright in an exhibit script prepared by the museum staff or in a scholarly essay written by an outside expert for a museum publication? The key to these questions is the work made for hire doctrine, an important exception to the general principle that the creator of a work is its author and initial copyright owner. The general rule is that copyright in a work made for hire belongs to the employer or to the person for whom the work was prepared, unless the parties have agreed otherwise in writing.

Consider the example of Harry Crawford, a curator of anthropology at the Seaside Aquatic Center, who hired Sally Lens, a freelance photographer, to take photographs of the center's newly installed exhibition *Sea Life of the World*. They did not bother to discuss who would own the copyright in the photographs of the new installation. Under the Copyright Act's ownership rules, initial ownership of the copyright in the photographs belongs to Lens as the author of the photographs because the parties did not agree otherwise in writing.

Under U.S. copyright law, there are two kinds of works made for hire: works "prepared by an employee within the scope of his or her employment" and certain types of works that are "specially ordered or commissioned" works.[117] The employer may be an individual, a commercial firm, or a nonprofit organization like a museum. Work made for hire status affects not only the initial ownership of copyright but also its duration. Unlike works created by individual authors, copyright protection for works made for hire lasts 95 years from the date of publication or 120 years from creation, whichever comes first. For obvious reasons, decisions that bear on work made for hire status should be approached with care.[118]

Identifying museum employees would not appear to be a difficult task. Museums employ directors, curators, conservators, computer programmers, exhibition designers, educators, security guards, and administrative assistants. While the employment status of these people may seem clear enough, it sometimes is difficult under copyright law to distinguish between museum employees and persons who simply provide services to the museum under contract, commonly called "independent contractors."

In determining whether an individual is a museum employee or an independent contractor, a court will closely analyze the relationship between the parties, including: the museum's right to control the manner and means of creating the work; the skill required; the provision of employee benefits; the tax treatment of the person; and whether the museum has the right to assign additional projects.[119] Other factors that a court might consider are whether the museum supplies the tools, the location of the work, the length of the relationship between the museum and the individual, the extent of the museum's discretion over the person's hours, and the payment method.[120]

Suppose that the registrar of the Running Brook Museum of Natural History hired James Anderson, a skilled computer programmer, to create a file retrieval program as part of its collections management system. The museum compensated Anderson handsomely and exercised general control over the project. However, consistent with museum policy for such projects, Anderson received no benefits (such as health insurance or paid vacations), and the museum did not withhold any payroll taxes. Anderson generally worked at home on his own computer. The museum was surprised to see Anderson's notice of copyright on the final product. Who owns the copyright in the computer program? On these facts, especially the treatment of benefits, payroll taxes, and place of performance of activities, a court probably would conclude that Anderson is an independent contractor. Under copyright's ownership rules, Anderson, not the museum, owns the copyright in the computer program. The museum might also have avoided some of its difficulties if it had specified in a written agreement with Anderson that the museum would own the copyright in the computer program, and Anderson would assign to the museum any rights he may have in the program.

Suppose that instead of hiring a computer programmer, the Running Brook Museum of Natural History assigned the project to a regular museum employee. Who owns the copyright? The general rule is that the employer owns the copyright in any work created by an employee working within the scope of employment. However, it is sometimes difficult to determine when a work is prepared within the scope of employment. It may even be necessary to evaluate the employee's

duties and responsibilities, the nature of the work, and whether museum resources and time were used in the preparation of the work.

Consider the case of the Einstein Science Center, which hired Lucy Smith as a security guard. During her lunch hour, Smith used equipment in the center's media lab to record an advertising jingle that she had composed over the weekend. The jingle turned out to be a big commercial hit. Is the museum entitled to any royalties? Probably not. Although Smith used museum equipment during the workday, composing advertising jingles generally is not considered part of a museum security guard's job. The advertising jingle, therefore, is not a work made for hire. As the author of the jingle, Smith, not the museum, is entitled to exploit the work.

To avoid scope-of-employment issues, the museum and a prospective employee may want to consider reaching an agreement in advance of employment, specifying in writing what types of works fall within and outside a particular job. This approach may be particularly useful for highly skilled museum workers who maintain an active professional life inside and outside the museum. Here is how the Mountaintop Museum of Art handled one such matter. Three years ago, the museum hired Antonio Bartoni, the world's leading authority on the conservation of Roman antiquities, to head its conservation laboratory. During his work at the museum, Bartoni prepared meticulous laboratory notebooks on the antiquities collection. Recently, he has been offered the opportunity to teach at the Wellington Institute in London, and he has expressed an interest in taking the laboratory notebooks with him. Who owns the copyright in the notebooks? While the Mountaintop Museum of Art probably owns the copyright in the notebooks (as works made for hire), the museum might have avoided any confusion over the matter by specifying in its employment agreement with Bartoni that preparing scientific reports and laboratory notebooks on the collections was within the scope of his employment, but that scholarly papers based on his laboratory experiments would be his own work product.

The Copyright Act provides for a special category of works made for hire, so-called "specially ordered or commissioned" works.[121] Such a work must fall into one of nine categories: a contribution to a collective work; part of a motion picture or other audiovisual work; a translation; a supplementary work; a compilation; an instructional text; a test; answer material for a test; or an atlas.[122] Assuming that the work fits one of these categories, the copyright law sets forth a simple ownership rule. If the museum (as hiring party) and the independent contractor expressly agree in writing signed by them to designate the work as a work made for hire, *and* if the work falls into one of the nine categories, the copyright belongs to the hiring party. If there is no written and signed agreement designating the work a work made for hire, the copyright belongs to the independent contractor.

The Gateway Museum of Science and Industry, for example, hired Digital Video Productions (DVP) to produce a computer animation film entitled *Tornado* in the Omnimax format for viewing in the museum's theater. The production agreement expressly provided that the software and animation sequences for the film were works made for hire. Because these works fall into one of the nine statutory categories (parts of an audiovisual work), and because the parties expressly agreed that they would be works made for hire, the Gateway Museum owns the copyright in the software and animation sequences in *Tornado*. DVP may not use these works in projects for other clients without first obtaining the museum's permission.

The creative efforts of museum employees, often working with outside scholars or experts, may result in a collective work that is eligible for a separate copyright. A collective work is a collection of independent, separately protectable works such as a periodical issue, an anthology, or an encyclopedia assembled into a collective whole.[123] The general ownership rule for collective works is that, in the absence of an express assignment of copyright, the author of each individual work retains copyright in that work. The compiler of the collective work owns the copyright in the creative "value added" to the work— typically the selection, coordination, and arrangement of the individual contributions plus a preface. What are a museum's ownership rights when it acts as an author of a collective work?

To illustrate these rules, consider the recent experience of the Museum of American Heritage, which published an exhibition catalogue, *Old Glory*, containing 200 historic images of the American flag. Robert Paterson, a professor at a local college, contributed the introductory essay on the history of the flag. The images were selected, arranged, and annotated by Malcolm Curtis, the museum's curator of political history. Who owns the copyright? The museum owns the copyright in the collective work, extending to its selection and arrangement of the individual contributions and to any separately copyrightable contributions by Curtis (as a work made for hire). Paterson owns the copyright in the introductory essay (unless, for example, the museum specially commissioned the essay as a contribution to a collective work). In the absence of a writing to the contrary, the museum is presumed to have acquired the privilege to publish Paterson's essay in this particular work. Thus, unless the museum receives authorization, it would not be permitted to reproduce Paterson's essay in its magazine. However, the museum would not need permission to reproduce Paterson's essay in a later revision of the catalogue.

Transfers of Copyright

Like tangible property such as a home or a wristwatch, copyrights (a type of intangible property) may be sold, left to heirs, or donated to a museum. Just as a landowner may freely divide a lot and sell portions to various persons, a copyright owner may divide, subdivide, and sell any of the exclusive rights of copyright.[124] But copyright's ownership transfer rules also differ in important respects from the rules that govern the world of tangible property. On a handshake, you can sell your wristwatch to your neighbor, but selling a copyright generally requires a written document. The prospective buyer of your watch probably will take it on faith that you own it, but the future copyright owner can check the records of the Copyright Office to see if any earlier copyright transfers have been recorded. Most people would be reluctant to buy a house if they thought the former owner could revoke the transaction 35 years later. Yet many people are surprised to learn that copyrighted works are routinely exchanged subject to such a "termination right" (see "Termination of Copyright Transfers").[125]

The Columbus School of Art Gallery, for example, owns the Joseph Hammond graphic art collection, original drawings by one of its most distinguished alumni and one of America's most famous illustrators. Many of the drawings have never been published, but others have appeared on the cover of *Tempus* magazine. Recently, attorneys for *Tempus* wrote to the museum claiming that the gallery's forthcoming merchandise line of the Hammond drawings would infringe the magazine's copyrights in the drawings, which it claims are works made for hire created when Hammond worked as an illustrator for the magazine. The gallery thought it had acquired copyrights in the Hammond drawings when the artist dropped them off at the museum years ago. Which view is correct?

Unfortunately, the gallery is mistaken about an important principle of copyright law. Under the 1976 Copyright Act, copyright ownership and ownership of the material object in which the object is embodied are entirely separate things.[126] The law goes on to say that the "[t]ransfer of ownership of any material object . . . does not of itself convey any rights in the copyrighted work embodied in the object" absent an agreement.[127] Thus, when the gallery took physical possession of the Hammond collection in 1965, it acquired nothing more than the material objects embodying the artist's work.

This does not mean that the gallery should simply take the *Tempus* lawyers' word for it. Before 1978, the copyright ownership transfer rules were quite different. Under state common law, authors and artists enjoyed a perpetual copyright in their unpublished works. However, it was generally understood that when an author or artist transferred an unpublished manuscript or work of art, the transfer was presumed to include the right of first publication. This common-law doctrine is often referred to as the "*Pushman* presumption," named after a New York case. However, for the presumption to work, the transfer had to be unconditional and without any mention by the artist or author of copyright (or any copyright notice on the work). Under such circumstances, the transfer of common-law copyright was presumed to be "automatic," unless the artist or author specifically reserved those rights. Any transfer of federal copyright, however, required a written document. In New York and California, at least for works of fine art, the *Pushman* presumption was reversed by statute in 1966 and 1976, respectively. The 1976 federal copyright law eliminated the common-law doctrine nationwide.

The Columbus School of Art Gallery might have an argument under the *Pushman* presumption that it at least owns the copyrights in the unpublished Hammond drawings. Of course, the gallery will need to prove that it meets all the requirements of the presumption and persuade a court to apply the old legal doctrine—not easy tasks. At the same time, on these facts, it looks like the gallery may not own the copyright in the published Hammond drawings. That is not to say that *Tempus* owns the copyright. The magazine will need to establish that it meets all the requirements of the applicable work made for hire rules or demonstrate that the copyright was transferred by written agreement. The magazine may find itself in a separate battle with the Hammond estate. There is a final possibility. Some of the Hammond drawings may have entered the public domain for reasons discussed earlier. Until all these legal issues are sorted out, the gallery's best course of action is to continue to serve as a good custodian for the collection and, of course, to make appropriate uses under the fair use doctrine (discussed in detail in "Fair Use and Other Limitations," later in this chapter).

After 1978, the rules for transferring copyright ownership became more transparent. The copyright owner may transfer ownership of any or all of the exclusive rights of copyright, in whole or in part, using a wide range of legal vehicles.[128] The transfer may be accomplished, for example, through an assignment, exclusive license, sale, gift, or bequest. The transfer of an ownership interest in copyright is sometimes called a "copyright grant." If the transfer is by assignment, the copyright owner transferring ownership is called an "assignor" and the party receiving the copyright grant is called an "assignee." As discussed more fully later in this chapter, documents transferring ownership in copyrights may be recorded in the Copyright Office (see "Recordation of Transfers"). The new owner of a copyright interest is entitled to all the protection and remedies of the original owner, including the right to bring a copyright infringement action.[129]

Formal Requirements

Documents that transfer an ownership interest in copyright must be in writing and signed by the person making or authorized to make the transfer.[130] By contrast, a nonexclusive license does not transfer an ownership interest in copyright; it merely grants the copyright owner's permission for another to use one or more of the exclusive rights under the terms and conditions of the license. Licenses often contain express limitations (such as time period and geographic restrictions). The copyright owner granting such permission is known as the "licensor," and the party receiving permission is known as the "licensee." Under a nonexclusive license, the copyright owner retains ownership and is free to permit others to use the same rights. Although nonexclusive licenses need not be in writing, the best practice is to always require a written document. Exclusive licenses must always be in writing.

In connection with its *American Photographic Millennium* exhibition, for example, the Western Museum of Photography granted the Eastern Publishing Company the exclusive right to publish the exhibition catalogue in North America during a five-year period. Can the Western Museum of Photography grant the Southern Publishing Company exclusive right to create and distribute a poster based on an image from the catalogue? Yes. The Western Museum only granted Eastern Publishing the exclusive right to reproduce and distribute the catalogue (a collective work) subject to the terms and conditions of the license. All other rights were reserved to the museum.

Recordation of Transfers

The documents transferring a copyright interest (whether by assignment, contract, exclusive or nonexclusive license, or any other legal vehicle) may be recorded in the Copyright Office, which will issue a certificate of recordation.[131] If the documents clearly identify the work, the Copyright Office recordation puts the world at large on notice of the facts of the transfer (even if no one ever reads the certificate). The principal advantage to recording a copyright transfer is to establish priority of ownership, which may be useful in resolving later conflicting transfers. This advantage applies only for works that are also registered with the Copyright Office. Priority decisions for unregistered works are made by the courts.

The case of James Swift provides an illustration. Shortly after Swift assigned copyright in his painting *Fool's Gold* to the Cosmopolitan Museum of Art, he sold the same rights to Denaro Duplicates, Inc. Who owns the rights? Under copyright's priority rules, the Cosmopolitan will prevail over Denaro Duplicates if the museum records the transfer during the one-month grace period following the transfer (two months for transfers made outside the country). After the grace period, it becomes a race to the Copyright Office, giving priority to the first to record. However, there are two circumstances under which Denaro Duplicates would not be able to establish priority (no matter when it filed with the Copyright Office): if it paid nothing for its rights in *Fool's Gold* (for example, if received as a gift or bequest) or if it knew of the prior transfer to the Cosmopolitan. Somewhat different priority rules would apply if Swift had granted a nonexclusive license to Denaro Duplicates.

Termination of Copyright Transfers

The copyright law includes an unusual rule (at least for property law) that may often be overlooked by museums. Under copyright's property transfer rules, an artist or author (or the creator's widow, children, or grandchildren) may "terminate" or revoke a grant of copyright during the five years following the expiration of a period of 35 years from the date of the original grant.[132] There is a special rule for terminating grants of the publication right. In such cases, the five-year window to terminate begins at the end of 35 years from the date of publication or 40 years

from the date of the grant, whichever comes first. There are also detailed rules for the termination of joint works and works owned by the author's heirs. In all cases, strict compliance is required.

To illustrate these rules, consider the case of the New Arts Gallery, which acquired the whimsical soft sculpture *Man and 12 Piglets*—as well as the copyright in the work, in a written agreement—from Jimmy Hearts' studio on January 2, 1978, for $100. Hearts was thrilled, because this was the first of his works to be included in a museum collection. At the time of the transaction, the purchase price was the last thing that he was thinking about. Even if he had been thinking about price, Hearts had no way of determining the work's commercial value since there was no market for his works at the time. Just a decade later, things were quite different. Early Hearts works were selling for tens of thousands of dollars at auction. Hearts began to look at the New Arts Gallery deal in a different light. After consulting with his attorney, he learned that he could "terminate" or revoke his transfer of copyright to the museum. Indeed, he found out that he could terminate transfers or licenses (whether exclusive or nonexclusive) of any copyright interests that he had made on or after January 1, 1978, except for works made for hire or works left in his will. Armed with this knowledge, two years before his death in 1990, Hearts wrote a letter to his wife in which he gave her his termination right in *Man and 12 Piglets*.

The New Arts Gallery must take this letter seriously, because all that Mrs. Hearts needs to do to revoke her late husband's transfer of copyright is to give the museum written advance notice stating the effective date of termination. The termination date may be any time during the 36th through the 40th year from the date of the original transfer. However, the museum must be given notice within the appropriate five-year window. Also, the museum must be notified at least two years but no more than ten years before the termination date.

Mrs. Hearts also will need to record the termination date with the Copyright Office. Conversely, the museum is not required to warn Mrs. Hearts about the expiration of the termination right. If she fails to timely exercise her right, it is lost.

If Mrs. Hearts does exercise her right in a timely manner, what happens next? On the date that she serves notice on the museum, she would become entitled to use the copyright interests that her late husband earlier transferred to the museum. In effect, she gets a second chance to license or assign the rights in *Man and 12 Piglets* and, of course, to be compensated accordingly. This special "copyright recapture" rule generally applies only to works that her husband or his agent personally transferred after January 1, 1978. There is nothing the museum could have done at the time of the original transfer of copyright to avoid later termination. By law, the artist could not have "contracted away" his termination right. However, Hearts and the museum could have agreed to an earlier termination date. Absent such an agreement, the appropriate statutory period will govern the exercise of termination rights.

The museum may continue selling its popular *Piglets* T-shirt, however. Mrs. Hearts' termination right in *Man and 12 Piglets* is subject to an important limitation. The museum may continue to use derivative works based on the sculpture (such as the T-shirt), subject to the conditions of the terminated grant. In this way, the "derivative works exception" to the author's termination right protects museums that have invested in the creation of derivative works. However, the museum's privilege is not absolute. It would not extend to other works by Hearts in the collections. Nor would the museum be permitted to prepare other derivative works based on *Man and 12 Piglets*. In other words, the museum must obtain Mrs. Hearts' consent before expanding its merchandise line to include *Piglets* tote bags and cocktail napkins. The public interest argument can be stretched just so far.

Infringement

The good news about copyright infringement is that there have not been many cases involving museums. But as the exclusive rights of copyright continue to grow in importance, museums may find themselves increasingly entangled in lawsuits, either as a plaintiff or as a defendant. In such an environment, museums must be aware of the basic framework under which copyright interests are enforced and defended.

Bringing an Infringement Claim

U.S. copyright law includes this sobering statement: "Anyone who violates any of the exclusive rights of the copyright owner . . . is an infringer of the copyright or right of the author, as the case may be."[133] What constitutes an infringement? Is all copying of a protected work an infringement? What are the defenses? Does it make a difference if the copying is inadvertent? What remedies are available? Can a museum be liable for the infringing actions of others? What follows is a brief introduction to copyright enforcement.

Consider the example of the American Zoological Gardens (AZG). In 1993, AZG introduced a line of popular soft sculpture products, Zoo Babies, produced under an exclusive license with the ABC Company. The Zoo Babies line includes Tommy the Tortoise, Freddie the Frog, and Gerty the Giraffe, each registered with the U.S. Copyright Office. Zoo Babies are sold with a birth certificate and educational brochure and are available for purchase for $5 at the AZG shop and through catalogue sales (print and online). Zoo Babies became an overnight craze, earning AZG significant revenues. Small wonder that AZG became alarmed when, about a year later, Kozy Kritters, Inc., a leading manufacturer of stuffed animals, introduced a nearly identical line of merchandise, Bean Bag Babies, at the National Toy Show in Chicago. AZG is beginning to consider its legal options.

Preliminary Considerations

At the outset, AZG will need to evaluate several preliminary matters. While the zoo would like quick relief, it has three years from the time of infringement to file its lawsuit in federal district court. Each work that AZG alleges to be infringed must be registered with the U.S. Copyright Office before an infringement action can commence.[134] Registration is mandatory in this case because AZG's copyrighted works are of U.S. origin. However, to recover statutory damages and attorney's fees, registration for all works, regardless of origin, must be made within three months of publication, or for unpublished works, registration must occur before the date of infringement.[135]

In the real world of copyright infringement litigation, the likelihood of collecting monetary damages and attorney's fees may be a key consideration in deciding whether to go forward with the lawsuit. Here, by promptly registering its products, AZG has preserved its legal options. As owner of all the exclusive rights in the Zoo Babies line, AZG is entitled to bring the infringement action. However, the right to sue also would extend to the ABC Company, AZG's exclusive licensee. AZG should review its licensing agreement with the ABC Company, which may address in greater detail the rights of the parties to bring a claim, a subject discussed more fully in chapter 4.

Early in the litigation process, AZG should develop a legal strategy that keeps its long-term interests in focus. The possible infringing conduct of Kozy Kritters may already have caused economic injury to the zoo and places at risk a continuing potential source of revenue. However, AZG must carefully evaluate the economic harm against the high costs of obtaining relief through copyright infringement litigation. Those costs include not only legal fees but also staff time and lost opportunities for the zoo. Viewed in this light, copyright litigation is probably best seen as a powerful sword, all the more potent when left sheathed.

AZG clearly will obtain no relief unless it demands it. An initial demand for relief usually takes the form of a cease and desist letter. Although there is no standard format for such letters, there are a number of common elements. First, the letter must clearly identify the allegedly infringed protected works, noting publication and copyright registration information. Second, the letter must clearly identify the alleged infringing use of the work. If permission was not requested, or requested and denied, the fact should be noted. Third, the letter should demand the end of all infringing conduct and the delivery or destruction of all infringing copies within a specified period. Fourth, the letter should make it clear that the copyright owner is prepared to take further action and will assert all applicable remedies under the Copyright Act.

Cease and desist letters are effective tools because they are backed up by remedies under the Copyright Act. Of these, injunctions—court orders prohibiting further infringements—are perhaps most important. The Copyright Act provides that a court may "grant temporary and final injunctions on such terms as it may deem reasonable to prevent or restrain infringement of a copyright."[136] Generally, for a court to issue an injunction, the plaintiff must establish that (1) it is likely to succeed on the merits of the claim, (2) it has no adequate legal remedy, and (3) it will suffer irreparable harm in the absence of injunctive relief.[137] Temporary injunctions are often granted when the plaintiff proves that it will likely prevail on the merits.

Evaluating the Merits of a Claim

AZG should ask its attorneys to prepare a brief memorandum clearly outlining the strengths and weaknesses of its possible infringement claim. Although copyright infringement cases can become extremely complex, a court must address two fundamental questions in each case. First, does the plaintiff own a valid copyright? Second, did the defendant wrongfully "copy" the protected expression of the copyright owner? AZG will need to introduce evidence on both questions to establish what attorneys call a prima facie case of copyright infringement (that is, evidence that is legally sufficient to permit a court to go forward with the case).

AZG will not be required to show that Kozy Kritters "intended" to infringe its copyright. Copyright infringement is known as a "strict liability" offense, which means that a person's infringing conduct alone may be enough to establish liability. However, as discussed more fully in the next section, inadvertent or so-called "innocent infringements" may be subject to reduced penalties. Once AZG has established the prima facie case of copyright infringement, Kozy Kritters will have the chance to rebut the evidence (for example, by arguing that it copied only uncopyrightable or public domain material) and to assert various defenses.

Proving copyright ownership and validity is usually the least complex issue in an infringement case. AZG would introduce into evidence the certificate of registration from the U.S. Copyright Office for each product alleged to be infringed. Such certificates constitute prima facie evidence of the validity and ownership of the copyright. Kozy Kritters then might attempt to show either that AZG does not own the copyright or that the work is not eligible for copyright protection. For example, Kozy Kritters might argue that there are only a limited number of ways of producing small, stuffed animals. When the idea of such toys "merges" with its expression, Kozy Kritters might argue, it would be unfair to provide a monopoly grant to AZG.

The centerpiece of a copyright infringement case is proving copying of protected expression. As you might expect, AZG is unlikely to have direct evidence (such as an admission) of actual copying by Kozy Kritters. More likely, AZG would introduce indirect, or circumstantial, evidence of copy-

ing. In the usual copyright infringement case, the plaintiff introduces evidence to show that the defendant had access to the protected work and used that access to copy it, as made clear by the substantial similarity of the two works. For example, AZG might point to the broad public display and circulation of its products, giving Kozy Kritters a reasonable opportunity to view copies of them. AZG does not need to show that Kozy Kritters actually viewed the zoo's products, just that it had the opportunity to do so.

Some courts have even held that if there is no evidence of access, copying may be inferred from a "striking similarity" between the two works. For example, one federal appeals court judge recently concluded that two bean-bag animals were so "strikingly similar" that the defendant retailer must have copied the work of the plaintiff manufacturer (even without any evidence of access).[138] Nonetheless, the defendant persisted, arguing that any similarity between the two animals was not because one was a copy of the other but because both were copies of real animals in the public domain, which are free for all to copy. Nonsense, said the judge after a close comparison of photographs of the two stuffed animals. The alleged infringing toy bore a "strikingly similar" appearance to the alleged infringed product and not to anything in the public domain.

How similar must two works be for a court to conclude that they are "substantially similar?" The answer to that question has long vexed the courts. As Justice Learned Hand long ago observed, "[O]bviously, no principle can be stated as to when an imitator has gone beyond copying the 'idea' and has borrowed its 'expression.'"[139] Nonetheless, the courts have devised some complex tests to determine whether two works are substantially similar. The precise test used often depends on the types of works at issue. Comparing stylistic differences in visual works of art obviously is quite a different task than analyzing the similarity of two computer programs. To oversimplify, most courts use a two-step process to determine (1) whether there is a similarity of ideas in the two works and (2) whether an "ordinary, reasonable person" would perceive a substantial taking of the protected expression.

In the Zoo Babies case, AZG should have little difficulty in proving copying of protected expression. Access should not be an issue because Kozy Kritters allegedly copied work in a mass-produced consumer product that could be purchased for $5. But remember that not all copying is infringement. To prevail, AZG must show that Kozy Kritters took "protected expression." Here, the court would exclude from its analysis any unprotected elements of the copyrighted work. For example, AZG would not be able to protect the idea of manufacturing a line of small stuffed animals because ideas are excluded from protection under copyright law. Nor would AZG be able to protect any functional elements of its product. Rather, the court would analyze the individual "expressive" elements of the two works (such as color, texture, and features), along with the "total concept and feel" of the works, to determine whether an "ordinary, reasonable person" would perceive a substantial taking.

Remedies

If AZG prevails in its infringement suit against Kozy Kritters, what remedies are available? Can the zoo or its licensee be compensated for their personal attachment to the original works? Can the museum's trustees and director be compensated for their emotional distress? In both instances, such relief is highly unlikely. Although infringement actions are expensive, time consuming, and stressful, the Copyright Act does not provide remedies for such personal losses. Rather, the copyright law provides for only two types of monetary recovery: actual damages and statutory damages.

Under the Copyright Act, the prevailing party in an infringement claim is entitled to recover actual damages. Actual damages include two elements: (1) damages suffered as a result of the infringement such as lost profits, lost business opportunities, and possible injury to the market value of the work and (2) the profits made by Kozy Kritters that are attributable to the infringement (but only to the extent not already taken into account in calculating AZG's lost profits). Awards of damages and profits serve different purposes. Damages are awarded to compensate the copyright owner for losses from the infringement; profits are awarded to prevent the infringer from unfairly benefiting from the wrongful conduct. However, AZG would be entitled to recover only those profits "attributable to the infringement." The courts are required to make an apportionment between profits that result from the infringement and other profits caused by different factors.

If proving actual damages turns out to be difficult, AZG may elect to recover statutory damages anytime before the final judgment is rendered. A judge has wide discretion in imposing statutory damages, which generally range from $500 to $20,000 for each infringement (but may go as high as $100,000 if the infringement is willful).[140] If the infringer proves that it was not aware and had no reason to believe that its acts constituted copyright infringement (so-called "innocent infringement"), the court may reduce the award to not less than $200 per copyright. When a suit involves infringement of more than one separate and independent work (as is the case here), the court must award minimum statutory damages for each work.

In sum, AZG probably will argue that the maximum damages—$100,000 per copyright, or $300,000—are appropriate because Kozy Kritters' infringement was willful. Kozy Kritters will argue that the minimum amount of damages, or $600, are appropriate because its infringement was innocent. Within this range, the final amount is within the sole discretion of the judge, who may consider the defendant's profits, the nature of copyright, the difficulty of proving actual damages, and the circumstances of the infringement, including the conduct of the parties, especially whether the infringement was willful. Finally, AZG also may be able to recover its costs and attorney's fees.[141]

Contributory and Vicarious Liability

Under certain circumstances, a person may be held liable for the infringing activities or conduct of others. There are two types of such indirect liability: contributory infringement and vicarious liability. Under the doctrine of contributory infringement, a person may be found liable for the infringing conduct of others when he has "knowledge of the infringing activity [and] induces, causes or materially contributes to the infringing conduct."[142] The classic illustration of contributory infringement may be too close for comfort for museums. Suppose that a museum rents its galleries for a fund-raising event that involves dancing. Suppose further that, without the museum's knowledge, the band performs musical works without paying the required royalties to the appropriate collecting society (an apparent infringement of the performance right). Under these facts, while the band may be liable as a direct infringer, the museum could also be found liable as a contributory infringer. The doctrine of contributory infringement also has been held to apply to the distribution of devices, including audiovisual equipment, if the devices have no substantial or commercially significant noninfringing uses.

Under the doctrine of vicarious liability, a person may be found liable for the direct infringing conduct of others when the individual has the ability to control the conduct of the infringing party and when the defendant financially benefits from the infringing conduct.[143] This is the case even when the defendant has no actual knowledge of the infringing activity. Suppose that the Post-Contemporary Museum (PCM) is held liable for the infringing conduct of its curator, Dan Scanner. Will plaintiff Upstart Art, Inc., also be able to recover against Donald Bankworth, chairman of PCM's board of trustees? Probably not. Unless Upstart Art, Inc., can establish that Bankworth was involved in the day-to-day activities of the museum and had the ability to control Scanner's conduct, Bankworth will not be vicariously liable for the infringing conduct of the museum's employee.

Fair Use and Other Limitations

Fair Use

Suppose that the Post-Contemporary Museum mounts an exhibition entitled *The Golden Age of American Art Cars: 1955 to 1975*, which examines a unique American popular artistic tradition. A highlight of the exhibition is art car designer John Martin's rhinestone-embedded 1962 Cadillac, with extended, flamelike tail fins. Luckily for the museum, Martin grants permission to the museum's staff photographer, Robert Shutter, to photograph him posed in front of his work. The museum decides to use the engaging image on the exhibition poster and catalogue and promptly registers the photograph with the U.S. Copyright Office. Shortly before the exhibition opening, the museum is disturbed to see Shutter's photograph reproduced in its entirety as a pullout centerfold in *Road Runner* magazine, which also includes a short article on the American art car movement. In response to an angry letter from the museum's director, the editor of *Road Runner* claims that its use of the museum photograph is covered under the fair use doctrine as critical commentary and news reporting. If the editor is correct, a judge might find that the magazine's conduct, which would otherwise constitute an infringement, is excused.[144]

For more than 150 years, judges have recognized that a certain amount of borrowing is a necessary part of the creative process and, therefore, must be permitted to achieve copyright's very purpose. The Supreme Court held that "[e]very book in literature, science and art, borrows, and must necessarily borrow, and use much which was well known and used before."[145] But where should judges draw the line between the interests of the author and those of the public? With a view toward providing guidance, in 1976 Congress incorporated four factors that judges had developed over the years to consider in determining whether a particular use is fair: (1) the purpose and character of the use; (2) the nature of the copyrighted work; (3) the amount and substantiality of the portion used in relation to the copyrighted work as a whole; and (4) the effect of the use upon the potential market for or value of the copyrighted work.[146]

Under the first factor, a court must consider "the purpose and character of the use," including whether the use is of a "commercial nature" or for "nonprofit educational purposes."[147] While the commercial use of copyrighted work tends to weigh against a finding of fair use, and nonprofit use tends to weigh in favor, there is nothing conclusive about these "presumptions." Moreover, the purpose and character of a use may be mixed. Under such circumstances, one federal district court stated: "When the use has both commercial and nonprofit characteristics, the court may consider 'whether the alleged infringing use was primarily for public benefit or for private commercial gain.'"[148] But probably more important is whether the use of a protected work "adds something new" to the work, transforming "raw material" into "new information, new aesthetics, new insights and understandings," or what has been recognized as "transformative" use.[149]

Road Runner's arguments that it used the Post-Contemporary Museum's photograph for the purposes of critical commentary and news reporting

are not convincing. The photograph clearly was not used for reporting on the museum's exhibition, which had not yet opened. Nor was the photograph used for the purpose of critical commentary. The article was about the art car movement, not about Robert Shutter's photography. Even if *Road Runner* could persuade a court that it used the photograph for criticism and news reporting, there is nothing transformative about the use. *Road Runner* added no "new information, new aesthetics, new insights and understandings." Rather, it simply copied the photograph as an illustration. Finally, the commercial nature of *Road Runner's* use is blatant, placing the image prominently in the centerfold of the magazine in an attempt to attract readers' attention. The first factor weighs against a finding of fair use.

Under the second factor, the nature of the copyrighted work, a court may recognize that certain works are "closer to the core of intended copyright protection than others," thereby making fair use more difficult to establish.[150] In evaluating this factor, a court may take into account whether a work is more factually based or fictional. Users of copyrighted factual works generally are more successful in asserting a fair use defense because of the public policy favoring the dissemination of information. At the other end of the spectrum, when a work is highly creative, imaginative, or original, the balance generally tilts against a finding of fair use. A court also will evaluate whether the work is published or unpublished. In order to preserve the copyright owner's rights to control first publication of his expression, courts generally tend to be less lenient when the use involves unpublished materials.

Under the second factor, *Road Runner* might argue that the Post-Contemporary Museum's photograph is not a creative work because it merely documents the artist in front of his car. In response, the museum would point out that the positioning of the designer in front of his work and the composition, lighting, and shading in the photograph (for example, highlighting the car's tail fins, its most impressive feature) are all creative choices of the photographer. Given the relatively low threshold of creativity required for copyrighting photographic works, a court probably would find that Shutter's photograph is a creative work, entitled to the highest level of protection. The second factor also tilts away from a finding of fair use.

Under the third factor, a court will evaluate "the amount and substantiality of the portion used in relation to the copyrighted work as a whole."[151] Generally, the greater the amount taken, the less likely it is that a court will find the use fair. But how much is too much? There are "no absolute rules as to how much of a copyrighted work may be copied."[152] Indeed, a court must evaluate the extent of borrowing from both quantitative and qualitative perspectives. Sometimes even a small amount taken may be unfair if the borrowed material is the "heart" of the work.[153] One federal appeals court recently observed that "courts considering the fair use defense in the context of visual works copied or displayed in other visual works must be careful not to permit this factor too easily to tip the aggregate fair use assessment in favor of those whom the other three factors do not favor."[154]

It is undisputed that *Road Runner* took the entire photograph. However, the question before the court will be whether in doing so, the magazine copied "more of the original . . . than necessary."[155] Courts have "recognized that the extent of permissible copying varies with the purpose and character of the use."[156] For example, when copying is done for the purpose of critical commentary and news reporting, courts have allowed significantly more leeway with the extent of the copying. *Road Runner* might argue that taking the entire photograph was necessary to inform its readers and comment on the art car movement in America. On these facts, such arguments are unpersuasive. The Post-Contemporary Museum

photograph, as noted above, is used as illustration rather than for critical commentary or news reporting. *Road Runner* appears to be using the museum's copyrighted image simply to save itself the expense of obtaining its own photograph.

The fourth factor is the "effect of the use upon the potential market for or value of the copyrighted work."[157] This factor was once considered the most important in determining fair use,[158] but the Supreme Court recently made it clear that "all [factors] are to be explored, and the results weighed together, in light of the purposes of copyright."[159] Under this factor, a court may evaluate not only "the extent of market harm caused by the particular actions of the alleged infringer" but also "whether unrestricted and widespread conduct of the sort engaged in by the defendant . . . would result in substantially adverse impact on the potential market for the original."[160] In analyzing the effect on the potential market for the original, courts are to consider "only traditional, reasonable, or likely to be developed markets." A court also can take into account the availability of a "convenient, reasonable licensing system" in evaluating the marketplace effect of the use.[161]

Under the fourth factor, the Post-Contemporary Museum would argue that the publication of its photograph in *Road Runner* caused immediate economic injury to the museum, which received no licensing fees from the magazine for the publication of the photograph. Perhaps even more significant for the museum is the harm to the potential market for the photograph, including derivative work markets such as posters. Because the photograph appeared as a pullout centerfold in the magazine, the museum should have little difficulty in establishing that the published photograph could easily serve as a market substitute for the poster, thereby adversely affecting the potential market for the original. Evaluating all four factors, a court probably would conclude that *Road Runner's* use of the museum's photograph was not a fair use.

Other Statutory Limitations

Archives and libraries benefit from a number of statutory limitations on the copyright owner's reproduction and distribution rights. Under these exemptions, a library or archives may copy certain protected works on request by users for purposes of study, research, or interlibrary exchange, and for archival preservation.[162] The exemptions do not apply to musical works; pictorial, graphic, and sculptural works; and films and other audio-visual works.[163] Though the copyright law specifically mentions nonprofit libraries and archives, the exemptions in section 108 would seem to apply to museums also and certainly to museum archives and libraries. To qualify for the exemption, an institution need not be nonprofit, although the copying must be done "without any purpose of direct or indirect commercial advantage." The collection must be open to the public, or, if not, it must be available to scholars conducting research in the specialized field, whether or not they are affiliated with the institution.[164]

The archives and library must comply with a number of other requirements and limitations. Each copy reproduced for private study or research must include the notice of copyright as it appears on the original work. If there is no such notice, the copy made by the library for study or research purposes must include "a legend stating that the work may be protected by copyright." The exemption only permits the making of single copies on an "isolated and unrelated" basis, as distinguished from "systematic reproduction or distribution of single or multiple copies." The term "systematic reproduction" is not defined, but it appears to cover the kind of copying that is a substitute for the purchase of journal subscriptions and article reprints.

Anthony Anderson, for example, a guest curator working on a contemporary sculpture exhibition at the Columbus School of Art Gallery, recently requested a copy of a journal article from the museum's library. The librarian responded that Anderson may make a copy of the article or other portion of a larger work for his private study, scholarship, or research if the museum has no notice that the copy will be used for any other purpose. The copy must become Anderson's property. The library also must display a copyright warning notice at the place where orders are placed and on its order forms. What if Anderson also requests a copy of the photograph of the sculpture he is researching? He is out of luck. The library copying exemption does not apply to pictorial works, so Anderson may need to obtain permission if the photograph is under copyright. Additional requirements apply if the request is for copying an entire work or a substantial part of it, the so-called "out of print" provision. Before honoring such a request, the museum library must conclude, on the basis of a reasonable investigation, that it cannot purchase a copy of the work at a fair price.[165]

The copyright law also contains exemptions permitting libraries and archives to make and distribute a limited number of copies for the purposes of preservation or replacement under certain circumstances. Suppose that a museum has a film archives that contains an important collection of motion pictures dating from the 1920s and 1930s. While some of the films are in the public domain, others are still under copyrights retained by the Hollywood studio. What steps, if any, may the museum take to preserve the deteriorating film collection? Until quite recently, the answer depended on whether a film was published. If unpublished, an archives was permitted to make a copy for the purposes of preservation and security (a "preservation copy"). If previously published, an archives was permitted to make a copy to replace one "that is damaged, deteriorating, lost, or stolen" (a "replacement copy"). However, before making a replacement copy, the museum must conclude that a replacement of the work is unavailable at a fair price after conducting a reasonable search.[166] Unlike the exemption for private study or research, the preservation exemption also covers the copying of motion pictures and other audiovisual works; musical works; and pictorial, graphic, and sculptural works.[167]

The Digital Millennium Copyright Act of 1998 (DMCA) updated these exemptions to permit libraries and archives to take advantage of digital technologies.[168] Prior to the enactment of the DMCA, preservation and replacement copies had to be in "facsimile form" (such as microfilm), and institutions were permitted to make only one copy. Under the new law, a library or archives may make up to three copies of an unpublished work for preservation or security purposes (or for deposit for research use in another archives or library) in digital and analog formats. A similar rule applies to making copies of damaged, deteriorating, lost, or stolen works. To ensure that copies of works continue to be accessible to the public, the DMCA also permits the making of replacement copies "if the existing format in which the work is stored has become obsolete."[169] A format is considered obsolete only if the equipment needed to exhibit the work "is no longer manufactured or reasonably available in the commercial marketplace." However, the making of digital preservation and replacement copies is subject to a significant limitation on their dissemination. In general, such digital copies may not be distributed "outside the premises of the library or archives."[170]

The copyright law also includes some important limitations on the public performance right, which may apply to certain museum educational programs and activities. One provision exempts performances by instructors or pupils during live, face-to-face teaching activities in nonprofit educational institutions.[171] To qualify for this exemption, the activity must first be nonprofit and educational in nature. A performance in the museum by a string quartet as part of a fundraising event or after a dinner for trustees would not be exempt. Second, the performance must be during "face-to-face teaching activities."

Broadcasts or other electronic transmissions of performances would not be exempt, a limitation discussed more fully in chapter 4. Third, the instructional activity must take place in a "classroom or a similar place devoted to instruction"[172] and involve members of a particular class. Fourth, in the case of a motion picture or other audiovisual work, the copy used for the performance must have been lawfully made. Here, although Congress apparently had schools in mind, the exemption could apply to museums if all the requirements were met.

There is a separate exemption for "educational broadcasting," transmissions of nondramatic literary works and musical works. To qualify, the instructional broadcast must be "a regular part of the systematic instructional activities of a governmental body or nonprofit educational institution."[173] Further, the broadcasts must be transmitted to classrooms or "similar places normally devoted to instruction." However, the exemption may be of only limited use to museums because it excludes performances for cultural or entertainment value.[174] Finally, there is an exemption for certain educational, religious, or charitable benefit performances. To qualify, the performance must be truly educational, religious, or charitable. No admission may be charged (or if there is an admission fee, the net proceeds must be used exclusively for educational or charitable purposes) and no compensation may be paid to the performers, promoters, and organizers.[175]

Chapter 2
TRADEMARK

Trademarks are extremely significant intellectual property assets of museums, although they are frequently ignored and often misunderstood. Like any other entity that offers valuable products and services to consumers, a museum invests considerable resources in building and maintaining its reputation not only within its area of focus and expertise but also with its general audience. An institution's trademarks are the objective symbols by which the external world identifies this effort. The museum's trademarks distinguish its collections, scholarship, and programs from those of other institutions and from the activities of other businesses and organizations. In addition, the museum's trademarks signify that all goods or services offered under these marks, whether T-shirts and posters or lectures and other educational programs, originate from and are controlled by a single source and are of consistent quality. These symbols are also critical to effective advertising, marketing and promotion of the museum's mission, programs, goods, and services.

To the extent that museum administrators have focused on intellectual property, copyright matters have received the lion's share of the attention. In contrast, most institutions deal with trademark issues in a reactive manner only after difficulties or conflicts arise. Museums that fail to act in managing and protecting their trademark assets risk jeopardizing their institutional reputations and the underlying goodwill that their trademarks represent.

Consider the following example: The City Museum of Art enjoys an excellent regional and national reputation for the quality of its collections and programs, which have developed over 50 years of continuous operation and careful stewardship. For an institution of its size and resources, the museum has an ambitious exhibition program, and it regularly organizes traveling exhibitions that are anxiously anticipated by the public, scholars, and other museums throughout the country and, in some instances, the world. The museum also has a fairly sophisticated merchandising operation focused on developing consumer products such as clothing, postcards, posters, catalogues, and other printed material, much of which prominently features the museum name and logo. The museum operates a retail store on its premises under the name CMA Museum Store. The museum, however, has not been entirely consistent in its use of this name in advertising and promoting the store. Indeed, local residents have come to refer to the store simply as the "City Museum Store."

Museum administrators learn that a local entrepreneur has unveiled plans to open a store in the city's main retail mall under the name City Museum Store. The store will feature a wide variety of merchandise, including art books, reproductions, and clothing, none of which will necessarily feature the name City Museum of Art, works from its collections, or merchandise offered in the CMA Museum Store. Nevertheless, the museum's administrators are very concerned about the mall store's threat to its retail income stream and its reputation generally, particularly given the likelihood that the public will assume there is some connection between the mall store and the institution. In fact, the museum has received a number of calls from members of the local press and public asking for more information about "the museum's new retail store at the mall."

The City Museum must now respond to this situation, but its administrators have more questions than answers: What are the museum's rights under these circumstances? Does the institution have legally protectable trademark rights in the name of the museum and/or its retail store, even in the absence of federal registrations for these marks? If so, can it rely on these rights to stop the retail store from operating under its proposed name? What actions can the museum take to stop this activity short of full-scale litigation? What defensive steps can it take to protect itself against such objectionable conduct in the future?

This chapter gives museum administrators a sense of the nature and scope of an institution's trademark rights and its options in light of these rights. More important, however, it identifies issues that all institutions should consider with respect to their trademark assets and provides guidance on steps that can be taken well in advance of disputes to avoid conflicts and to strengthen the institution's position should a dispute regarding trademark rights arise.

Purpose of Trademarks and Their Relevance to Museums

A trademark is a distinctive word, name, symbol, slogan, or some combination of these elements used to identify one party's products and distinguish them from those of others.[1] When a mark is used to identify and distinguish a service, it is called a service mark. For instance, an exhibition title may serve as a service mark when identifying the exhibition and related educational programs. In contrast, when the exhibition title is featured on merchandise (i.e., goods) it functions as a trademark.

Like copyrights and patents, trademarks and service marks (collectively referred to as "trademarks" or "marks") are forms of intellectual property. Each type of intellectual property, however, serves a different function. Copyright protects an author's proprietary interest in his or her work and precludes others from, among other things, copying the work. Copyright protects the original way an idea is expressed, but not the

idea itself. Patent protects a new and useful process or machine and provides the inventor with the exclusive rights to make, use, and sell a patented invention.

Trademarks, by contrast, cannot be used by their owners to stop others from copying goods or services or to exclude others from making or using the same or similar goods or services. Rather, trademarks indicate the source of goods and services. They also guarantee the quality of the goods or services bearing the mark and, through advertising, create and maintain a demand for the product or service. In practice this means that copyright may protect the artistic elements or design qualities of a museum's logo from copying, while a trademark may protect the name and logo from use by others in a confusingly similar manner.

Trademark law, therefore, protects the museum's monetary and reputational interests while also protecting the public from confusion. Museums as trademark owners have the right to use their marks in connection with particular products and services, and they may prevent others from using these or similar marks in a manner that might confuse consumers as to the source, origin, or quality of products or services.

For museums, trademark rights may arise in many ways, some of which may be more self-evident than others. Of primary significance to every museum is the name under which it operates. This name, in all likelihood, serves a trademark function because it is a symbol identifying the wide range of services the museum offers to the public, from educational programs to restaurant and retail services. Certain goods and services may be identified by and offered to the public under their own trademarks. For instance, museum stores and restaurants may be identified by distinctive logos or names in their advertising or promotion. Specialized museum programs, such as community outreach or school programs, also may be associated with particular names, logos, or slogans that have source-identifying trademark significance. Titles of exhibitions and publications may also function as protectable trademarks.

Establishment of Trademark Rights and Bases for Protection

Common-Law Rights

Trademark rights are established through the actual use of a mark to identify the goods and services of one party and distinguish them from those offered by others. These "common-law" rights are independent of the rights granted under either the federal or any state trademark registration system. Therefore, even without the benefit of registration, a museum has rights in a mark as soon as it begins using the mark publicly to identify its services or products, provided the mark is distinctive, that is, not "generic" or "merely descriptive" of the goods or services it identifies.

A common-law user's rights in a mark vis-à-vis the rights of third parties are governed by priority of use, meaning that the first party to use the mark in a particular geographic area in connection with the particular goods or services is the "owner" of the mark and the "senior user."[2] The holder of common-law rights in a mark can protect the mark within its established geographic area of use (which can range in size) against later or "junior" users. Thus, to successfully challenge a junior user, a senior user must establish the following elements: (1) ownership of a distinctive mark; (2) prior use of the mark in overlapping geographic marketing areas; and (3) sufficient relationship among the goods and/or services of the respective parties to generate some sort of consumer confusion as to source, sponsorship, or affiliation.

Federal Registration

Trademark rights arise from use of the mark in commerce. Although not a prerequisite for acquiring trademark rights, federal registration does afford a trademark owner important legal benefits and procedural advantages. The benefits of owning a mark registered on the Principal Register of the U.S. Patent and Trademark Office (PTO) include the right of nationwide priority from the filing date of the application for registration.[3] A federal registrant can prohibit all subsequent use of confusingly similar marks adopted after the registrant's filing date in any area of the United States in which the registrant uses or has immediate plans to use the mark.[4] A federal registration, which lasts for 10 years and may be renewed,[5] also provides the owner with presumptive evidence of the validity of the registration, ownership of the mark, and the exclusive right to use the mark nationwide in connection with the goods and services identified in the federal registration.[6] In addition, a federal registration may provide successful plaintiffs in a trademark infringement action certain monetary remedies that may not be available under common law.[7] (See "The Federal Registration Process: Initial Considerations," later in this chapter.)

State Trademark Protection

Most states have a system for the registration of trademarks used in that state, although state trademark registration generally does not offer the same benefits as federal registration. Moreover, state registration is not likely to add significantly to the scope of protection already afforded the trademark owner through common-law use. Generally, a mark cannot be registered in a state unless and until that mark has actually been used in connection with the sale of goods or services in that state.

The principal benefit of state registration is that it provides notice to anyone who checks the state registration records that the mark is owned by the registrant. This notice may lead most would-be users of the same mark to choose another mark rather than risk a potential dispute. If the mark is federally registered, this notice is effected nationwide, and state registration is generally not necessary.

Some state laws do provide additional benefits or expand certain rights provided under the federal trademark statute (the Lanham Act).[8] For instance, in certain states, successful plaintiffs in infringement actions may recover their attorneys' fees even in the absence of a finding that the case is "exceptional," as is required under federal law.[9] Owning a state trademark registration may also prevent third parties from acquiring a state registration for the same or an arguably similar mark.

Compared with federal registration, obtaining state registration is usually a relatively expeditious and inexpensive process. It is an obvious alternative for institutions that are active in only one state, when federal registration is too costly or time consuming or when it is unavailable because the institution is not using the mark in interstate commerce. (See "What Is Actual Use?" later in this chapter.)

Scope of Trademark Protection

All trademarks are not created equal. The more distinctive the mark is, the more successful it will be in readily distinguishing the products or services of the institution from those of others. In contrast, a mark that is merely a descriptive term commonly used by museums cannot be immediately distinctive of a particular museum's products or services and, therefore, will require a greater investment of resources in order to generate market recognition and protect against unauthorized use, if at all.

When developing new trademarks for a museum's use or when analyzing the degree of protectability of an existing trademark, one must understand what differentiates a strong mark from a weak one. In general, marks can be divided into three broad categories: (1) those that can function as marks as soon as they are used; (2) those that can function as marks only after continuous and exclusive use; and (3) those that can never function as marks. An important conceptual tool in judging the relative strengths of marks is known as the "spectrum of distinctiveness."[10] The four categories into which a trademark might fall—arbitrary/fanciful, suggestive, descriptive, and generic—are arranged along the spectrum from highly distinctive, protectable marks to nondistinctive, legally unprotectable terms.[11]

Inherently Distinctive Marks

Terms that do not describe any aspect of the product or service that they identify are considered to be inherently distinctive and the strongest marks in terms of legal protectability. These marks are generally classified as either "arbitrary" or "fanciful" and function as trademarks immediately upon use. Fanciful marks are composed of coined words or symbols (for example, KODAK or EXXON), or archaic terms that are not particularly well known. The mark AVISO used by the American Association of Museums to identify its monthly newsletter is an example of a fanciful trademark.[12] Other examples of highly distinctive "coined" marks include the following:

- The mark NEWSEUM used to identify museum services featuring the historical and technological accomplishments of journalism[13]

- The mark GEOVATOR used by the Houston Museum of Natural Science in connection with a simulated elevator ride for amusement and educational purposes[14]

Arbitrary marks are composed of words with English-language meanings unrelated to the products they identify (for example, APPLE computers).

The following are examples of arbitrary marks used in the museum context:

- The mark CULTURE VULTURE used by the Phoenix Art Museum to identify coloring books for children[15]

- The mark *TRACKS* used by the Cleveland Museum of Natural History to identify a monthly newsletter[16]

Suggestive Marks

Suggestive marks are also considered inherently distinctive and, therefore, are also entitled to protection immediately upon use. Because of their suggestive nature, however, they are entitled to a narrower scope of protection than arbitrary or fanciful marks. A suggestive mark does not immediately describe the goods or services it identifies or their nature or features. Instead, a suggestive mark requires the consumer to exercise some modicum of thought or imagination to discern the nature, characteristics, or function of the goods or services (for example, COPPERTONE for sun protection products or SWEET DREAMS for mattresses or hotel services). The distinction between suggestive marks and descriptive marks is not clearly defined, as reflected by the difficulty courts often have in determining whether a mark is immediately protectable against use by others (suggestive) or not protectable without evidence of what is known as "acquired distinctiveness" (descriptive), a quality discussed below.

Examples of suggestive marks in the museum field include the following:

- The mark the SCIENCE PLACE used by the Southwest Museum of Science and Technology in Dallas to identify museum services[17]

- The mark COMPUTER CLUBHOUSE used by the Computer Museum in Boston to identify instructional materials in the field of art and computers[18]

Descriptive Marks

Terms that directly describe a product or service or its characteristics, functions, or qualities are considered to be nondistinctive and, therefore, not immediately protectable.[19] Because a descriptive term has a direct link to the products or services it purports to identify, one party cannot claim the exclusive right to use the term. However, even if a given symbol or word is not inherently distinctive, it can become legally protectable if the owner can show that the mark has acquired distinctiveness. Acquired distinctiveness, also referred to as "secondary meaning," occurs when the public has come to associate an otherwise descriptive term with the goods or service of one particular party.[20]

Arguably, the most valuable trademark asset of any museum is the institution's name. In many instances, however, the name of the institution is likely to be considered descriptive of the goods and services offered by the institution. Examples include the following marks used to identify museum and related educational services:

- The mark THE COMPUTER MUSEUM owned by the institution of the same name in Boston[21]

- The mark MUSEO ITALOAMERICANO owned by the institution of the same name in San Francisco[22]

- The mark ROCK AND ROLL HALL OF FAME AND MUSEUM owned by the Rock and Roll Hall of Fame Foundation, Inc., in New York[23]

As these federally registered marks demonstrate, the presence of a descriptive term in the name of the museum does not mean that the institution's most valuable trademark asset is not protectable. The mark THE MUSEUM OF MODERN ART is but one example of a descriptive mark that unquestionably satisfies the standard of acquired distinctiveness through long-standing and continuous use of the mark by the Museum of Modern Art in New York.[24] The notion of acquired distinctiveness is no less applicable to institutions that serve local or regional markets as opposed to national markets. For such institutions, the extent to which an otherwise descriptive trademark can be protected is directly correlated to the scope of the relevant market and whether or not distinctiveness has been acquired within that market.

Other marks requiring proof of secondary meaning for protection include geographically descriptive marks, personal name marks, and titles of single artistic or literary works and laudatory terms.[25] There are countless examples of institutions with marks that include geographic designations and/or personal names. Here again, the degree to which an institution may protect marks that include such components depends on whether the relevant mark has acquired distinctiveness. For example, the mark ST. LOUIS CHILDREN'S MUSEUM or the marks associated with venerable institutions such as the PHILADELPHIA MUSEUM OF ART and THE ART INSTITUTE OF CHICAGO, although "primarily geographically descriptive," are certainly protectable based on their longstanding use and significant public recognition in their respective domestic markets and internationally. Trademarks that incorporate personal names, such as THE FIELD MUSEUM, THE HIGH MUSEUM OF ART, THE SOLOMON R. GUGGENHEIM MUSEUM, and THE FRANKLIN INSTITUTE, are protectable for the same reasons.[26]

Generic and Other Unprotectable Terms

A generic term is incapable of functioning as a mark, regardless of how long or how extensively it has been used by one party. Certain terms may be inherently generic for a type of product or service (such as credit card or telephone), and certain coined terms may become generic over time (such as aspirin, cellophane, and escalator). Because the name of the actual goods and/or services and the generic term are the same, a generic term can never distinguish the products and/or services of one party from those of any other entity providing the same or similar goods and/or services. For instance, the term "museum store" may arguably be considered a generic term when used to describe an institution's retail operations. Although there is no legal prohibition against adopting a generic term as the name of the institution's products or services, the museum gains little value from doing so, as the mark is not protectable in any way against use by others.

Other types of words or symbols that can never function as marks, regardless of how long a party has made exclusive use of the term, include "deceptively misdescriptive" and "primarily geographically misdescriptive" terms.[27] Deceptively misdescriptive terms misrepresent a characteristic of the goods or services that could materially affect a consumer's decision to purchase them (for example, "metalized" for radio resistors that are not in fact made of metal). Primarily geographically misdescriptive terms are terms that lead consumers to conclude that a product originates from a geographic region other than that from which it actually originates (for example, "Italian-made" for neckties that are not made in Italy).

ASSOCIATION OF
SCIENCE-TECHNOLOGY
CENTERS
INCORPORATED

figure 1   figure 2   figure 3

Format and Subject Matter of Trademarks

Trademarks and service marks are not the only types of marks that may be relevant to museums. Certification marks and collective marks both have direct application. In addition, those who manage and protect a museum's trademark assets should also be familiar with the important distinction between trademark and trade name use, the use of proper names as trademarks, the use of buildings as trademarks, trademark protection for exhibition and program titles, and the concept of "trade dress."

Certification Marks

While trademarks and service marks identify the source of particular goods and services, certification marks certify particular characteristics of goods or services provided by others.[28] A certification mark may identify characteristics such as regional origin, method of manufacture, product quality, and service accuracy. Certification marks differ from trademarks in two important respects. First, and most significantly, a certification mark may not be used by the owner of the mark to identify its own goods or services—a restriction often referred to as the "anti-use by owner" prohibition. The mark is instead licensed to third parties who use it in connection with their own goods and services. Second, a certification mark need not be associated with the goods and services of any one party. Rather, it may attest to the origin, quality and/or unique charac-

teristics of goods or services being offered by various parties. One of the most recognized certification marks is the GOOD HOUSEKEEPING SEAL OF APPROVAL. The AAM accreditation mark (fig. 1) is a prominent example of a certification mark in the museum field. The AAM mark certifies that the institution displaying the mark has satisfied certain requirements and meets professional standards of the museum field as articulated and judged by AAM.

Collective Marks

Members of a group or organization may use a collective mark to identify and distinguish their goods or services from those offered by others who are not members.[29] One type of collective mark, called a collective membership mark, indicates membership in a group or organization. A collective membership mark identifies the group's members, but it is not necessarily used in connection with the offering of goods and/or services.

From a functional standpoint, collective marks are often difficult to distinguish from certification marks. However, those authorized to use certification marks need not be members of the organization that owns and controls the mark. In addition, the so-called "anti-use by owner" prohibition applicable to the certification mark generally does not apply to collective marks. Accordingly, an association name or emblem can be used in such a way as to be both a collective membership mark and a trademark of the organization. For example, the mark AMERICAN ASSOCIATION OF MUSEUMS may

Association of Art Museum Directors

figure 4   figure 5

be used by members to indicate membership in the organization. AAM itself also uses this mark as a service mark to identify the variety of services it offers to the museum field. Figures 2 through 5 are other examples of marks in the museum field that function in an equivalent manner.

Distinguishing Trade Names from Trademarks

The name that an institution uses to identify itself is referred to as its "trade name." A trade name may or may not also serve as a trademark. A trade name refers to the business or organization as a whole, and it is used on corporate documents, bank accounts, invoices, and letterhead. When the name identifies a museum in this way—in a corporate sense rather than in a marketing or promotional sense—it has some degree of protection under state and local corporate and fictitious business name registration laws. Moreover, although trade names are not by themselves considered trademarks for purposes of the federal trademark statute, they may still be protected under federal and state unfair competition laws against unauthorized use by third parties.[30]

One common misconception with respect to trade names is the belief that having rights to a trade name automatically confers rights to use it as a trademark. A fictitious business name filing with the relevant state authority (usually the secretary of state) allows the public to identify the entity operating under the assumed business name. It does not confer trademark rights beyond providing some evidence that a particular name has been used at least as early as the filing date of the fictitious name registration. Similarly, filing articles of incorporation or qualifying to do business in a particular state do not necessarily confer trademark rights.

Rather, a trade name is not entitled to trademark protection unless it is used to identify the source or origin of particular products or services sold or offered by that institution. In this regard, a trade-

mark functions as an extension of the owner's trade name, carrying within it the identity of the source of its goods and/or services as well as the reputation and goodwill of the owner. The distinction between trade names and trademarks often blurs when the entity and the services it offers are associated with the same name. This convergence would appear to be the rule rather than the exception for museums. To the extent that a museum uses its corporate name to identify its products and services, the museum's trade name will in all likelihood have a parallel trademark function. Indeed, a search of the Patent and Trademark Office (PTO) records reveals well in excess of 200 references to valid federal registrations or currently pending applications for registration of marks that include the term MUSEUM used to identify educational services.

Proper Names as Trademarks

A mark consisting in whole or in part of a living or deceased person's surname can function as a source identifier and may be registered with the PTO, provided the proper consent is obtained from the individual or his or her heirs.[31] Personal name marks, however, fall into the category of marks that are not inherently distinctive and are, therefore, not protectable or registrable without a showing of acquired distinctiveness.[32]

Moreover, although some courts have held that the names of historical figures are unprotectable for some uses, most view it that historical names are protectable if they are recognized as symbols of origin. Depending on the nature of their use, historical names may or may not require a showing of acquired distinctiveness to be protectable. For instance, when used in connection with automobiles, the name LINCOLN is considered arbitrary. In contrast, the hypothetical mark ABRAHAM LINCOLN MUSEUM is suggestive and/or descriptive of the service offered under the mark by that institution and will, therefore, likely require a showing of acquired distinctiveness.

Accordingly, a museum with a trademark that incorporates a personal name may protect its rights in the mark against third parties who attempt to trade or capitalize on the goodwill or reputation of the institution by adopting a similar mark to that of the institution. However, the museum may not be able to restrict all uses of that proper name, particularly uses by individuals who have the same or similar names.[33] Trademark law has traditionally recognized an individual's special right to use his or her name in connection with his or her business. Although this right was once considered "sacred" or "absolute," courts now tend to balance this right with the public interest of protecting against consumer confusion. When infringement is alleged by one of two parties that are using the same or a highly similar personal name mark, a court will consider who first began using the name as a trademark, whether the second use began in bad faith (with the intention of passing off goods or services as those of the first user), and how similar are the goods and services offered. Unless there is evidence of bad faith, a court may not necessarily impose an absolute restriction on the second user, and may require instead that the second user modify its mark or restrict usage to a certain geographic area.

Consider the hypothetical example of the Woodard Museum in New York City, named for its deceased founder and principal benefactor, Harold Woodard. The museum features the works of the lesser-known French impressionists and operates a small retail store offering reproductions of some of the works on posters, T-shirts, and cards. Paul Woodard, the great-grandson of Harold Woodard, owns a poster store in Chicago doing business under the name Woodard Gallery. One day Paul Woodard decides, based on the success of his Chicago business, to open a store in New York City just down the block from the Woodard Museum. The museum director learns of Paul Woodard's plans and becomes concerned that the poster store will interfere with retail business at the Woodard Museum or detract from the museum's fine reputation.

A court may prohibit Paul Woodard entirely from using the name Woodard if it finds Paul's actions to be in bad faith (motivated by the desire to trade on the museum's goodwill and consumer recognition). As an alternative, a court may require Paul to take some action to avoid consumer confusion between his store and the Woodard Museum's retail operations. Moving the poster store's location or adding a disclaimer on all promotional material announcing that the Woodard Gallery is "not affiliated with the Woodard Museum" might serve this purpose. In most cases involving personal name marks, courts balance the individual's right to use his or her name with the public interest in preventing consumer confusion. It should be noted, however, that courts may not always allow multiple users of the same mark even when the junior user has a legitimate claim to that name. If the senior mark is well known, a court may decide that consumer confusion is likely regardless of the junior user's good faith and efforts to prevent confusion.

Trademark Rights in Artists' Names

Personal name marks may have particular relevance to art museums. When an artist affixes his name to a work of art, the name may simply serve the informational purpose of identifying the individual who created the work. The artist's name arguably also serves a trademark function in that it identifies the source of an artistic "commodity" and may distinguish one artist's works from those of others. The line between trademark (that is, source-identifying) use and informational (that is, descriptive) use is often difficult to draw, and courts and the PTO have long struggled to define precisely where that line is.

It is clear, however, that an artist's name affixed to a work of art may function as a trademark and may be registrable with the PTO under certain circumstances.[34] Moreover, a well-known artist's signature alone may be featured in broad-ranging merchandising efforts involving consumer products from T-shirts to ceramics. Such use of an artist's signature apart from a work of art (that is, as a brand) suggests that the respective goods were made with the sponsorship or approval of the artist (or his or her heirs) and is, therefore, protectable as a trademark.

Even without a federal registration, an artist may prevent others from using his name or distinctive logos on products that he has not created or authorized. Consider, for example, a situation in which an entrepreneur sells items featuring images that prominently display a facsimile signature of a well-known artist. These images, while bearing some stylistic resemblance to the artist's work, were not in fact created by the artist. The artist may have an actionable claim under federal trademark law or state unfair competition law because the goods are being falsely represented as depicting works by that artist. A similar claim may be available if a merchandise item features a reproduction of a work that the artist did create, but the appearance of which has been unsatisfactorily altered by the entrepreneur. (See chapter 1, "Exclusive Rights and Their Limitations: Moral Rights," for a related discussion of Visual Artists Rights Act provisions granting creators of certain works of fine art the right of "attribution.")

As a general rule, however, an artist cannot (on trademark grounds) object to a museum's use of his or her name in connection with a work (or a reproduction of a work) provided such use merely involves a truthful statement that the person is the author of the work.[35] As such, whenever the museum reproduces a work of art (under license or otherwise), the museum may use the artist's name in a manner that accurately conveys the fact that the artist is responsible for the work without risk of liability. The museum should not, however, use an artist's name, signature, or logo in connection with artwork that he or she did not create, or in connection with merchandise items in a manner that falsely implies that the work was created, authorized, or endorsed by the artist (or his or her estate).

Museum Buildings as Trademarks

In the eyes of the public, a museum's building may come to symbolize the goods and services offered by the institution in the same way that the museum's name and logos serve as source-identifying trademarks.[36] It is well established that the design or appearance of a building can be protected from confusingly similar use under the theories of trademark or trade dress. The Principal Register of the PTO includes registrations featuring the designs of approximately 100 buildings, among them such landmark structures as the Chrysler Building in New York,[37] the New York Stock Exchange facade,[38] the Golden Dome of Notre Dame University,[39] and the castle building of the Smithsonian Institution.[40] (See chapter 1, "Subject Matter of Copyright: Types of Works Protected" for a discussion of copyright protection of buildings and building designs.)

Consider the hypothetical example of an art museum located in a medium-sized midwestern city that erects a new building designed by a world-renowned architect. The building is unlike any other in its overall conception and design. In the few short years since its construction, it has received significant international attention and acclaim. Understandably, the museum has capitalized on the distinctive look of its building and has expended considerable resources in developing merchandise featuring drawings and photographs of the structure, from posters and postcards to T-shirts and neckties. The museum recently learned, however, that a local professional photographer has been selling posters featuring a photograph of the museum with the name of the institution in large type at the bottom of the poster. Although the museum's administrators cannot object to individuals taking photographs and making renderings of the building for their own personal use, they are concerned about possible confusion among the public between the photographer's and the museum's products.

The question of the protectability of a distinctive museum building as a trademark was recently addressed in a case involving the Rock and Roll Hall of Fame and Museum in Cleveland, Ohio, on facts paralleling this example.[41] In that case, a photographer sold posters featuring the museum building without the museum's consent, and the museum sued, claiming that the posters infringed its trademark rights in its distinctive building. The posters sold by the photographer consisted of a photograph of the building against a sunset with the words "Rock N' Roll Hall of Fame Cleveland" in the border below the photograph.

Although the lower court had prohibited the defendant's continuing sale of the offending posters, the appellate court reversed this decision, finding that the museum had neither proven that it had used the building as its own source-identifying trademark nor that the defendant's use of the building was an infringement. Critical to the court's holding was the observation that, although the museum had used drawings and photographs of its building design on various goods, no particular rendition had been used with any consistency. Rather, the museum had depicted the building in various media and had used images showing the building from differing angles. According to the court, these disparate uses did not create "a consistent and distinct commercial impression as an indicator of a single source of origin or sponsorship."[42] The court concluded that when it viewed the photographer's poster, it did not "readily recognize the design of the Museum's building as an indicator of source or sponsorship. What we see, rather, is a photograph of an accessible, well-known, public landmark."[43] The court went on to reason that if the defendant's use of the photograph was not an infringement of the museum's trademark rights, then the words "Rock N' Roll Hall of Fame" used in the poster's caption were nothing more than a description of the building itself, and thus constituted a fair use of the plaintiff's registered trademark.

Although the court in the Rock and Roll Hall of Fame and Museum case acknowledged the possibility that a distinctive building design can serve a trademark function in the museum context, the lesson of this case, in the words of the court, is that "[c]onsistent and repetitive use of a designation as an indicator of source is the hallmark of a trademark."[44] In other words, institutions that wish to protect their trademark rights in a distinctive building must be consistent in their own use of images of their building. Whether the image is a photograph, line drawing, or logo based on the museum's facade, or is being used to advertise the museum and its services or in connection with merchandise, the building should be portrayed from a single, consistent angle and perspective.

Organizations with national scope and those with extensive merchandising or licensing programs may wish to consider seeking federal registration of particular renditions of their distinctive building designs.[45] Museums may obtain federal registrations even when the building in which the museum is housed is owned by a public entity, such as the local, state, or federal government. State registration may also offer an easy and relatively inexpensive means of achieving and reinforcing protection for institutions whose activities are limited to particular states or regions. The museum should recognize, however, that even if it develops protectable trademark rights in its building design, it will not be able to enforce these rights against certain uses, such as noncommercial fair uses.[46]

Trademark Protection for Exhibition and Program Titles

Although a museum name is arguably the institution's most valuable trademark asset, titles of exhibitions and programs may also be important assets protectable under trademark law. Indeed, trademark law may provide the only source of intellectual property protection for these assets, as copyright does not apply to titles.[47] As with other marks, the scope of protection will depend in large part on the relative trademark strength of the title. A more descriptive mark (for example, OCEANS OF THE WORLD used in connection with an exhibition on oceanic marine life) is less protectable than a more distinctive alternative (for example, BLUE WONDER used to identify the same exhibition). The degree of protection afforded to exhibition titles in particular may be subject to an additional caveat. Unlike other marks, the titles of single works (such as books, plays, motion pictures, songs, and records) are not immediately protectable as trademarks without proof of secondary meaning and consumer recognition, even when the mark is highly distinctive and not otherwise suggestive of its subject matter.[48] This limitation also may apply to exhibition titles, particularly if the title is used only to identify the actual exhibition and related services and not broader merchandising and licensing efforts involving apparel, posters, postcards, and other consumer products.

The Principal Register of the PTO contains many examples of exhibition and program titles that function as trademarks:

- A federal registration for the mark ROCK 'N' SOUL: SOCIAL CROSSROADS used to identify "museum services, and educational services, namely, conducting educational workshops, seminars and exhibitions related to the study of popular American music," owned by the Smithsonian Institution[49]

- A pending application for federal registration of the mark PREHISTORIC JOURNEY used to identify "educational and entertainment services, namely, museum exhibitions and educational material related thereto . . . in the field of earth sciences and early life on earth" and related consumer items, owned by the Denver Museum of Natural History[50]

- A federal registration for THE LIVING WORLD used to identify "educational services, namely conducting classes, seminars and demonstra-

tions in the fields of zoology, biology, conservation and ecology . . . ; organizing educational exhibitions concerning animals, plants, conservation and ecology," owned by the Zoological Subdistrict of The Metropolitan Zoological Park and Museum District in St. Louis[51]

The investment in time and resources required to obtain a state or federal trademark registration may not be warranted unless the exhibition is permanent, anticipated to run for a significant period, or coupled with merchandising and licensing efforts featuring the exhibition title. It is important to remember, however, that a museum may have protectable common-law trademark rights in an exhibition title even without a federal or state trademark registration.

For instance, a regional science museum organizes a national traveling exhibition entitled *The Hubble Telescope: Keyhole to the Universe*. After the tour begins, the organizing museum learns that an educational film production company has produced a film by this same title that is scheduled to be shown at several institutions on the exhibition tour. The organizing museum also learns that a clothing manufacturer has offered to sell T-shirts featuring the exhibition title and an image of the telescope in the gift shops of many institutions on the tour.

Even without a federal registration, the organizing museum has likely developed common-law trademark rights in THE HUBBLE TELESCOPE: KEYHOLE TO THE UNIVERSE mark. It may be able to exert those rights against the film production company to prevent the distribution and showing of the film using the mark THE HUBBLE TELESCOPE: KEYHOLE TO THE UNIVERSE. Clearly, if the film is simultaneously released and shown at museums on the tour, the public is likely to assume that the film and the production company responsible for it are somehow sponsored by, affiliated with, or connected to the exhibition. Moreover, even if the organizing institution does not intend to use the exhibition title on merchandise or license to others the right to do so, the unauthorized use of the mark on T-shirts may cause consumers to assume otherwise. Products bearing the title may also appear to be approved by, sponsored by, or affiliated with the organizing museum. As such, the sale of T-shirts may also be prevented.

Trade Dress Protection

In addition to being identified by a word, logo, slogan, or design, a product may become known by its distinctive packaging or color, and services may become known by a distinctive decor or other characteristic. The overall image or impression conveyed to consumers through the use of unique product configuration or packaging is known as trade dress. Trade dress may be protected in the same manner and to the same extent that trademarks are protected. The distinctive colors on Kodak film packaging and the unmistakable shape of the Coca-Cola bottle are among the most recognizable examples of trade dress. To assert a claim for infringement, the owner of the trade dress rights must demonstrate that (1) the public recognizes the trade dress to identify and distinguish the source; (2) the trade dress is not dictated by utilitarian concerns (also known as the "functionality" limitation); and (3) consumers are likely be confused as to the source, sponsorship, ownership, or affiliation of the products or services because of the similarity in the respective trade dress. If a trade dress satisfies the threshold requirements of federal registration, it may also be registered with the PTO (for example, the shape of LIFESAVER candy).[52]

A museum may have protectable trade dress rights to the extent that its products and services are identified by distinguishing, nonfunctional characteristics. These characteristics may range from a unique interior decor or exhibition display configuration to specialized packaging used in retail operations. Trade dress rights, however, may also have particular relevance to art muse-

ums due to the potential application of trade dress rights to works of visual art. Although visual artists generally resort to the copyright law as the primary means of protecting their financial interest in their works, some artists have successfully invoked the federal trademark law, particularly trade dress concepts, to protect their unique styles.[53] Therefore, museum merchandising activities that involve creating or offering products invoking the style of a given artist, even if direct copying of a work or elements of a work are not involved, are not without risk. This risk is heightened when the artist whose style is being emulated sells his or her works in volume to a broad audience. In these cases, the artist's work is more likely to have acquired "secondary meaning" such that the artist's style could be considered an indicator of source.[54] The risk of consumer confusion is also heightened in such instances because purchasers of reproductions like posters and calendars (as compared to purchasers of original works of art) arguably have less expertise in discerning differences among works and may, therefore, be more likely to be confused as to their origin.

Works of Art as Trademarks

One should be careful to distinguish between trade dress rights in a particular distinctive artistic style, as discussed above, and trademark rights that may arise from using a particular artistic work as a source identifier. As a general rule, a work of art, like any other visual symbol or design, may function as a trademark if it is used in the promotion of goods or services. Suppose, for instance, that a corporation purchases a large outdoor sculpture, displays it in front of its corporate headquarters, and develops a company logo based on the sculpture with the approval of the artist. To the extent that the image featuring the sculpture becomes known by the public as the symbol of the corporation, it is likely protectable as a trademark. By the same token, if an institution known for a particular work in its collection chooses to develop and feature a logo based on that work in all museum promotional and educational materials, that image may in fact represent a protectable trademark asset of the institution. Without this sort of purposeful "brand" cultivation, however, works owned by an institution (and images or logos based on them) do not serve as trademarks of the institution simply by virtue of the museum's ownership of the objects themselves.[55]

The question of whether a particular work of art or a series of works (as compared to the distinctive style of an artist) can function as a protectable mark identifying the creator's own services and products raises a slightly different issue. Because a trademark must become associated with a good, service, or business in order to acquire secondary meaning, artistic works may not receive trademark protection if they are used for purely artistic as opposed to commercial purposes. The federal trial court in *Hughes v. Design Look, Inc.* addressed this precise question in a case involving the works of Andy Warhol.[56] In that case, the artist's estate attempted to enjoin on trademark grounds, among others, the production of a calendar featuring 12 images created by Warhol. In rejecting the plaintiff's claim that the particular Warhol works were protectable as the trademarks of Warhol and his estate, the court relied on the fact that there was no evidence that the specific images used by the defendant were ever used by the artist to identify the source of any particular goods or services. According to the court, simply showing that the images have come to signify Warhol is not sufficient to prevail on a trademark claim. As such, the lesson of *Hughes* would appear to be that artists who only sell singular, original works may find it difficult to secure protection from trademark infringement, whereas artists who sell works in volume, or in connection with other goods (such as posters, calendars, or other consumer products), may be more likely to receive protection.[57]

The Federal Registration Process: Initial Considerations

Whether to Seek Federal Registration

Although federal registration gives trademark owners important legal benefits and procedural advantages, registration is not a prerequisite for acquiring and enforcing trademark rights.[58] In light of the time and expense associated with filing and successfully prosecuting a federal trademark application, a museum may choose instead to rely on its common-law trademark rights for all but the most important of the institution's marks.

The decision whether to seek federal registration will depend on the actual and intended geographic scope of the use of a given mark; how long the institution intends to use the mark; the strength and fundamental protectability of the mark; and the likelihood that the PTO will issue a registration for the mark given existing registrations for arguably similar marks. Legal counsel can play an invaluable role in helping the institution analyze these factors and assess the costs and benefits of seeking federal registration for particular marks.[59]

Marks that will only be used for a limited period, including perhaps those identifying temporary or special exhibitions and associated programs, may not warrant federal registration. In contrast, the name of the museum and any related logo or design treatment that has or will be widely used for a significant period of time to identify the museum may be appropriate for federal registration. Similarly, a federal registration should also be considered with respect to marks used in connection with broad merchandising, retailing, or licensing efforts.

Even if the institution caters to a regional audience and does not anticipate broader national activity, a federal registration may be beneficial. Indeed, as discussed in greater detail in chapter 3, ownership of a federal registration may be necessary in order to take advantage of certain Internet domain name dispute resolution procedures. Therefore, for those institutions interested in expanding their reach through digital technology—the Internet in particular—federal registration of trademarks becomes increasingly advisable.

Role of Trademark Counsel in Selecting, Searching, and Registering Trademarks

Working with experienced trademark counsel in selecting, clearing, and applying for registration of marks may be critical to successful registration and protection of a museum's marks. Although it is certainly possible for an institution to navigate its course without the assistance of counsel, the cost and duration of the process may be minimized and the scope of the museum's rights maximized if handled by experienced trademark counsel from the outset. The decision will ultimately turn on the importance of the mark to the institution. It should be remembered, however, that even in instances when the mark is not of paramount importance or may be used for a limited time (for example, a temporary exhibition title), without undertaking the proper due diligence, the museum's use of the mark may subject the institution to a risk of liability if such use impinges on the rights of third parties.

Although seeking the assistance of counsel at the early stages clearly involves a commitment of resources, it is often more cost-effective and efficient than turning to counsel only after difficulties arise. For instance, because only certain types of marks may be registered, experienced trademark counsel can help educate those within the institution responsible for creating or selecting a mark about what types of marks will face the fewest obstacles during the process. Selecting marks with these considerations in mind not only can lower the cost of obtaining a federal registration but also may prevent future problems in enforcing the museum's trademark rights. Moreover, counsel

may add significant value both in crafting the scope of the search and in analyzing the results. While a museum may choose to minimize its costs by conducting its own preliminary availability searches or commissioning full trademark searches without assistance of counsel, the ultimate decision about whether to proceed with a particular mark is best made with the benefit of expert analysis of the risks revealed by the searches. Legal counsel may also be relied upon to draft, file, and prosecute applications for federal registration. For instance, obstacles to obtaining a federal registration may be avoided through careful crafting of the descriptions of goods and/or services covered in the application. Accordingly, it is advisable to draft the initial application with potential dangers and obstacles in mind rather than risk incurring the considerable expense of responding to a substantive Office Action by the PTO refusing registration or a third-party challenge to the use and/or registration of the mark. Successful prosecution of a federal application, particularly if substantive objections to registration are raised, requires the experience of counsel.

The following sections provide a broad outline of the process of "clearing" marks to ensure that they are available for use and/or registration by the museum and describe in general the process of applying for, maintaining, and renewing a federal trademark registration. These sections are intended to familiarize readers with the critical steps to and highlight how legal counsel can facilitate the process. For institutions that choose to conduct their own clearance without the assistance of counsel (or with limited assistance), more detailed guidance on the clearance and registration processes are provided in appendixes A and D.

Selection of Marks and Classification of Goods and Services

There is an inherent tension between the natural tendency to choose a mark that readily describes the product or service with which it is used and the long-term benefits of choosing an arbitrary, fanciful, or even suggestive mark, which will be accorded a greater degree of protection.[60] Selecting a mark that has a direct association with the product or service it represents (that is, a weak mark) may yield the short-term benefits of immediate consumer recognition. In the long run, however, the rewards may be greater if the necessary time and effort are spent to develop a strong mark.

Identifying or selecting a mark is the critical first step in the registration process. The attributes of the mark selected will often determine how difficult it will be to obtain a registration and will, therefore, affect the costs of the process. It is also important at the initial stages to determine the precise goods and/or services to which the mark will apply. Because marks are specific to goods and/or services, meaningful research to determine availability cannot be conducted until the goods and/or services have been identified.

Trademark Availability Searches

Once a mark has been selected, it is critical to conduct an investigation—generally referred to as a "clearance" or "availability" search—to ensure that the mark is available for use and/or registration. Failure to conduct such a search may lead to a conflict with a senior user of an identical or confusingly similar mark.

Searches of varying degrees of completeness are available. Which search to conduct will depend on a number of factors, including the importance of the mark to the institution, time constraints, and costs. As a preliminary step, it is often advisable to conduct a relatively inexpensive computer search of the PTO records, which will quickly reveal whether a proposed mark is clearly unavailable or whether a more thorough search is advisable. Internet searches relying on several different search engines may also identify common-law users of a proposed mark and provide some insight into the nature and scope of such use.

Because trademark rights arise with use, a more comprehensive search may be advisable to uncover prior users of a mark who have confined themselves to a small geographic area and have not previously sought or obtained a federal or state registration. Therefore, even if the preliminary search does not identify any conflicts, a more comprehensive search should, depending on the circumstances, be considered before moving forward. Comprehensive searches, offered by several commercial search firms, review federal and state trademark registries, various trade and telephone directories, corporate name databases, and domain name registries. Detailed guidance on trademark availability searches, including the types of searches available, identification of the commercial firms that offer these services, and the approximate cost, can be found in appendix A.

Federal Registration Requirements and Procedure [61]

Bases and Requirements for Registration

A museum that either is actually using or has a bona fide intent to use a mark in interstate commerce may apply for a federal trademark registration.[62] It is advisable to apply to register a mark at the earliest date possible because the filing date serves as the "constructive use" date of the mark.[63] For example, when the application is filed based on the intention to use a mark (commonly referred to as an "ITU" application), and actual use commences after another party has used the same or a confusingly similar mark, the applicant will nonetheless have priority based on the constructive use dating from the earlier filing date, when and if the application matures to registration.

As a general rule, in order for a mark to proceed to registration on the PTO's Principal Register (whether originally filed as a use-based or an ITU application) the mark must ultimately satisfy the following criteria: (1) It must be actually used in interstate commerce; (2) it cannot be generic or merely descriptive (which may be overcome by a showing of "acquired distinctiveness)"; and (3) it may not be confusingly similar to a mark covered by a registration. A mark cannot be registered with the PTO if it includes the name of a living person without his or her consent; immoral or scandalous matter; or matter that may disparage, falsely suggest connection, or bring an individual, institution, belief, or national symbol into contempt or disrepute.[64] In addition, marks composed of a flag or coat of arms or other insignia of the United States, any state or municipality, or a foreign nation may not be registered.[65]

What Is Actual Use?

"Actual use" of a trademark generally consists of affixing the mark to a product or its packaging and selling the product in interstate commerce.[66] This means the mark must be used on a product or service that crosses state, national, or territorial lines or that effects commerce crossing such lines. It should be noted that the use of a trademark in connection with advertising a good, without actual sales or affixing the mark to the product itself, does not constitute use of a trademark. "Actual use" of a service mark may consist of the advertising or sale of currently available services to the public under the mark.

PTO Application and Review Process

A federal trademark application consists of: (1) a written application form (see appendix B); (2) a drawing of the mark; (3) specimens showing use of the mark (for use-based applications); and (4) the required filing fee. The application must include a description of the goods and/or services to be offered under the mark, and each good or service must fall with one of the 42 categories specified in the International Schedule of Classes of Goods and Services (see appendix C). The current application fee is $245 per class of goods or services. The application for federal registration, with its associated filing fees, is submitted to the PTO in Arlington, Virginia.

After filing an application with the PTO, there is a delay of approximately 9 to 12 months before the PTO takes initial action. Trademark applications are reviewed by a PTO examining attorney for compliance with certain statutory and regulatory requirements. Two major components of the examination are distinctiveness of mark and the similarity of the marks to other marks with earlier filing dates.[67] The examining attorney will either approve the mark for publication or, more commonly, issue an Office Action noting issues that the applicant must resolve before the application can move forward. If and when the examining attorney is satisfied that the mark appears to be registrable, the PTO will publish the mark in its *Official Gazette*, which provides notice to any party who may wish to oppose the registration of the mark. If no party files an opposition or request for extension of time within which to oppose the registration of a mark within 30 days of publication, the PTO will issue a registration for use-based application.[68]

For an ITU application that successfully passes the PTO examination/review process and the publication period, a Notice of Allowance is issued.[69] The applicant must make actual use of the mark within six months from the date the Notice of Allowance is issued by filing a Statement of Use, or the application will be deemed abandoned.[70] If the applicant cannot demonstrate actual use of the mark within six months, the party can, on showing "good cause," extend the period to show use of the mark for up to an additional two and one-half years. An applicant may, therefore, have a total of three years within which to "reserve" a mark that it eventually intends to use. After the party commences use of the mark and provides appropriate evidence of such use to the PTO, the PTO grants a registration.

Appendix D provides more detailed discussion of the particular components of a trademark application, guidance on suitable specimens of use, descriptions of goods and services likely to be applicable to the museum context, and more extensive review of issues that may arise in the course of the PTO's examination process.

Supplemental Register

If a mark is refused registration on the Principal Register on the ground that it is nondistinctive (that is, merely descriptive, geographically descriptive, or primarily a surname), and the mark has not yet acquired distinctiveness, the mark may be registered on the Supplemental Register.[71] A pending use-based application for registration on the Principal Register may be amended to seek registration on the Supplemental Register. Often the suggestion to amend an application for registration on the Supplemental Register is made by the examining attorney who has refused registration of the mark on the Principal Register.

The benefits of a registration on the Supplemental Register are not as great as with the Principal Register. For instance, applications for marks that are based on the applicant's intent to use the mark cannot be made directly to the Supplemental Register. Registrations on the Supplemental Register are not considered evidence of the validity of the registered mark or the registrant's ownership or exclusive right to use the mark.

Registration on the Supplemental Register does, however, afford the registrant the right to use the federal registration symbol (®). In addition, a registration on the Supplemental Register should appear in the trademark search reports commissioned by third parties and would therefore give notice to others of the registrant's claim in the mark. A registration on the Supplemental Register may be cited by the PTO as a bar to registration of confusingly similar marks and could serve as a deterrent to third parties seeking to use and/or register a similar mark. A registration on the Supplemental Register can also be used as a basis for filing applications in foreign countries pursuant to certain international treaties.[72]

Timing

The federal registration process may, in some instances, be completed in less than two years. The process can and often does take much longer, however, particularly if the examining attorney initially refuses registration of the mark on substantive grounds. Moreover, an opposition proceeding can add a year or more to the registration process, and the outcome of this litigation-type proceeding is often difficult to predict.

Maintaining and Renewing Federal Registrations

An institution that successfully obtains a federal registration for a mark must remember that the PTO imposes ongoing maintenance and renewal requirements that must be satisfied or the PTO will cancel the registration.

Declaration of Continued Use (Section 8 Affidavit)

During the sixth year after the registration issues (between the fifth and sixth anniversaries of registration), the registrant must file with the PTO an affidavit or declaration attesting to current use of the mark or showing that its nonuse is due to special circumstances and not to any intention to abandon the mark (this process is referred to as a Section 8 filing).[73] If a trademark owner fails to file this declaration with the PTO during the sixth year, the PTO will automatically cancel the registration. Along with the Section 8 filing, the trademark owner must provide a specimen showing current use of the mark in commerce. The museum should carefully monitor the time for submitting the Section 8 filing. For those museums that rely on counsel to file and prosecute applications, notice of relevant deadlines may also be provided by their attorneys.

Declaration of Incontestability (Section 15 Filing)

If a registered trademark has been in continuous use for five years (that is, the fifth anniversary of the registration date has passed) and has not been subject to any third-party challenges, the trademark owner may file a declaration with the PTO attesting to these facts (this process is referred to as a Section 15 filing).[74] This declaration can be made simultaneously with the Section 8 filing discussed above.[75] Once a Section 15 filing is approved by the PTO, registration becomes conclusive evidence of the registrant's exclusive right to use the mark in connection with the goods and/or services listed in the registration certificate.[76]

Renewal

If a trademark is properly monitored and used in commerce, and is not abandoned by the trademark owner, protection for the mark will last indefinitely under common law. However, a federal trademark registration currently only lasts for 10 years from the date on which the registration was granted (not the filing date) and must be renewed during the final six months of the registration period.[77] As long as the trademark continues to be used, administrative formalities are satisfied, and no judicial decisions canceling the trademark registration have been issued, the registration may continue to be renewed for additional 10-year periods indefinitely. Museums should keep track of their renewal deadlines. If a museum relies on counsel to file and prosecute the application, the counsel responsible for the marks may have docketing systems to attempt to ensure that the museum is reminded of the deadlines.

Proper Trademark Usage

Guidelines for Usage

A trademark (registered or not) lasts only as long as it identifies the source of goods and/or services to the public. Museums that do not take affirmative steps to control and police the use of their marks by third parties and within the institution itself may find that the mark can no longer serve as a source identifier. The first step in protecting a mark is to ensure that it is used in a manner consistent with its source-identifying function. The following guidelines should be followed, when applicable, to ensure proper trademark usage and protect the integrity of the institution's marks.

- *Make the mark typographically distinct.* It is important to distinguish a mark from its surrounding text. Thus, whenever possible, the museum should use a distinctive typeface or other features such as quotation marks, all capital letters, or at least capitalization of the first letter of the mark.

- *Distinguish the mark from the museum's corporate or institutional name.* Because a museum's corporate name may also function as a trademark, when appropriate, the name should be used in a manner that reinforces its trademark function. For example, the mark should appear apart from and perhaps in differing typographic style from the institution's address to avoid suggesting that the name is being used not to identify goods or services but merely as a trade name identifying the institution. Trade names per se are not registrable at the PTO and, hence, do not enjoy the protection afforded registered marks. Moreover, trade name use will not support an application for federal registration.[78]

- *Use the registration symbol whenever the registered mark is used.* Once a mark is federally registered, the registration symbol (®) should be displayed when possible with the mark each time the mark is used to identify the goods and/or services contained in the registration certificate. At a minimum, it should be used at least once in each publication or printed piece, preferably the first time a mark appears on a page (either printed or electronic) or product surface.

It is important to note that the registration symbol should not be used in connection with a mark until the mark has been federally registered.[79] For unregistered marks (including marks that are the subject of pending applications for federal registration and state registrations), the owner may display the ™ symbol in connection with the display of trademarks or the ℠ symbol in connection with the display of service marks. Use of these symbols alerts the public that the museum is aware of its rights in the mark. Other forms of notice are also acceptable; there is generally no statutory formulation, except with respect to federally registered marks. If a mark is registered in a state, but not federally, the term "registered" may be used. For instance:

Federally registered: MUSEUM TO GO ®
State registered: MUSEUM TO GO*
(*MUSEUM TO GO is the registered trademark/service mark of The Franklin Institute)

It is also advisable to have a trademark attorney periodically review samples of all publications and promotional materials (such as exhibition catalogues, brochures, membership materials, and Web sites) to ensure that such materials reflect proper trademark usage.

- *Clarify ownership of the mark.* If it is not readily apparent who owns a trademark—for example, if the museum's letterhead is not being used or the association with the institution is not otherwise apparent from the nature of the use—a notice of ownership should be given. The marks owned by third parties should also be properly noticed if used by the institution in marketing, development, or advertising materials (for example, a corporate sponsor's logo).

- *Develop guidelines for consistent use of the museum's marks by others.* With respect to use of the institution's marks by parties outside the museum, the museum should include express language in any agreements it enters into with sponsors, licensees, associated institutions, and others governing the proper use of the mark and providing for preapproval and review mechanisms.

Dangers of Nonuse

If a trademark owner does not actively use a mark for three years, the mark may be presumed to be abandoned.[80] Therefore, to avoid being subject to an abandonment claim, the museum should keep track of marks that fall into disuse and avoid prolonged periods of nonuse for any marks that it does not intend to abandon.

Failure to control use of a mark by third parties may also result in the loss of trademark rights. Allowing others to use the mark without control over the nature and quality of the goods and/or services offered—called "naked licensing" or "tolerated infringement"—may eventually be fatal to the trademark owner's rights. Monitoring third-party use and establishing standards for the use of the museum's marks are particularly important in the licensing context (see chapter 4).[81]

In contrast, courts do not equate a trademark owner's failure to sue apparent infringing users with active consent or implied licensing of those who use the mark. Nevertheless, if an owner does not enforce its rights in a mark, the mark may lose its significance as an indication of source. Similarly, although delay in enforcing trademark rights may not result in abandonment, such a delay may provide an infringer with grounds to assert an affirmative defense and thereby restrict the trademark owner's remedies against that particular infringer.[82]

Trademark Enforcement

Unauthorized third-party use of a museum's trademark, or a mark confusingly similar to the museum's mark, may inflict significant damage on an institution's reputation and goodwill and directly affect its commercial and financial interests. All museums, regardless of size and scope, must be proactive in their efforts to detect and prevent misuse of their marks. This section provides guidance on steps that museums can take to monitor and police their marks. It outlines the possible claims and associated remedies available to a museum in enforcing its trademark rights.

Likelihood of Confusion Standard

Those within the institution responsible for developing and implementing an effective trademark enforcement strategy must understand what types of third-party activities are actionable. The standard for determining whether trademark infringement exists is known as the "likelihood of confusion" test. This test involves assessing whether a third party's use of a given mark is likely to cause the public to be confused as to the source, affiliation, or sponsorship of the goods or services in question.[83] The standard is not whether the allegedly infringing mark has actually caused or is certain to cause confusion, but whether there is a "likelihood" that confusion will arise.

The likelihood of confusion standard is applicable not only in trademark infringement litigation in state and federal courts but also in other contexts. For instance, the PTO applies this standard when judging applications for federal registration. Moreover, the issue of likelihood of confusion is at the core of many opposition and cancellation proceedings before the Trademark Trial and Appeal Board (TTAB).

A number of well-established factors are considered by the courts when determining if a likelihood of confusion exists.[84] The following are among the most common and significant:

- *Strength of the mark:* The more distinctive the mark, the less similar the marks and the goods or services need to be to find a likelihood of confusion.

- *Similarity of marks:* Marks are compared in terms of their sight, sound, meaning, and overall commercial impression. Marks need not be identical to give rise to likelihood of confusion.

- *Similarity or relatedness of goods or services:* The more related the goods or services sold by the two parties, the greater the likelihood that confusion exists between similar marks.

- *Similarity of marketing channels:* The greater the similarity between the target consumers, marketing media, and the channels used to distribute goods and services under similar marks, the greater the potential for confusion.

- *Sophistication of consumers:* The more sophisticated the purchasers, the more likely that they will be able to discern differences in products and services and the less likely that similar marks will be confused. Sophisticated consumers (including professionals or those spending considerable sums for the relevant products or services) are assumed to exercise greater care in purchasing decisions.

- *Instances of actual confusion:* Evidence that the use of the two marks has already led to consumer confusion may be a persuasive indicator that future confusion is likely. Conversely, the absence of actual confusion over a long period of concurrent use may indicate that future confusion is unlikely.

- *Wrongful intent:* Likelihood of confusion is presumed when it is shown that the infringing party deliberately intended to trade off the goodwill associated with another party's mark by adopting a similar mark. Knowledge of the other party's prior use will not alone establish wrongful intent, as long as the alleged infringer believes in good faith that the marks and goods and services are distinguishable or other mitigating factors exist.

- *Likelihood of expansion:* If a trademark owner can demonstrate that expansion of its use of a mark into an alleged infringer's market is likely or natural, or if consumers are likely to assume that such expansion will occur or has occurred, the likelihood of confusion is more probable.

Strategies for Policing and Monitoring Marks

In addition to defensive steps to ensure that the museum's marks are being used properly by the institution itself (and by its licensees, if applicable), museums must also take affirmative steps to ensure that no third parties use the museum's marks, or arguably similar marks, in such a way as to give rise to a likelihood of confusion. Failure to effectively police a mark may limit the museum's ability to exert its rights offensively or, in the worst case, may undermine the source-identifying function of the mark to such a degree that the trademark may be deemed abandoned.[85] Effective monitoring can be accomplished through a variety of means, which may include the following alternatives.

Watching Services

The most comprehensive way to monitor an institution's marks is to commission a watching service. Watching services offer regular monitoring of common-law trademarks as well as international, federal, and state trademark applications and registrations. The principal benefit of these services is that they give trademark owners early notice of the use or attempted registration of identical or confusingly similar marks. Many trademark owners choose to limit the watching services to federal applications, but common-law monitoring is advisable for an institution relying exclusively on watching services to alert it of infringing uses of its marks.

Watching services are offered by various commercial trademark search firms and differ in scope and cost.[86] A museum may commission the service directly from the search firm, or it may have trademark counsel commission the service, receive and monitor reports, and notify the institution if references of concern are identified. In light of the costs, a museum may decide to engage watching services for only its most valuable trademark assets (such as the name of the institution) and rely on in-house monitoring for other marks.

In-House Monitoring

Monitoring can also be conducted by museum personnel either exclusively or in conjunction with a commercial watching service. The PTO publishes all marks in its *Official Gazette*. Museums may subscribe to and monitor the *Official Gazette* on their own, but they must keep in mind that regular and consistent monitoring is necessary because parties wishing to oppose applications have only 30 days from the date of publication to file an opposition or seek an extension of time to oppose.[87] In-house monitoring of the Internet is also recommended. By typing variations of the museum's word marks into several search engines and reviewing the resulting Web sites, the institution may obtain valuable information regarding the nature and scope of third parties' use of terms comprising the museum's marks. Effective trademark monitoring and policing also involve educating personnel in all museum departments about the need to inform the appropriate administrators or outside counsel of any similar or confusingly similar marks they encounter in the marketplace.

Judging the Risks Presented and Role of Counsel

Once evidence of objectionable third-party use of a museum mark is uncovered, the nature and scope of the third party's use must be carefully investigated. To assess effectively the degree of risk presented by an apparent infringement and determine the appropriate response, if any, the following information is needed: (1) the identity of the infringer; (2) its resources; (3) the exact goods and/or services the mark is being used in connection with; (4) the date the third party's use of the mark began; and (5) the marketing channels used to sell the product.

Museum officials can glean this information through their own independent efforts, including commissioning a private investigation,[88] or through the assistance of counsel. Much of it may now be obtained over the Internet. This information is critical to assessing whether the museum is in fact the senior user of the mark and whether there is a likelihood of confusion between the museum's goods and/or services and those of the other entity. In some instances, the investigation may reveal that instead of having superior rights, the museum is in fact the junior user of the relevant mark. Under these circumstances, the museum and its counsel should consider the best course of action to eliminate or minimize the risk of liability in the event that the other entity becomes aware of and/or objects to the museum's use of the mark.

Even when an institution chooses to obtain factual information about the third party's use independently, seeking the advice of counsel immediately upon or shortly after discovering a seemingly troublesome third-party use is highly advisable. Counsel experienced in trademark law can be invaluable in assessing whether and to what extent the third-party use presents risk to the museum's rights; what action(s) may be taken against the third-party use; the costs and benefits of particular actions; and the museum's likelihood of success. As discussed in connection with the clearance of trademarks, except for those few institutions with in-house counsel, seeking the assistance of outside trademark counsel will require a commitment of resources. However, attempting to proceed without the benefit of expert analysis may subject the institution to unforseen costs and exposure, particularly if the museum's assessment of the relative rights of the

parties turns out to be wrong (for example, if the third party is in fact the senior user and responds to the challenge by bringing an infringement action against the museum).

Cease and Desist, "Line-Drawing," and "Information-Seeking" Letters

After discovering a third party's use of a mark that appears likely to cause confusion with a museum trademark and confirming through independent research that the museum has superior rights, the museum may wish to send the third party a cease and desist letter. The cease and desist letter provides notice of the museum's rights in the mark and may give the third party the opportunity to resolve the matter without requiring further action by the museum. Depending on the strength of the museum's position and the degree of aggressiveness with which it wishes to pursue the matter, the letter may come from either a senior administrator (the director, the chief financial officer), or the museum's trademark counsel.

Each cease and desist letter should be specifically tailored to the situation at hand, but it will typically contain some or all of the following elements:

- Identification of the sender (the museum administrator or counsel and descriptions of the institution's mark and the confusingly similar mark

- Details of the institution's rights in the mark, including the dates of first use, pertinent federal or state registration information, and relevant background information communicating to the recipient the value and strength of the museum's mark(s)

- Brief discussion of how the third party's use is likely to cause confusion, deception, or mistake among the public as to source, sponsorship, or affiliation

- Summary of the legal claims and remedies available to the institution

- Demand that the third party cease use of the mark and provide written assurances within a given period of time that such use has ceased and will not recur

In certain instances, particularly if the facts indicate that the objectionable conduct may be unintentional and poses minimal risk to the institution's rights, the letter may encourage the third party's cooperation by referring to possible alternative means of resolving the matter, including negotiating a licensing arrangement, providing the third party a fixed time within which to change its mark, or paying a royalty on the third party's prior sales and remaining inventory.[89]

Less aggressive forms of communicating with the third party may be appropriate under some circumstances. For instance, if the risk of confusion between the third party's mark and the museum's mark appears minimal, but if expanded use (whether geographic, potential additional uses, or otherwise) by the third party would risk significant confusion, the museum may opt to send a less aggressive "line-drawing" letter. This letter puts the third party on notice of the museum's rights, may acknowledge that the museum has no objection to the third party's use provided the status quo is maintained (or some other condition is met), but cautions that any future expansion or evidence of actual confusion will be met with objection by the museum.

When the museum appears to have superior rights, but the nature and scope of the third party's use cannot be determined conclusively, the museum may wish to send a nonconfrontational "information-gathering" inquiry. With any form of communication, however, there is always a twofold risk: (1) If the third party turns out to have rights superior to those of the museum, the notification may only prompt offensive action against the museum, and (2) the third party may

file its own suit seeking judicial determination that its conduct is not infringing (a "declaratory judgment action"). In light of these risks, museums are well advised to seek the advice of experienced trademark counsel before contacting any potential adversary.

If a museum receives a cease and desist letter or a milder form of objection asserting that its use of a mark impinges a third party's rights, the museum should notify trademark counsel immediately. The information necessary to evaluate the museum's potential liability in a defensive situation parallels that needed if the museum is exerting its own rights.[90] On being informed of any claim or potential claim, it may also be advisable to notify the museum's liability insurance carrier, even when the initial communication is not adversarial and the likelihood of an amicable resolution appears great. A museum should never ignore a cease and desist letter. To do so may subject the institution to a claim of willful infringement, giving rise to a risk of increased damages in the unfortunate event that the dispute matures into litigation and judgment is entered against the museum.

Trademark Enforcement Litigation

Disputes over trademarks are resolved short of litigation in the vast majority of instances. There may be situations, however, when the parties are unable to resolve their differences amicably and a trademark owner has no option but to seek relief through litigation. Generally, trademark owners have two options for seeking redress and protecting their rights. If the remedy sought is cessation of the objectionable use of a mark by a third party (with associated monetary recovery for damage done to goodwill and reputation), the museum must bring an action in state or federal court. If the remedy sought relates to ownership or respective rights to the federal registration of a mark, a litigation-type administrative proceeding may be brought before the Trademark Trial and Appeal Board (TTAB) of the PTO. Depending on the circumstances of the case and the outcome desired, judicial and TTAB proceedings may be brought in tandem and proceed on a parallel course, or the party on the offensive may choose one avenue or the other.

Bases for Liability: Enforcing Rights in Federal or State Court

Many potential theories of liability are available to a museum in challenging an unauthorized use of its mark by a third party. Because these theories often overlap, more than one theory can often be asserted based upon a set of facts. In short, these theories are geared toward protecting the trademark owner from a third party's unauthorized use of its trademark that may cause significant damage to the trademark owner's reputation and goodwill, as well as toward protecting the trademark owner from commercial and monetary harm.

Infringement

Trademark infringement actions may be brought under the federal trademark statute to redress the unauthorized use of the trademark owner's registered or unregistered mark in a manner that is likely to lead to consumer confusion.[91] Trademark owners, including museums, generally must guard against two forms of confusion. One form involves the use of a confusingly similar mark by a third party in connection with goods or services identical to or highly related to those of the museum in such a way that it may cause members of the public to choose the infringer's goods or services when they meant to select the museum's goods or services. The other form of confusion, arguably more relevant to museums, arises when a third party's use of a mark falsely suggests a connection or affiliation with, or sponsorship by, the museum, or causes the public to blame the museum when dissatisfied with the quality of the goods or services offered by the third party. The potential for damage to the institution's reputation may arise even when the third party provides "noncompeting" goods or services.

The typical remedy awarded in a successful trademark infringement action brought under the federal trademark statute is an injunction,[92] which is essentially a court order requiring a defendant to stop its current and any future infringing activity. The scope of the injunction will often depend on the circumstances of the case (for a discussion of injunction standards, see chapter 1, "Infringement: Preliminary Considerations"). Monetary damages are also available in some cases and typically include the defendant's profits and/or the plaintiff's actual damages. These monetary damages may also be multiplied by a factor of three ("treble damages") at the discretion of the court in egregious cases. Finally, a court may also award attorneys' fees in exceptional cases, such as where bad faith, malice, or willful infringement has been established.[93]

Dilution

If a museum owns a mark of considerable renown, it may bring a federal dilution claim when unauthorized commercial use of the same or a similar mark might weaken or harm the museum's mark, even when there is no competition between goods or services and when there is no likelihood of confusion.[94] As a threshold matter, the federal dilution statute requires that the mark be "famous" in order to maintain an action for dilution. Under the statute, fame is measured by such factors as the degree of distinctiveness of the mark, the duration and geographic extent of its use, and the nature and amount of use of the same or a similar mark by other third parties.

Dilution may occur by "blurring" (that is, when the unauthorized use lessens the ability of the famous mark to serve as a unique source identifier of the trademark owner's goods or services) or by tarnishment (that is, when the trademark owner's mark is used in a degrading or unsavory manner, therefore creating a negative association with the trademark owner's goods or services in the mind of the public). Injunctive relief is generally the sole remedy for dilution. However, in cases where a willful intent to dilute is shown, significant damages may be awarded.

False Advertising/Disparagement

A museum can bring a false advertising or disparagement claim if another party makes a false or misleading assertion about the museum's products, services, or commercial activities that is likely to result in damage to the museum (either reputational or commercial).[95] To succeed, a claimant must show a false or misleading assertion that was material to the purchasing decision, as well as a likelihood of damage due to the false or misleading assertion. The remedies available for an action for false advertising or disparagement are essentially the same as those available for trademark infringement.

Counterfeiting

The most blatant and egregious form of trademark infringement is counterfeiting. A counterfeit mark is a mark that is identical to, or indistinguishable from, a registered trademark and is applied to the same goods or services covered by the genuine mark's trademark registration. For example, if a museum sells T-shirts in its retail store bearing the museum's federally registered logo, and outside, a few blocks away, a street vendor sells unauthorized T-shirts bearing an identical copy of the museum's logo, the museum may have an action for counterfeiting against the vendor under the Lanham Act, and perhaps against others involved in the manufacture or distribution of the T-shirts. The Counterfeiting Act of 1984 may also be used to impose criminal penalties, including substantial fines and incarceration.[96]

To seek redress under the anticounterfeiting provision of the Lanham Act, the museum must have a federal registration on the Principal Register, and the defendant must be applying the counterfeit mark to the same goods or services covered by the genuine mark's trademark registration.[97] The Lanham Act contains strong remedies against counterfeiting, including mechanisms for the seizure of goods bearing counterfeit marks and the award of damages and attorneys' fees.[98]

State Actions/Remedies

State remedies provide a means of trademark enforcement when the infringer is not using the offending mark in interstate commerce, as required for actions under the Lanham Act.[99] In addition, many plaintiffs bringing actions under the Lanham Act also bring claims under state statutes and common law; federal and state remedies are not mutually exclusive. Indeed, many states have their own dilution statutes. Unlike the federal dilution law, state dilution statutes often provide relief even if the infringed mark is "famous" only statewide and may not require the same degree of "fame" as required under the federal counterpart. However, a state dilution action is barred against a defendant who holds a federal registration for the mark that is the subject of the challenge.

The standards for trademark infringement under state law are generally the same as for an infringement action under the Lanham Act. Many states also have unfair competition laws that encompass many different kinds of unfair behavior that run contrary to accepted business ethics or public policy. In addition to injunctions and compensatory damages, remedies that are also available under federal law, many states allow recovery of punitive damages.

Trademark Trial and Appeal Board Proceedings

A trademark owner who may be damaged by the issuance or existence of a trademark registration can institute two litigation-type proceedings at the PTO to enforce its rights: (1) oppositions against applications for registration[100] and (2) cancellation actions filed against marks that are already registered.[101]

Opposition to Registration

A Notice of Opposition may be filed at the Trademark Trial and Appeal Board (TTAB) seeking a declaration that the proposed registration of a mark is improper.[102] If, for instance, the museum's trademark monitoring activities reveal the filing or publication of an application for federal registration for a mark that is arguably confusingly similar to a museum mark (or that is arguably descriptive or generic), the museum should consider and discuss with counsel the possibility of taking such action. Time is of the essence because oppositions must be filed within 30 days of publication of the application in the PTO's *Official Gazette*.[103]

The most common ground for opposing a registration is likelihood of confusion with an opposer's registered trademark or common-law mark. To oppose the registration of a mark on the ground that it is confusingly similar to that of the museum, the museum must show that it has superior rights (that is, earlier use or a trademark registration with a filing date earlier than the applicant's first use). It is important to emphasize that the museum may rely on its superior common-law trademark rights and need not hold a federal registration to oppose the registration of another mark. In deciding the matter, the TTAB will evaluate the two marks to determine whether coexistence of the marks is likely to cause confusion. To this end, the TTAB will apply a variation of the likelihood of confusion test discussed in greater detail earlier in this section (see "Likelihood of Confusion Standard").

Cancellation of Registration

Cancellation proceedings are adjudicated by the TTAB and may be brought by a party, including a holder of common-law trademark rights, alleging that it will be harmed by an existing federal registration of a mark.[104] Unlike oppositions that are used to preclude an applicant from obtaining a federal registration, the cancellation proceeding is used to attack a federal registration that has already been issued. Cancellations are procedurally equivalent to oppositions and may be brought on the same grounds.

The opposition and cancellation proceedings determine only whether the challenged party is entitled to a federal registration. The TTAB has no power to award damages or injunctive relief and can make no determination of the right to use the mark. Final decisions of the TTAB in both opposition and cancellation proceedings may be appealed to the U.S. Court of Appeals for the Federal Circuit, or the appealing party can pursue other appropriate relief (including injunctive relief, damages, and other means of relief) by filing a civil action in U.S. District Court.[105]

Museum as Defendant: Risks from Direct and Secondary Liability

Museums must not only be concerned with protecting their own trademark assets, but they should be equally vigilant in ensuring that the marks of others are used properly and only with authorization. It is a well-settled principle of trademark law that a retailer or dealer that does not itself manufacture goods that bear an infringing mark, but merely sells them, may be liable for trademark infringement.[106] Under this rule, a museum may be liable even without knowledge of or reason to suspect that the goods it sells are infringing, although such "innocent" infringement is less likely to result in severe monetary sanctions. Therefore, all institutions with retail operations featuring the goods of others must take steps to ensure that the suppliers and manufacturers with whom they deal are beyond reproach. In negotiating contracts with suppliers and manufacturers, the museum would be wise to demand, in its written agreements, indemnification or other assurances that the products purchased or offered by the institution for resale do not infringe the rights of others.

In addition to liability for "direct infringement," related theories of liability allow a trademark owner to bring a claim of trademark infringement against not only the entities directly responsible for the infringement (including the retailer or distributor of the goods), but also against other parties with more attenuated relationships with the infringer. Although secondary liability is not specifically mentioned in the federal trademark statute, courts have held that its provisions encompass secondary liability causes of action and that remedies provided thereunder are applicable.[107] Thus, a museum may avail itself of the theories of "secondary liability" in offensive actions against infringers of the museum's marks, but these theories are equally applicable if the museum's conduct, or the conduct of parties with certain relationships with the institution, are at issue.

Vicarious Liability

As a general rule, a museum will be held vicariously liable for the infringing actions of its employees (and perhaps even independent contractors, if the institution exercises sufficient control over a contractor's activities) when those actions are committed by the employee acting with the scope of his or her duties.[108] Under such circumstances, the museum's lack of knowledge of the infringing activity will not necessarily absolve it from liability.

Consider the following example: The museum hires an employee to design and maintain its Web site. The employee incorporates into the Web site a federally registered icon used to identify an Internet search engine without the search engine owner's permission. The employee's actions may constitute actionable trademark infringement because the use of another's trademark may suggest that the search engine owner and the museum are affiliated in some way when in fact they are not. The infringing conduct of the employee may be attributed to the employer-museum under traditional theories of agency law because the employee committed the infringement in the course of his employment.

Contributory Infringement

A charge of contributory infringement may also be brought against a party that encourages infringement of a mark or knows (or has reason to know) of the infringing activity by the other but does nothing to stop it.[109] A museum may have contributory liability exposure for many activities that arguably are ancillary to its core services. The museum may, for example, lease space to third parties who in turn sell goods (for example, for craft shows) or provide services on the museum's premises (for example, as part of a restaurant or other food service). When the museum serves primarily as a landlord and does not exercise direct control over the third party, it may nevertheless be held liable for the infringing conduct of the third party if the museum knows or should have known of such conduct. To protect against this risk, the museum may consider including an indemnification provision in its standard facilities lease agreement. The museum, however, has no independent duty to investigate whether its "tenants" are infringing another's trademark.[110]

Settlement of Trademark Disputes

At some stage in a trademark dispute—either after a cease and desist letter has been sent, opposition/cancellation proceedings instituted, or an action brought in federal or state court—the parties may decide that settlement is the preferred option in light of the expense and time required to pursue the matter further. The contours of a settlement agreement will depend on various factors, including the relative strength of the parties' positions, their respective resources, and the importance of the marks to the parties. Institutions considering making or entering into a settlement proposal should do so only with the benefit of expert legal advice. Settlement agreements can be structured in innumerable ways, but some standard approaches include the following:

- *Capitulation by defending party*. Under some circumstances, the party defending its use and/or effort to register a mark may simply agree to cease from all use and/or further attempts to register the mark at issue, with or without admitting liability for its previous conduct. For the party asserting superior rights in a mark, this is usually the preferred outcome to any dispute. The settlement agreement should be drafted to provide for cessation of the objectionable use, and it may require the allegedly infringing party to destroy all infringing goods in its possession and withdraw any pending applications for registration of the mark (either state or federal) by a certain date. The settlement agreement may also include provisions by which the parties agree in advance to a damage amount should infringing use be discovered in the future. Under certain circumstances, a phase-out period may be granted to the capitulating party.

- *Purchase of rights.* In some cases one party may wish to purchase the trademark rights and related goodwill held by the other party. This approach may be particularly effective for trademark owners who plan to expand their use of a mark into new geographic markets or in connection with new goods or services but are faced with the existence of third parties who may have conflicting rights. Negotiations for the purchase of trademarks can be very complicated. Unlike the purchase of commodities, the purchase of trademarks involves very complex and unquantifiable factors and may require the services of independent valuation experts. In addition, trademark assignment, if not done with considerable care, may result in loss of the very rights that the parties purported to transfer.[111]

- *Coexistence agreements.* The parties may also consider entering into a coexistence agreement, which may allow both of them to use their marks in specific geographic areas or in connection with particular noncompeting goods or services. The negative aspects of a coexistence agreement, particularly for a party holding a

federal registration for the mark at issue, is that it reduces the scope of that party's trademark rights. Specifically, by affirmatively acquiescing to the use of an arguably infringing mark by one third party, the trademark owner may have difficulty objecting to subsequent use of the mark by others.

- *License agreements.* A license is different from a coexistence agreement in that the licensee recognizes the licensor's ownership of (and thus exclusive rights to) the mark. Under a license agreement the junior party may be permitted to continue its use of a mark, subject to "quality control" procedures and other conditions specified by the trademark owner.[112] Beyond those two characteristics, licenses can take many forms—royalty or royalty-free, limited time or perpetual, limited in geographic scope or not, limited to specific products or services or not. (See chapter 4 for further discussion of licensing agreements.)

Permitted Uses and Defenses to Trademark Infringement

Trademark owners, even those relying on common-law rights, have the right under trademark law to prevent junior users from using the same or similar marks in a manner likely to cause confusion, suggest an affiliation, or disparage or damage the trademark owner in some way. This protection is not absolute, and the extent of its scope is delineated by several countervailing considerations that can restrict a trademark owner's ability to enforce its rights against certain parties under certain circumstances. Permitted third-party uses, as well as affirmative defenses to the enforcement of trademark rights, may limit the ability of a museum to take action against every objectionable use of its marks. Certain uses described below (for example, fair use and nominative use) are, in their truest sense, not to be viewed as defenses to infringement. Rather, they are deemed noninfringing, permitted uses in the first instance because they do not create a risk of consumer confusion. By contrast, the affirmative defenses described in this section (for example, acquiescence and fraud) arise as a consequence of the trademark owner's own actions, or failure to act, and are asserted by a defendant as a shield in situations when the defendant's conduct otherwise results in consumer confusion.

Fair Use

Although the owner of a trademark has the right to prevent third-party use of the identical mark or a similar mark in a manner likely to cause consumer confusion, that trademark owner cannot prevent the use of a mark by others if the mark is used in its descriptive sense.[113] In other words, third parties are free to use the words or symbols that constitute the protected trademark of an institution provided that such elements are used purely descriptively and not as an identifier of goods or services. In effect, fair use allows parties to use an otherwise protected mark to accurately describe their own products or services in order to inform consumers of what they offer. For example, a children's museum using the mark THE WORLD OF WONDER in connection with a particular program or exhibition may not be able to prohibit another party (even a commercial enterprise) from using the phrase "A world of wonder awaits you" as an advertising slogan, even if the museum's mark has acquired distinctiveness. Courts apply the following criteria in evaluating whether a given use is fair: (1) whether the mark is used in good faith and not for the purposes of capitalizing on the success and reputation of the trademark owner; (2) whether the mark is used in a nontrademark sense and not as source identifier; and (3) whether the mark accurately describes the third-party user's products or services.[114] If all three criteria are satisfied, use of the mark may be deemed fair and therefore noninfringing.

Nominative Use

Third-party use of a museum's mark to identify the museum's goods or services (as opposed to those of the third party) may constitute a permissible nominative use of that mark.[115] Nominative trademark use arises in a variety of situations, such as comparative advertising, advertising used by an entity whose goods or services relate to those of the trademark owner, news reporting, and dissemination of consumer protection information. Permissible nominative trademark use is often characterized as nonconfusing because this type of use arguably does not suggest sponsorship or endorsement by the trademark owner. Courts have suggested that permissible nominative use can only be asserted when the products or services of the trademark owner are not identifiable without use of the mark and when the third party uses only the amount of the mark necessary to reference the trademark owner's goods or services.[116]

First Amendment Considerations

Another form of permitted use arises in the context of artistic or literary works that reference or incorporate the trademarks or service marks of others. Certain forms of artistic or literary expression may incorporate trademarks owned by others for the purpose of engaging in social commentary or criticism. When a trademark is used in this way—as part of a noncommercial, communicative message rather than as a source-identifier—the artist's First Amendment right to freedom of expression trumps the trademark owner's proprietary interest in protecting its goodwill in the mark. Such uses, therefore, are likely immune to claims of trademark infringement or dilution, and an institution displaying and reproducing works featuring appropriated marks would be similarly protected.[117] This is precisely why Andy Warhol and Jasper Johns were able to freely incorporate the Campbell's soup and Savarin coffee trademarks into their respective works without the fear of infringement liability, and why museums are free to continue to display such works without risk of liability.

Parody is a particular form of artistic expression protected by the First Amendment. A claim of parody is not really defense to trademark infringement, but a claim that the relevant consumers are not likely to be confused as to source sponsorship or affiliation. In the words of a federal appeals court, "[a] non-infringing parody is merely amusing, not confusing."[118] However, as with parodies of a copyrighted work, to qualify as a noninfringing parodic use of a trademark, the trademark itself and/or the trademark owner must be the target of the parody. In other words, if a mark is appropriated not to parody a product or the company symbolized by the mark, but as a means of communicating some other message, then the use is unlikely to be considered a protected "parody."[119]

It should be noted that even when the use of a trademark can fairly be characterized as a non-commercial "artistic" or "parodic" use, the protections of the First Amendment are not absolute. The issue of whether the use is likely to confuse consumers will remain a critical issue. In such cases, if confusion is likely to result, a court may restrict such use in the interest of preventing consumer deception, notwithstanding the strong countervailing First Amendment considerations. Moreover, even in the absence of actual or likely consumer confusion, there may be circumstances in which the use of a trademark in a controversial, unsavory, or derogatory context may result in damage to the value of the mark or its owner's goodwill. In extreme circumstances, particularly where the unauthorized use is commercial, such use may also be actionable under state or federal dilution statutes or under common-law claims including passing off, misappropriation, defamation, and disparagement.

Defenses to Infringement

Defenses to conduct that may otherwise constitute trademark infringement may arise as a consequence of the trademark owner's own actions or failure to act and may serve to shield an infringer from liability.[120] Defenses that arise from a trademark owner's failure to act include laches and abandonment. Defenses that arise as a function of the trademark owner's affirmative actions include acquiescence and fraud.

When a trademark owner knows of a potentially infringing use of its mark but delays taking action against such use for a significant period of time, he may be barred from asserting a claim under the equitable doctrine known as "laches." If successfully asserted, laches can be used to prohibit the award of certain remedies, to overcome a motion, or to defeat an entire infringement suit. Abandonment may be asserted if a trademark owner has either failed to enforce its rights against other users of confusingly similar marks or has stopped using a mark for some period of time without an intent to resume use. In these instances, the mark may be deemed abandoned because it is no longer capable of distinguishing the goods and services of the owner from the goods and services of others. Depending on the circumstances surrounding a mark's abandonment, the mark may be used by the general public or by a subsequent third-party user claiming rights in the mark.

Acquiescence is similar to laches but requires an additional finding that the trademark owner, by some sort of action, communicated to the alleged infringer that the owner would not take steps to prohibit the challenged use. This additional element makes the defense of acquiescence difficult to assert successfully and is available only in unusual circumstances. Another defense, fraud on the PTO, can be asserted when a plaintiff claims to have superior trademark rights to those of a defendant but has obtained a federal registration through fraudulent means (for example, a false claim of date of first use in the application for federal registration). A successful allegation of fraud may not act as an absolute defense in an infringement action, but it can lead to cancellation of the registration.

Joint Ownership and Transfers of Trademark Rights

Joint Ownership

As with most other forms of property, a trademark may be owned by more than one entity. Joint ownership of a trademark may be appropriate when two museums collaborate on a special exhibition or an ongoing project, particularly if each museum wants to use a variation of its own mark in connection with the joint effort. Consider, for example, a situation in which two museums, the East Museum and the West Museum, launch a long-term traveling exhibition featuring works from the collections of each museum to appear in exhibition venues in different cities throughout the United States. The museums plan to promote this project under the mark EAST-WEST MUSEUMS: MASTERWORKS ON VIEW and decide to file an application for federal registration of this mark as joint owners. Before filing this application, the museums should take into account several considerations particular to joint ownership of a mark, including possible shortcomings of these types of arrangements.

Joint ownership of a mark would appear to impinge on the basic function of a trademark: to identify goods and services originating from a single source. Use of the same mark by multiple parties can lead to consumer confusion and the appearance that the goods or services at issue are not subject to some form of centralized quality control. For this reason, any joint ownership arrangement must be very carefully circumscribed and set forth in a written agreement

between the parties. This agreement should address issues such as upholding quality control, avoiding consumer confusion, and responsibilities for use and ownership of the mark during the exhibition and, if appropriate, on termination of the relationship. This last issue, if not adequately addressed at the outset of the joint ownership arrangement, can become the most problematic aspect of joint trademark ownership. Museums contemplating registration of a jointly owned mark should also consider that all documents filed at the PTO (including the application and all maintenance and renewal documents) will need to be either executed or verified at some point by both owners.

A museum contemplating shared use of a mark may consider creating other arrangements whereby joint use would be permitted without some of the difficulties of joint ownership. One possible arrangement is the creation of a joint venture or other independent legal entity that would assume ownership of all contractual obligations and intellectual property relevant to the joint enterprise. For example, several museums interested in producing a collective catalogue that features their respective retail merchandise may form a consortium to jointly develop and own the trademarks used to identify and promote the catalogue. It is important to note, however, that creating a different legal entity to act as applicant and owner may not work in the scenario described above involving the East-West project; if the marks EAST MUSEUM and WEST MUSEUM are federally registered, the PTO will cite these applications against any confusingly similar application filed by the jointly formed legal entity. In this situation, therefore, a trademark application listing each entity as a joint owner may be the better solution.

Potential problems of joint ownership may also be solved through license agreements. License agreements may be the best types of arrangements for museums that do not wish to be legally tied to another institution through joint trademark ownership or a formal joint venture arrangement. For example, a museum may want to enter into an arrangement with a credit card company or bank to create an affinity credit card featuring a new museum logo designed especially for use in connection with the card. The museum may not want to own the new logo jointly with the credit card company and may also want to avoid the potential liabilities associated with a formal joint venture. By entering into a carefully drafted license agreement with the company, the museum maintains ultimate control over its own marks while not exposing itself to various potential business risks.[121]

Assignment of Trademarks

A museum that wants to transfer ownership of a mark to a third party or to acquire a mark from a third party may implement such transfers through a written trademark assignment. A written assignment is required to document the transfer of ownership of a federal registration or pending application at the PTO and, though not required, is strongly recommended to memorialize transfer of any unregistered marks. Several general rules govern the assignment of rights in a mark.[122]

First, because a trademark symbolizes the goodwill of the business with which it is associated, a trademark cannot be assigned without simultaneous conveyance of such goodwill. Not adhering to this rule, known as the prohibition on assignments in gross, can render a transfer null and void and, ultimately, can lead to abandonment of the mark intended to be transferred. To prevent such an occurrence, trademark assignments should explicitly state that all marks are being transferred along with the goodwill of the business to which they pertain. When appropriate, physical assets of the business in which the trademark is used should also be transferred. At the very least, the goods offered by the transferee under the mark should be related to, if not the same as, those previously offered under the same mark by the transferor.

Second, applications for federal registration filed on an intent-to-use basis cannot be assigned before an acceptable allegation of use has been filed.[123] Although an application subject to such an assignment will not be refused registration, it will be subject to cancellation by any third party that can establish untimely assignment. It is important to note, however, that the prohibition on assignment of ITU applications does not apply to most situations in which a mark is being conveyed to a successor to the business of the applicant to which the mark pertains.

Finally, as explained above in part, any trademark assignment that involves a federal registration or a pending application for federal registration should be recorded with the PTO within three months of execution. Recordation will put any prospective subsequent purchaser on notice of the proper owner of the mark. The form for recording assignment of a federally registered mark or a pending use-based application and information regarding filing fees and procedures are available on the PTO's Web site at www.uspto.gov/web/forms/index.html#trademark.

Chapter 3
MUSEUMS AND THE WEB

The number of museum Web sites on the Internet is large, and growing rapidly. One online directory lists more than 10,000 museums in 120 countries, with a new museum added to the list almost every day.[1] The number of virtual visitors to museum Web sites is skyrocketing, sometimes exceeding the number of visitors to the actual museums. Just a few years ago, many museums viewed their Web sites as nothing more than electronic brochures, offering the usual visitor information such as hours, current exhibitions, and visitor services, a little institutional history, a floor plan, some highlights from the collections, and perhaps even a virtual tour of selected galleries.

Today, museums are beginning to appreciate the tremendous potential of the Internet. Museum educators are offering and obtaining a wider range of educational materials, developing Web features for students and teachers, and interacting with users through discussion lists and chat rooms. Curators conducting research in specialized fields are taking advantage of the rich textual and visual resources from the great museum collections of the world, which are gradually becoming available online. Museum directors are planning online exhibitions (as stand-alone or supplementary shows) to reach wider audiences. One museum director notes that the Internet holds the promise of immersing "the casual viewer in a world of imagination and creativity in stark contrast to the flotsam of commercial stimuli that continues to overwhelm online networks."[2] At the same time, the potential of the Internet for increasing earned income has not been lost on museums, which are beginning to offer new online stores, services, and publications. Such ventures hold the great promise of increasing a museum's revenues and heightening its visibility in cyberspace, establishing brand loyalty for cultural products and services.

While the Internet presents new opportunities for museums, it also presents new challenges. Unauthorized use of museum digital assets is cheap, easy, and quick in the digitally networked environment. Not surprisingly, museums are looking for ways to reduce the risk of unauthorized reproduction, alteration, and distribution of digital content. How can copyrights, contracts, and technological measures be used to protect museum digital assets in cyberspace? As both content providers and service providers, museums also risk inadvertently infringing the intellectual property rights of others on the Internet. What defenses and "safe harbors" are available to museums to limit or mitigate such legal risks? Finally, the Internet is home to other electronic entrepreneurs who are all too eager to take for their own commercial advantage the symbols, goodwill, and reputation of museums doing business in the digital marketplace. How can museums safeguard the trademarks that identify their goods and services, protect themselves against "cybersquatters," and otherwise insulate themselves from unfair business practices on the Web?

One thing is certain in the law of the Internet: It will be different tomorrow. At the same time, the new information technologies will continue to outpace the law. Thus, for many years to come, critical legal issues will be grinding through the judicial and legislative processes. Still, museums need advice today about how to avoid liability and protect their interests in cyberspace. In this spirit, this chapter is a brief introduction to the growing body of cases and laws that apply to the Internet. The focus is on copyrights, trademarks and domain names. (Contracting and licensing issues in the digital environment are discussed in chapter 4.) However, museums should also be aware that other bodies of law apply with equal force in the online environment, including the laws that govern trade secrets, defamation, invasion of privacy (see appendix E), and freedom of speech. Moreover, international implications, such as the vastly different U.S. and European notions of privacy, will continue to have an uncertain impact on the field.

Copyright and the Internet

Just a few years ago, some doubted whether copyright law would play a meaningful role in cyberspace. Designed initially to protect the creation and distribution of tangible works in a print world, copyright law seemed outdated, ill-suited to protect digital works on the Internet. In such a dynamic environment, how would copyrights be enforced? What would constitute a violation of a copyright owner's reproduction, distribution, public display, or public performance rights?

It is becoming clearer that copyright law will play a vital role in cyberspace, with its bedrock principle of "balance" recently reaffirmed by Congress in the Digital Millennium Copyright Act of 1998.[3] Under U.S. law, copyright owners may control and use their protected works on the Internet by exercising their exclusive rights, such as the rights of reproduction, distribution, adaptation, and public display. Moreover, the recent World Intellectual Property Organization copyright treaties recognize the copyright owner's right of "transmission and access" or the right of communication to the public "by wire or wireless."[4]

Online Rights

Museums operate in an information-rich environment. Museum professionals routinely transfer files from one computer to another, post messages to bulletin boards, create hypertext links, and upload or download information. While just part of a day's work, such online conduct by its very nature involves copyrights. Many of the exclusive rights discussed in chapter 1 apply with equal force in the networked environment.

Reproduction

The reproduction right, perhaps the most fundamental of copyright's bundle of six exclusive rights, is the right to make or authorize others to make copies of original expression in a material object.[5] A reproduction may occur any time digital content is fixed in almost any permanent storage device, including disks, tapes, or the random-access memory of computers.[6] In the online environment, the digital representation of photographs on a bulletin board service[7] and the placement of files of copyrighted clip art on a Web site[8] have been found to involve the reproduction right. When a user uploads a copyrighted work to a service provider's computer or downloads a protected work from a Web site or a service provider's computer, the reproduction right is implicated because such conduct generally involves the making of copies at some time during the transmission process.[9] However, under current law, the simple act of browsing would not appear to trigger the reproduction right. Even if implicated, browsing is undoubtedly protected under the fair use doctrine.[10]

Adaptation

The Copyright Act gives the copyright owner the exclusive right to prepare a derivative version of a work such as a translation, dramatization, or art reproduction (sometimes called the adaptation right).[11] The purely mechanical process of digitizing certain protected works, however, would not appear to implicate the right to prepare derivative works.[12] By the same token, the manipulation of digital images may result in infringing images, without authorization or the application of the fair use doctrine.[13]

Distribution

The Copyright Act gives the copyright owner the exclusive right to publicly distribute a protected work by sale, rental, lease, or lending.[14] The application of the distribution right in the online environment continues to present courts with conceptual difficulties. Unlike a distribution in the material world, no physical media are transferred when a work is transmitted electronically. Indeed, on completion of the transmission, both the sender and the recipient end up with a copy of the transferred file. For example, the sale and transmission of a digital postcard through an online museum store is a significantly different transaction from the sale of the same postcard in the museum's shop. In light of those differences, there is some uncertainty about the application of the distribution right in cyberspace.[15]

The application of the first sale doctrine on the Internet also is not clear. The first sale doctrine is an important limitation on the copyright owner's distribution right (see chapter 1, "Exclusive Rights and Their Limitations"). Under this doctrine, once "a particular lawful copy" of work has been sold or otherwise distributed, the right is exhausted. For example, a museum could not prevent the purchaser of an exhibition catalogue from disposing of that particular copy by reselling it to a secondhand bookstore. Suppose, however, that a museum distributed the same catalogue through an online transaction. Would the buyer, under the first sale doctrine, be permitted to retransmit that particular lawful copy? The answer would appear to be no, because no material copy of the work ever changed hands, as it did in the actual transaction. However, the application of the first sale doctrine in cyberspace remains an unsettled and contentious question. In any event, it is clear that an unauthorized retransmission of such a protected work probably would violate the museum's reproduction right because it would involve making a copy of the work without permission.

Public Performance

The Copyright Act gives the copyright owner the exclusive right to perform certain works in public.[16] In broad outline, all of the following may be public performances: a performance at a place open to the public; a performance by trans-

mission to a place open to the public; and a performance by transmission to a dispersed audience, either in time or in place.[17] In the online environment, the public performance right has raised particularly difficult legal issues. Suppose that a museum, as part of a virtual exhibition, electronically transmits a protected audiovisual work. At first glance, the transmission would appear to fall within the third category of public performance. On closer inspection, however, there is a whole range of problems. What constitutes a "transmission" by the museum?[18] Is the simple act of placing the files on the museum's server available for downloading sufficient to constitute a public performance? Or must the images and sounds be received? If the files must be received, must they be immediately converted into sounds and images (isochronous transmission)? Or may the transmissions be either faster or slower than the originally fixed performance (asynchronous transmission)? Such questions will keep attorneys and the courts busy for a long time.

Public Display

The Copyright Act gives the owner of a protected work, and persons authorized by the owner, the exclusive right to display the copyrighted work publicly.[19] Once viewed as important primarily to museums and galleries, the public display right probably will become much more significant in the online environment. In one early case, for example, a court held that the posting of 170 copyrighted images on a bulletin board service was a "public display" because the audience consisted of a "substantial number of persons outside of a normal circle of family and its social acquaintances."[20] More recently, another court found violations of the public display right in connection with the operation of a bulletin board service that contained more than 10,000 digital graphic files, of which more than 400 were exact reproductions of copyrighted photographs.[21]

Like the public performance right, however, the precise contours of the public display right in cyberspace have yet to come into sharp focus. Will merely permitting subscribers to a bulletin board service to browse copyrighted images stored on the system constitute a public display?[22] If a museum merely serves as a "conduit" for content originating on other sites, will it be insulated from violations of the public display right?[23] For obvious reasons, museums should closely monitor legal developments affecting the display right on the Internet.

Theories of Infringement

Suppose that the American Science Museum and Planetarium (ASMP), a science museum serving the western United States, is expanding and renovating its Web site, initially conceived as an electronic brochure for the museum. The project is now viewed as a critical element of the museum's strategic plan. Specifically, according to director Kate Goodhart, the expanded Web site will broaden and enrich ASMP's educational activities, provide supplementary, electronic service for ongoing exhibitions, and be a new vehicle to promote the museum and increase earned revenues. To help realize this vision, the museum recently contracted with a new service provider, the ABC Company. Goodhart refers to the expanded Web site as the SkyMuseum.

Suppose further that Bob Simpson, ASMP's webmaster, is a fervent fan of the *Star Blaster* television and movie series, which chronicles the adventures of the *U.S.S. Horizon* and its crew as they travel through space during the 23rd century. To help launch SkyMuseum, Goodhart gave Simpson permission to post digital files from Simpson's *Star Blaster Companion*, a guide that contains "everything the *Star Blaster* fan needs to know about the series."

Simpson's book includes a concise history of the *Star Blaster* series, lengthy quotations taken from various *Star Blaster* films and television programs, plot summaries of individual episodes, original commentary and criticism, and images of some of the show's most beloved characters, including Captain Quirk, Mr. Stock, Obey Kanobey, and Princess Liza. All of the materials were taken from *Star Blaster* publications, including some guides published or licensed by the studio, such as *The Star Blaster Encyclopedia* and *The Official Star Blaster History*. Recently Simpson added prerelease audio and video clips from *Star Blaster: The Next Adventure*, soon to be released by WonderPlex Studios, which he obtained from an unidentified source. Although the digital scanning and audio recording in these long segments is amateurish, Simpson is convinced that the new materials will attract thousands of visitors to the museum's Web site, ensuring a successful launch. Many of them, Simpson believes, are likely to become regular users of SkyMuseum resources, including its extensive science fiction collection.

The attorneys for WonderPlex Studios look at the matter somewhat differently, of course. With the imminent release of *Star Blaster: The Next Adventure*, they began a worldwide campaign to crack down on unauthorized uses of the studio's copyrights and trademarks, including the unauthorized use of protected materials on Web sites. As part of the campaign, WonderPlex lawyers recently sent a letter to Goodhart requesting the immediate removal of the allegedly infringing video and audio clips.[24] Although the tone of the letter is more informational than confrontational (it explains the studio's large investment in its film and television properties), Goodhart understood the possible consequences of failure to take down the challenged materials. WonderPlex will bring a copyright infringement suit, alleging violations of its reproduction, distribution, derivative work, public display, and public performance rights. What theories of infringement might apply to the museum's online conduct?

The Copyright Act states: "Anyone who violates any of the exclusive rights of the copyright owner . . . is an infringer of the copyright."[25] To prevail in a direct copyright infringement claim, the copyright owner must establish that he owns a valid copyright and that the defendant copied original elements of the work.[26] It makes no difference if the copyrighted work is in analog or digital format. Nor does it matter whether the alleged infringing copying, adaptation, distribution, public performance, or public display occurred online or in a nonelectronic environment. To succeed in a copyright lawsuit, the plaintiff must simply prove that the defendant had access to a protected work and used such access to copy it, as evidenced by the substantial similarity of the original and allegedly infringing works. The intent of the alleged infringer is not relevant. Copyright infringement is a "strict liability" offense, which means that conduct alone may be enough for a court to find liability.

Under those traditional standards of direct copyright liability, a significant amount of online conduct could be potentially actionable. How are museums to know when they are subjecting themselves to liability or failing to adequately protect their rights in cyberspace? Although there are no absolute answers, recent Internet cases suggest that some volitional act by the defendant must be present for a finding of direct copyright infringement liability.[27] For service providers, the Digital Millennium Copyright Act requires a volitional act for a finding of direct liability.[28]

In addition to direct liability for copyright infringement, there are two theories of indirect liability. Under the theory of contributory infringement, an individual may be liable for the direct infringing conduct of another if the individual has knowledge of the infringing conduct and "induces, causes, or materially contributes to the infringing conduct."[29] Under the theory of vicarious liability, a person may be liable for the direct infringing conduct of another if the individual "can control and financially benefits from the infringing conduct."[30] Both theories of indirect liability have been applied in cyberspace, typically

to service providers. How might a court apply these theories to the American Science Museum and Planetarium's online conduct?

By placing the unauthorized *Star Blaster Companion* on ASMP's server, available for downloading by users, Bob Simpson has exposed the museum to liability for direct copyright infringement. Specifically, loading the unauthorized audio and video clips onto the hard drive of the ABC Company's computer probably violated WonderPlex's reproduction right, and making these materials available for downloading by others without the permission of WonderPlex probably violated the studio's right to distribute, publicly display, and publicly perform these works.

What about WonderPlex's claim of direct infringement against the ABC Company? Although ABC also made unauthorized copies of the protected works, it probably will not be liable for direct copyright infringement. Although copyright infringement is a "strict liability" offense (conduct alone is enough), the courts generally require some awareness of the infringing conduct, selection and control of content, or some volitional act by a service provider before imposing liability for direct infringement. In this example, none of these elements seem to be present. For example, one federal court ruled that a service provider was not liable for direct copyright infringement when it only provided the means to copy, distribute, or display protected clip art placed on its server by a nonprofit organization for downloading by its members.[31] The court reasoned that the service provider was merely acting like the owner of a public copying machine used by a third party to copy protected material.

What about WonderPlex's indirect liability claims? ABC Company probably will not be liable for contributory infringement because it did not appear to know of the infringing activity on the museum's Web site or "induce, cause, or materially contribute to" the infringing conduct.

Moreover, the fact that ABC neither monitored nor exercised any control over the selection of content on the museum's Web site is significant. Nor does it appear that the ABC Company would be vicariously liable for ASMP's infringing conduct. First, there is no direct or contributory infringement. Second, even if the museum were liable, the board would not be vicariously liable unless it could be established that a board member had a direct financial interest in the infringing activity and the right and ability to supervise the activity that caused the infringement.

Fair Use in the Online Context

If the American Science Museum can establish that its use was a fair use, it will not be liable under any of the theories of infringement discussed above. For more than 150 years, the fair use doctrine has provided an important means to ensure an appropriate balance between the exclusive rights of copyright owners and the interests of the public. Under this doctrine, discussed more fully in chapter 1, the courts must analyze four factors in determining whether a particular use is fair: (1) the purpose and character of the use, including whether it is for commercial or nonprofit purposes; (2) the nature of the copyrighted work; (3) the amount or proportion of the original work used; and (4) the effect of the use on the potential market for or value of the copyrighted work.[32] How would a court evaluate each element of the museum's fair use defense?

The first statutory factor looks to the purpose and character of the use, beginning with an evaluation of whether the online conduct is primarily commercial in nature or aspires to serve broad public purposes.[33] In the *Star Blaster* example, the online conduct falls somewhere between the two poles. The museum would argue that Simpson was motivated largely by a desire to help others understand the *Star Blaster* phenomenon and to attract new visitors to the SkyMuseum site, itself an educational undertaking. Although Simpson's materials on the *Star Blaster* series (including his original commentary and criticism) do not fall within the traditional notion of an educational work, a court would likely be reluctant to make subjective judgments about the quality of a work that might tilt the scales of fair use.[34] The counterargument is that the posting of the unauthorized *Star Blaster Companion* was simply an attempt to promote the SkyMuseum site without paying the customary licensing fees. As one court observed: "[T]he crux of the profit/nonprofit distinction is not whether the sole motive of the use is monetary gain but whether the user stands to profit from the exploitation of the copyrighted material without paying the customary price."[35] Because it is not clear whether ASMP's online conduct was primarily commercial or educational in nature, the weight of the first factor probably will turn on whether Simpson's work was transformative.

A work is transformative when it adds something new to another work "with a further purpose or different character, altering the first with new expression, meaning or message."[36] In this example, the lengthy quotations, the images of popular characters, and the detailed synopses of individual episodes—all taken directly from *Star Blaster* publications—point away from a finding of a fair use. Nor does the incorporation of original commentary and criticism on the *Star Blaster* series necessarily lead to a finding of fair use. Illicit copies are not protected merely by placing them in the midst of noninfringing materials. As Judge Learned Hand pointed out, "no plagiarist can excuse the wrong by showing how much of his work he did not pirate."[37] On balance, the first factor weighs against a finding of fair use.

The second factor looks to the nature of the copyrighted work, recognizing that certain works are "closer to the core of intended copyright protection than others."[38] Fair use is generally construed more broadly with respect to factual and published works than with respect to fictional or unpublished works. In this example, the copied *Star Blaster* materials are creative works of fiction entitled to the highest protection.[39] Moreover, some of these materials were disseminated over the Internet without authorization prior to their theatrical release, interfering with the copyright owner's right to control the first distribution of a protected work. The second factor does not support a finding of fair use.

The third factor looks to the amount and substantiality of the use in relation to the copyrighted work as a whole. This fair use factor generally excuses copying when no more of the work is used than is absolutely necessary for the particular use. However, there are no rigid numerical guidelines that inform the analysis under this factor. Rather, a court must evaluate the use from both qualitative and quantitative perspectives. The copying of even a small amount of protected expression may not be a fair use if it amounts to the "heart" of the work.[40] In the *Star Blaster* example, by relating synopses of key episodes, displaying long dramatic sequences, and encapsulating the plot and characters of many episodes, the museum may have taken the heart of the work.[41] The third factor tilts away from a finding of fair use.

The fourth factor looks to the effect of the use on the potential market for a value of the copyrighted work. In the online context, the fourth factor has been particularly significant. One court stated: "To negate fair use one need only show that if the challenged use 'should become widespread, it would adversely affect the potential market for the copyrighted work.'"[42] Economic harm may arise because the infringing work serves as a market substitute for either the original or a derivative work.[43] Although the *Star Blaster Companion* cannot serve as a market substitute for the *Star Blaster* television programs and movies, it can interfere with WonderPlex Studio's market for derivative works. In fact, as noted earlier, Wonder-Plex already publishes or licenses a number of

guidebooks, including *The Star Blaster Encyclopedia* and *The Official Star Blaster History*. The fourth factor does not favor a finding of fair use. Because all four factors for determining fair use favor WonderPlex, a court would have little difficulty in concluding that the American Science Museum's use is not a fair use.

Luckily, like many of the episodes in the *Star Blaster* series, the museum's walk on the wild side of the Internet had a happy ending. Shortly after the *Star Blaster* materials were posted to the ASMP's Web site, three studio executives held a conference call with Kate Goodhart. The executives said that their principal objective was to obtain immediate removal of the infringing video and audio clips from the Web site. They explained the studio's marketing program for *Star Blaster: The Next Adventure* and the company's interest in eliminating amateur scanning and audio recording of their products. At the same time, the WonderPlex executives were aware of the importance of the museum's science fiction collection and the appropriate place of *Star Blaster* works within it. They went on to say that, after the removal of all infringing materials from the Sky-Museum site, the studio would be willing to license to ASMP selected *Star Blaster* media files at very reasonable rates provided that specific copyright management information would appear on all museum Web pages that include *Star Blaster* licensed materials. Goodhart agreed to remove the audio and video clips and said that the museum would consider the licensing offer.

Digital Millennium Copyright Act of 1998

On October 28, 1998, the Digital Millennium Copyright Act of 1998 (DMCA)[44] was signed into law, implementing recent World Intellectual Property Organization copyright treaties and updating U.S. copyright law for the information age. It may take some time to evaluate the DMCA's impact on the museum community, for it will take years for the courts to interpret this complex piece of legislation. Nonetheless, it is fair to predict that the DMCA will have a significant effect on the online conduct of museums—as content providers, service providers, or users of materials in the networked environment.

The DMCA does not expand a copyright owner's panoply of rights under U.S. law but does include provisions that provide for enhanced protection for such rights. As service providers on the Internet, museums should be familiar with the safe harbor provisions, which clarify the circumstances under which a museum might limit its liability for its online conduct and for the presence of infringing material on its computer network (see the next section). As content providers on the Internet, museums should become familiar with the DMCA's anticircumvention and copyright management information (CMI) provisions. The law provides for protection against the circumvention of certain technological measures (such as passwords and encryption technology) that protect copyrighted works on the Internet. The DMCA also protects against the alteration or removal of CMI, which is defined to include much more than standard copyright notice information. Finally, as copyright users, museums should have a basic understanding of the special liability limitations for libraries, archives, and educational institutions that use digital works (discussed in chapter 1, "Fair Use and Other Limitations").

Safe Harbors on the Internet

The DMCA's definition of "service provider" is very broad: "a provider of online services or network access, or the operator of facilities therefor." How does this definition apply to museums? The answer is not entirely clear. There is a strong argument that many museums, which are not generally in the business of providing online services, will not be regarded as service providers under the DMCA. For example, a museum that maintains a "passive" Web site, such as a site without subscribers, may not be a service provider for DMCA purposes. Nonetheless, the

act's definition is broad enough to encompass museums' online activities. For example, a museum that provides Internet access to subscribers or hosts chat rooms or other museums' Web sites may qualify as a service provider. When functioning as a service provider, a museum may be able to use the DMCA's exemptions to limit its liability. But the DMCA may also require the museum, as a service provider, to block access to a site or take down challenged materials from the Internet.

The DMCA does not change existing copyright infringement liability principles. Instead, it limits service providers' liability for online conduct in certain categories of activities, sometimes called "safe harbors," as long as the service provider meets all conditions for the exemption. Each limitation operates as a complete bar on the award of monetary damages and restricts the availability of injunctive relief (court orders that command or prohibit some act). If the activity falls within a safe harbor, the service provider qualifies for the limitation on liability. But if the activity does not fall within a safe harbor, the service provider is not necessarily liable for copyright infringement. Rather, a court would apply the normal copyright infringement principles and defenses, including the fair use doctrine, to determine liability.

To qualify for any safe harbor, the service provider must meet two general conditions. First, it must adopt and reasonably implement a policy for terminating the accounts of subscribers who are repeat infringers. Second, it must accommodate and not interfere with "standard technical measures" used to identify and protect copyrighted works (such as watermarking). While nothing in the law is intended to discourage service providers from voluntarily monitoring their services, it does not require a service provider to do so or to affirmatively seek information about copyright infringement on its service.

In addition to the overall conditions, each safe harbor contains specific conditions that must be met. A service provider must designate an agent to receive such notices in its service and must register this agent with the Copyright Office.[45] The written notice must identify the allegedly infringing material in sufficient detail to permit the service provider to locate the material, the reference, or the link.[46] Once a service provider receives a notice that substantially complies with these requirements, it must act expeditiously to remove or block access to the challenged material. If the service provider in good faith removes or blocks access to material that it has cached, stored at a user's request, or referred users to, either because it has received notice from the copyright owner or because it otherwise becomes aware of the infringing nature of the materials, the DMCA insulates the service provider from liability for such removal or blocking.

The DMCA also includes detailed "notice and put-back" provisions, which are designed to protect users' rights when the removal or blocking of materials was the result of a mistake or misidentification of the challenged material.[47] First, a service provider must take reasonable steps to provide notice of such action to a subscriber. Second, a subscriber has the opportunity to contest a complaining party's notification of infringement by filing a counternotification, which attests that the challenged work was removed by mistake or misidentification. On receipt of such a notice, the service provider must send a copy to the complaining party. Third, a service provider is required to place the subscriber's material back online between 10 and 14 business days after receiving a counternotification, unless the matter is referred to a court.[48] Let's take a closer look at these safe harbors and their application to the online activities of museums.

Caching Information

"Caching," a commonplace activity on the Internet, occurs when an online service provider makes a temporary copy of requested materials so that it can deliver that copy to subsequent users more quickly than would be possible if the service

provider returned to the original source. The caching of substantially all of the contents of a remote server by a service provider to meet the needs of subscribers is sometimes called "proxy caching." By contrast, browsers automatically save copies of recently accessed Web pages on a user's computer through a process known as "local caching." The purpose of local caching is to permit the user to return readily to the last several Web pages viewed. Local caching, a ubiquitous function of all browsers, generally is regarded as raising few liability issues even though copying occurs. Libraries, educational institutions, and museums may engage in proxy caching in an effort to better serve their students, faculty, and visitors. Does such temporary copying expose museums to liability? Consider the application of the caching safe harbor to the American Science Museum and Planetarium's online activities.

One of the museum's services is to store and disseminate scientific information in response to requests from visitors, students, and scholars in the area. Often the ASMP serves as an intermediary between originating sources on the East Coast and end users on the West Coast. To facilitate access, the museum temporarily caches, or stores on its own server, previously requested information and Web pages. To speed up repeated access to the same data, the museum simply downloads the information from its server rather than return to the original source. Is the museum potentially liable for copyright infringement because of caching?

A museum that engages only in acts of intermediate and temporary storage made through an automatic technical process for the purpose of making the materials available to persons who subsequently request it may be able to take advantage of the liability limitation for system caching. To qualify for this safe harbor, the American Science Museum must: (1) not modify the retained material; (2) follow any rules on "refreshing" the material imposed by the originating source; (3) not interfere with the technology that returns certain information ("hit" information) to the originator; (4) limit access to any cached materials according to the conditions (such as password requirements) imposed by the originating source; and (5) remove or block the cached material consistent with the notice and take-down provisions if the material has been removed or blocked at the originating site.[49] If the museum follows these basic rules, it should be protected from liability for caching information.

Storing Information at the Direction of Users

Museums sometimes provide storage space on their servers for a user's Web site, a chat room, or another forum in which information may be posted at the direction of users. What if the posted information turns out to infringe another person's copyright? Until the enactment of the DMCA, these acts of generosity exposed museums to the risk of copyright infringement suits. Now, the DMCA's safe harbor for system storage limits the potential liabilities for such online conduct as long as the museum complies with a complex set of procedural requirements.[50]

To illustrate these new rules, consider the case of the recently founded Museum of Digital Art (MODA), which collects, displays, and disseminates computer-related art. One of the most popular features of MODA's Web site is its award-winning online magazine, *Digital Art Showcase*, which includes a forum that allows subscribers to post their most recent digital works. Dan Scanner, an up-and-coming computer artist, recently posted his whimsical *Halo Dolly*, which combines visual elements from a 14th-century Italian Renaissance drawing with a photograph of the world's first cloned sheep. To increase MODA's online revenues, the editor of *Digital Art Showcase* used *Halo Dolly* on the cover page, with Scanner's permission. As predicted, subscriptions to the online magazine skyrocketed. Bob Woolrich, who claims to own the exclusive rights in the famous photo-

graph of Dolly, was upset. He fired off an e-mail to MODA demanding the removal of the allegedly infringing work. The editor, who believes that Scanner has transformed the photograph, adding new expression and meaning to the work, decided to ignore Woolrich's demand.

As a service provider storing information at the request of users of its bulletin board, MODA is under no obligation to monitor its service or affirmatively seek out information about the possible infringing conduct of its users. However, to qualify for the exemption, a service provider must act promptly to remove or disable access to infringing material once it obtains "actual knowledge" or becomes aware, based on facts or circumstances, of infringing materials or activities on its network.[51] By doing nothing in response to Woolrich's e-mail, MODA risks losing its liability limitation as a service provider under DMCA. However, MODA would retain all defenses, including the fair use defense, in any subsequent copyright litigation. MODA also can lose the protection of the system storage safe harbor if a court determines that it received a "financial benefit directly attributable to the infringing activity."[52] Under these facts, a court in all likelihood would conclude that this element was satisfied.

Suppose that MODA decided to remove the challenged work, and it later turned out that Bob Woolrich was not Dolly's photographer after all. Would MODA then be potentially liable for improperly removing Scanner's work from *Digital Art Showcase*? It appears that MODA complied in good faith with the DMCA's notice and take-down provisions and, therefore, would be insulated from liability to its subscribers and third parties. If MODA received a notification that it had removed the challenged image because of a mistake or misidentification, and if it complied with the DMCA put-back provisions, the museum would be insulated against liability to Scanner.

Information Location Tools

Information location tools, which range in size from massive online directories like Yahoo to more modest lists of recommended sites, are an essential feature of the Internet. Yahoo's directory alone, which might be considered an electronic card catalogue to the World Wide Web, contains more than 800,000 online locations. Large museums, as important centers in the global network of cultural heritage information, often include extensive lists of Internet resources to help visitors navigate through this massive body of information. Could such well-intentioned acts lead to unanticipated liabilities? Consider the case of the Cosmopolitan Museum of Art.

The Cosmopolitan Museum of Art recently added a link to MODA. Consistent with the Cosmopolitan's policy, Paul Browser, the museum's webmaster, paid a brief cataloguing visit to the MODA site, where he happened to notice Scanner's engaging image, *Halo Dolly*. Two weeks later, the Cosmopolitan received an angry letter from Bob Woolrich demanding that the museum sever its link to MODA, which Woolrich claims is infringing his copyright in his underlying photograph, perhaps the world's most famous sheep. Browser had his doubts about the claim but, consistent with museum policy, he decided to play it safe by removing the link.

By promptly removing the challenged link, Browser preserved the Cosmopolitan's eligibility for the information location tool safe harbor.[53] Under the DMCA, the term "information location tool" is used broadly to include directories, indexes of online sites, and references to other online materials such as a list of recommended sites. Although the issue is not entirely free from doubt, the Cosmopolitan list of recommended sites probably is an information location tool. To qualify for the liability limitation, the museum must follow the DMCA's notice and take-down procedures, which include a requirement that it lacks "actual knowledge" of the infringement on the linked site or is not aware of facts or circumstances from which infringing activity on the linked site would be apparent. To put the matter another way, the Cosmopolitan was under no obligation to seek out information about possible copyright infringements on the MODA site, but it would not qualify for the safe harbor if it turned a blind eye to an obvious infringement, sometimes called a "red flag."[54]

Browser actually saw Scanner's intriguing image when he visited the MODA Web site, but that would not constitute actual knowledge or a red flag. During a brief cataloguing visit, Browser could not be expected to determine the copyright status of Scanner's work, which could require the analysis of such complex copyright issues as duration, licensing, and fair use. Nor did the Cosmopolitan receive a financial benefit directly attributable to the possible infringing activity on the MODA site (another requirement). Finally, because the Cosmopolitan promptly removed the challenged link, it satisfied the last requirement to qualify for the information tool safe harbor. If the Cosmopolitan linked to the Barbary Coast Pirate Museum site, where visitors could freely download photographic images, designs, illustrations, and music, the outcome might be different. That is the kind of sophisticated "pirate site" that the law's safe harbor was designed to exclude. If the Cosmopolitan avoided all the telltale signs and linked to such a pirate site, it will find no safety in this safe harbor.[55]

Protection Against Circumvention of Technology

Museums are beginning to use technological measures, or copyright protection systems, to regulate access to and control the use of protected works in digital format. The same technological measures are also available to persons who control works that museums may seek to use. In fact, one of the most contentious issues during the legislative process leading to the enactment of the DMCA involved measures to prevent the circumvention of copyright protection systems. Congress sought to strike a balance between the legitimate interests of copyright owners while enabling the kinds of uses by individuals and institutions that have been so important in fostering the creation of new works in the United States.

Technological protection measures have become a new reality for museums working in an electronic environment. In general, such measures operate by: (1) controlling access to a protected work; (2) preventing the unauthorized exercise of the owner's rights; and (3) displaying identifying information about the work, including information about the creator, copyright owner, and terms of use of the work. Under current technology, museums may adopt a number of measures to protect their digital assets. A watermark (formed by switching particular bits in a digital image) permits the owner of the image to identify the image later. Digital fingerprints can be created within an image file. Software can be used to restrict access to authorized users and monitor the number of users and nature of use. Copyright identification information can be displayed in connection with a work or embedded directly into the pixels of a digital image with a link back to the museum. Images and data also can be protected through encryption.

Of course, even the most sophisticated technological measures are vulnerable to tampering. In such a case, what legal recourse, if any, would a museum have? The two new World Intellectual Property Organization copyright treaties[56] require signatories to provide "adequate legal protection and effective legal remedies against the circumvention of effective technological measures used by authors in connection with the exercise of their rights under this Treaty or the Berne Convention and that restrict acts which are not authorized by the authors or permitted by law." How were these words implemented in U.S. law?

The DMCA contains a provision that prohibits conduct that would circumvent technological measures (such as encryption) that control access to a copyrighted work.[57] Congress said that such a provision was needed to prevent the "electronic equivalent of breaking into a locked room in order to obtain a copy of a book."[58] During the legislative process, members of the nonprofit community and others expressed concern that such a measure may have a substantial adverse effect on users' ability to make noninfringing uses of technologically protected works. As a consequence, Congress delayed the implementation of this provision until two years after the effective date of the DMCA and mandated a rulemaking proceeding to evaluate the impact of the provision on the user community.[59] Once the provision becomes effective, it is subject to an exception for users of particular classes of works if they are or are likely to be adversely affected by the provision in making noninfringing uses of encrypted works.

The DMCA also contains a provision that prohibits certain types of devices. More specifically, the act prohibits any technology, product, service, or device that (1) is "primarily designed or produced" to circumvent technology that effectively controls access to a copyrighted work; (2) has "only [a] limited commercially significant purpose or use" other than to circumvent such technology; or (3) is marketed for use in circumventing such technology.[60] There is an exemption to this provision that permits nonprofit libraries, archives, and educational institutions to circumvent technological measures solely for the purpose of making a good-faith determination whether to acquire a work.[61] This exemption only applies when a qualifying institution cannot obtain a copy by other means and only lasts as long as necessary to make the determination.

Third, the DMCA contains provisions designed to ensure the integrity of copyright management information (CMI). [62] CMI includes a broad range of information that currently has or is likely to have increasing significance to museums managing their rights in the information age. Any of the following may constitute CMI: information that identifies the copyrighted work, including title, author, and copyright owner; information that identifies the writer, performer, or director of a work; terms and conditions for the use of a work; and identifying numbers or symbols that accompany the above information (including hypertext links).[63] For the DMCA's protections to apply, the CMI must be conveyed in connection with a copyrighted work. The DMCA prohibits the distribution of false CMI, the intentional removal or alteration of such information, and the distribution or importation of copies of works with the knowledge that such information has been removed or altered.[64]

To illustrate the potential importance of the DMCA's rules governing CMI, consider the recent experience of the American Science Museum and Planetarium, which developed a method for producing more accurate star images by combining digital information from another planetarium that operates a telescope. To disseminate the images more widely, each museum agreed to place the images on its Web site, including hypertext links back to the contributing institutions. To obtain additional rights management information for higher-resolution images, the visitor need only click on the appropriate link. As a practical joke, Dan Scanner manipulated a substantial number of images in the database to include an image of Tinkle Bell (a character developed by WonderPlex Studios) and placed the altered files on his server for downloading by visitors to the Peter Pan Lost Boys site. To conceal any possible copyright infringement, Scanner removed ASMP's hypertext links and copyright management information. Does the museum have any legal recourse?

Dan Scanner probably has run afoul of the DMCA's provisions protecting the integrity of CMI. To fall within DMCA's definition of CMI, the information must be "conveyed" in connection with the protected work.[65] The term "conveyed" is used in the broadest sense. To satisfy this threshold requirement, the information need

only be accessible in conjunction with, or appear with, an embodiment of the work. When Scanner placed the altered images on his server, he probably satisfied this requirement.

By intentionally altering and removing protected CMI, Scanner's practical joke may turn out to have serious consequences. To make matters worse for Scanner, he also probably violated the DMCA's prohibition on distribution of illegally modified works. The museum would argue that Scanner made the altered materials available for downloading (a distribution) with the intent to "induce, enable, facilitate, or conceal an infringement" of any of the exclusive rights of copyright.[66]

If ASMP prevails in its copyright infringement lawsuit, it will be able to take advantage of the DMCA's civil remedies for alteration and removal of CMI and for distribution of illegally modified works. Such remedies are in addition to any remedies for the infringement of the protected images themselves.[67] Under the DMCA, a court may impose treble damages for repeat offenders, and, conversely, may reduce or remit damages for a nonprofit library, archives, or educational institution when such an institution was not aware and had no reason to believe that its acts constituted a violation.[68]

Trademarks and Domain Names

Museums are increasingly using digital technologies, most notably the Internet, as effective merchandising and promotional tools. For instance, a museum may use the power of the World Wide Web to inform the public of its current or upcoming exhibitions, disseminate information about its collections, provide details of membership benefits, or offer retail merchandise. Although the promotional benefits are clear, the Internet also presents museums with significant challenges in protecting their trademarks and maintaining the goodwill and reputation symbolized by those marks.

Trademark owners and other Internet stakeholders have been struggling with the unique problems this vast network presents with regard to the establishment, maintenance, and protection of trademark rights. Museums must be particularly vigilant in monitoring and protecting their marks online, because perceived associations with unsavory or overtly commercial enterprises may irreparably damage a museum's reputation.

Courts attempting to resolve these issues face significant challenges, because in many cases the Internet does not lend itself to the application of traditional trademark law principles. For example, electronic communications are not bound by any geographic boundaries, while trademark rights have traditionally been obtained at the national level. The law regarding trademark rights online is still evolving.

The legal issues arising from the intersection between trademarks and Internet domain names have been the most hotly contested. This section describes the structure of the domain name system and summarizes procedures for securing domain names as of the writing of this guide. It also highlights the two avenues currently available to trademark owners to challenge third-party use of their trademarks as domain names: administrative procedures offered by domain name registration authorities and traditional trademark litigation in the courts. Finally, this section discusses a relatively new phenomenon giving rise to potential trademark infringement or dilution claims: use of third-party trademarks in metatags, or hidden code of World Wide Web pages.

While this section provides a brief overview of the legal issues and procedures currently involved in obtaining and enforcing trademark rights online, readers should be aware that due to the rapidly changing nature of the electronic environment, the law and procedures applicable in this context are constantly changing. Museums must keep abreast of developments that may supersede the information that follows.

Internet Domain Name Basics

Purpose of Domain Names

The Internet (including the World Wide Web) is a global network of "host" computers connecting other networks and computers. Every network connected to the Internet has a unique numerical site address that identifies its "location," called its Internet Protocol (IP) number. Each IP number generally corresponds to an easy-to-remember alphanumeric combination, called a "domain name."

The domain name may have a multitude of functions for a museum. On one level, it may serve as the address for the museum's World Wide Web site, accessible to the public by reference to a Uniform Resource Locator (URL), such as www.museum.org. Thus, the domain name is used to attract Internet users to the institution's Web site through Web browsers such as Netscape and Microsoft Internet Explorer. Moreover, the domain name may also be used to receive electronic mail, such as janedoe@museum.org, when Jane Doe has an account with a museum's computer network. In addition to serving as the institution's electronic address, the domain name may also have a broader, source-identifying function and may therefore be protectable as a trademark.

Basic Domain Structure and Authorities

Generally, domain names have two primary components: an alphanumeric name followed by a zone designation. These components are known as domain levels and are separated by periods (for example, museum.org). Top-level domains are referred to by their Internet zone designations and were originally designed to identify the type of entity associated with the particular domain name—for example, .com identifying commercial entities; .org identifying nonprofit organizations; .edu identifying educational institutions; and .gov identifying governmental entities. Although applicants for registration in the .edu and .gov domains generally must be educational institutions or government agencies, respectively, registration in the remaining top-level domains is now open to all entities, although these domains were originally intended to identify particular types of organizations. The second-level domain consists of the characters immediately to the left of the top-level domain (for example, "museum" in the domain name museum.org).

The vast majority of Internet domain name registrations in the United States are handled by the Internet Network Information Center (InterNIC), a cooperative effort of the National Science Foundation, AT&T, and Network Solutions, Inc. (NSI). InterNIC is managed by NSI, a for-profit provider of domain name registration services, under to a federal contract to provide a centralized directory of Internet domain names. At present, NSI acts as sole registrar for the most popular generic top-level domains—.com, .org, .net, and .edu—but NSI's contract with the U.S. government expires in September 2000.

The Internet Corporation for Assigned Names and Numbers (ICANN) has been formed to assume responsibility for domain name system management currently performed under a federal contract by NSI, the Internet Assigned Number Authority (IANA), and other entities. ICANN will ultimately decide whether to expand the number of generic top-level domains (to include others, for example, like .store, .arts, and .biz) and will develop new approaches for preventing and resolving trademark disputes involving domain names.

The formation of ICANN marks a transition from governmental to private-sector control of the domain name system. However, as the original registrar of domain names in the most popular generic top-level domains, NSI will likely remain a central player in the domain name registration process for years to come. For this reason, museums that currently have or are considering the development of an Internet presence should understand the contours of NSI's policies and procedures.

In addition to the generic top-level domains handled by NSI, there are also approximately 200 country-specific top-level domains, such as .uk (United Kingdom) and .jp (Japan), discussed in greater detail below. Country code top-level domain registration is administered on a national basis. The .us domain is the official two-letter country code for the United States.

Domain Name Selection, Clearance, and Registration

To enable Internet users to find a museum's Web site quickly and easily, the museum's name (or a widely recognized variation of its name) is the obvious choice to serve as the institution's second-level domain name. A museum can register its second-level domain name in as many applicable top-level domains as it wishes, including .net, .org, and .com, and others to be designated, as well as in any appropriate country code domains. Although many museums are recognized as educational institutions under state corporate law and for taxation purposes, the .edu domain generally is limited to four-year, degree-granting colleges and universities.

The museum can check the availability for registration of a given domain name and/or variations of that name in the .net, .org, and .com top-level domains by conducting a search at the Web site www.whois.net.[69] The Whois search will determine whether another party has already registered the exact domain name being searched. If a domain name has been previously registered, the search will provide information regarding the identity and address of the registrant. Museums relying on the Whois directory should be aware that the information it contains is provided by the domain name registrants and is not independently verified, so it may not be entirely accurate or up to date. Commercial search firms can also provide information regarding domain name availability, although they often charge fees for this service.[70] For example, the American Science Museum and Planetarium engaged such a firm to determine the availability of SkyMuseum as a possible domain name for its expanded Web site. After learning that the domain names SkyMuseum.org, SkyMuseum.net, and SkyMuseum.com were available for registration, Bob Simpson, the museum's webmaster, registered all three with NSI.

Museums may register domain names in the .com and .org generic top-level domains online with NSI (www.networksolutions.com). The procedure is fairly straightforward and requires the applicant to fill out and submit the application form electronically using a template provided by NSI. Hard-copy applications by facsimile or mail are not acceptable; all applications must be processed electronically. The museum's service provider may also apply for the domain name registration on the museum's behalf.

NSI issues domain name registrations on a first-come, first-served basis. NSI does not examine a proposed domain name to determine whether its use will infringe the trademark or other proprietary rights of third parties, nor does it determine whether the applicant has the right to use the domain name. NSI's sole purpose is to ensure that two parties do not use the same domain name. Moreover, unlike state or federal trademark registration, there is no use-in-commerce requirement for the issuance of a domain name registration.

Because of numerous disputes between domain name registrants and trademark owners, NSI has required applicants to make certain representations designed to reduce such conflicts. Applicants must represent that (1) registration of the domain name, to the best of the applicant's knowledge, does not infringe or interfere with a third party's rights; (2) the domain name is not being registered for any unlawful purpose; and (3) all statements on the application are true. These requirements are intended to discourage "cybersquatting"—the practice of registering domain names based on famous marks owned by others in order to extort money from the legitimate trademark owners. However, representations made by the applicant are only meant to protect NSI from potential liability and generally cannot be relied upon by third-party trademark owners whose rights may be violated by the registration of domain names that are arguably confusingly similar to their trademarks. NSI also has a Domain Name Dispute Policy that may be available to resolve conflicts between domain name registrants and trademark owners (see "NSI Domain Name Dispute Procedures," later in this chapter).

Defensive Domain Name Registration

By registering a domain name, the domain name holder, or registrant, is able to record and thereby reserve the name in a database maintained by the domain name registrar (NSI or one of the country code top-level domain name registrars). Any party that later attempts to register or reserve the identical name in that top-level domain will be unable to do so, thus ensuring the name's uniqueness within that top-level domain.

Under the current system it is possible for two unrelated entities to register with NSI and use the same second-level domains (for example, "cosmopolitanmuseum") in differing top-level generic domains (www.cosmopolitanmuseum.net and www.cosmopolitanmuseum.org). This can lead to considerable confusion among Internet users. Further, it is also possible for a museum in the United States to have a valid domain name registration under the .org top-level domain (www.cosmopolitanmuseum.org) while a completely unrelated entity may have the same second-level domain name registered under a country top-level domain (www.cosmopolitanmuseum.fr).

One way for a museum to minimize the risk of such confusion, and perhaps preclude the registration of arguably similar domain names by cybersquatters, is to register its domain name in all three top-level domains (.com, .org, and .net). The museum should also consider registering variations of its chosen domain name, as well as its most prominent trademarks, in each top-level domain.

Returning to the example of ASMP, Bob Simpson decided to retain the museum's current domain name, asmp.org, for use in connection with the expanded Web site because many visitors to the site were already familiar with this address. Moreover, as a precaution, Simpson registered asmp.com and asmp.net. As it turns out, ASMP is also informally known as "AMSCI" by the public. Accordingly, Simpson registered in three top-level domains: amsci, am-sci, and theamsci. All these domain names will be used to direct visitors (via hot links) to the SkyMuseum, the primary locus of ASMP's Web page.

In addition to registering variations of a museum's name and/or trademarks in each top-level domain, institutions should also consider registering their second-level domain names in any country top-level domain where Internet users might seek out the museum's Web site. Each country has its own rules and regulations governing registration. Some allow any entity to register an available domain name in their top-level domains, while others have more stringent rules about who may register and often limit that privilege to entities domiciled within national borders. The museum will need to contact the domain name registration authority in each country of interest for information on registering a domain name.

There is currently no centralized international domain name registration body, but there are two important Regional Internet Registries (RIR)—Réseaux IP Européens Network Coordination Centre (RIPE NCC) for Europe and the surrounding areas[71] and Asia-Pacific Network Information Centre (APNIC) for the Asia-Pacific region.[72] In addition, commercial registration services may offer assistance with registering an institution's domain name in multiple foreign domains.[73]

Entities can also register under the .us domain as long as they adhere to the more complex naming structure for this domain: companyname.locality.statecode.us. Moreover, the .us domain offers a recommended naming structure (subdomain) unique to museums: museumname.mus.statecode.us. Detailed information regarding the .us domain, including application materials and procedures, can be found at the U.S. Domain Registry at the Information Sciences Institute, University of Southern California (www.isi.edu/in-notes/usdnr).

Registrability of Domain Names with the PTO

Some domain names simply identify a party's Internet address, while others serve a broader source-identifying function. The distinction is analogous to toll-free telephone numbers. Toll-free numbers consisting only of digits serve merely to locate a party, while those that feature brand names or other terms may serve as trademarks (for example, 1-800-GO-U-HAUL).

Over the past several years the U.S. Patent and Trademark Office (PTO) has issued a series of policy statements regarding the registrability of domain names as trademarks and service marks. The PTO's current position is that a domain name is registrable as a trademark if the domain name is being used to identify the source of one's goods or services and to distinguish those goods or services from those of another, but *not* if the domain name is merely being used as an Internet address.[74] Courts that have considered this issue have agreed that domain names can function as trademarks.[75]

For example, a Web site that simply contains basic promotional material with brief descriptions of a museum's collections, programs, or location, with the domain name only displayed as part of the URL on the upper-right corner of the screen, will likely not be registrable as a service mark with the PTO. In contrast, a content-rich Web site, including virtual tours of exhibitions, searchable databases of the institution's collections, or retail merchandise, with the domain name prominently displayed at the top of the home page, would more likely have its domain name qualify for service mark protection. Generally, the more distinctive the presentation of the Internet domain name within the site or in the institution's traditional printed promotional materials, and the further the domain name is removed from other address-like information appearing with the domain name (such as the name and location of the institution), the more likely the domain name will be perceived to function as a service mark by the PTO.

In applying to register a domain name as a trademark with the PTO, one cannot use the term "Internet" in describing the goods and services that the mark identifies, because of an ongoing dispute about the proprietary nature of the term.[76] The principal service offered by a museum through its Web site may be identified as "providing information and educational services regarding [subject] via a global computer network."

In many instances, however, seeking federal registration for a domain name, particularly when it features a mark already covered by a federal registration, may be unnecessary. Consider the example of the Einstein Science Center (ESC), which owns a federal registration for the mark EINSTEIN SCIENCE CENTER for use in connection with educational and retail services. The Einstein Science Center also holds a domain name registration for einsteinsciencecenter.org and offers on its Web site virtual tours of its exhibitions as well as a selection of retail merchandise.

In this example, the domain name is likely being used as a trademark and service mark in connection with the same services covered by ESC's federally registered mark. Securing a registration for the domain name, therefore, would provide ESC with little additional protection. If, however, the center's federal registration covered restaurant services instead of retail services, ESC would be well advised to seek federal registration for EINSTEIN SCIENCE CENTER covering retail services as well, as they fall outside the scope of its current federal registration.

By the same token, museums also should consider seeking federal registration for domain names that feature terms either not previously used by the institution as trademarks or not protected by currently valid federal registrations. The Smith Art Center, for example, wants to develop a Web site and tries to register variations of its domain name with NSI, only to discover that other institutions with similar names have already registered all suitable variations in each top-level domain. Because the Smith Art Center is known for its unique location on top of one of its city's highest hills, the center decides that artonthehill.org might make a fine domain name. The center has not previously used the Art on the Hill slogan in connection with any of its programs.

In this case, the Smith Art Center may wish to seek federal registration for ART ON THE HILL to protect the institution's trademark rights in the slogan. Moreover, should the Smith Art Center later discover that a commercial art gallery owner in the same city registered and has begun to use artonthehill.com, the center would not be able to take advantage of NSI's domain name dispute resolution procedures and challenge the gallery's domain name registration without a federal registration, as discussed below in greater detail.

Conflicts Between Domain Names and Trademarks

Trademark law permits different entities to use similar or identical marks provided there is no likelihood that consumers will be confused as to the source, sponsorship, or affiliation of the parties' respective goods or services. Generally, the risk of confusion may not exist—for instance, when the entities are in different lines of business or are located in nonoverlapping geographic market areas. However, these tenets of trademark law are largely inapplicable in the Internet context. Top-level domain names give no clear indication as to domain name owners' line of business, and the global nature of the Internet undermines the notion of geographic market areas.

Understandably, most organizations and businesses prefer to use their trademarks as second-level domain names. Use of such "intuitive" domain names helps Internet users locate the organization's Web site with a minimal amount of searching. The desire of parties to use their trademarks as domain names and to restrict third parties' ability to use identical marks as domain names has resulted in significant conflict between trademark owners and domain name registrants. Many different types of domain name disputes have arisen. Most fall into one of three categories:

- Parties who have registered another entity's trademarks as second-level domain names with the intention of selling the domain names back to the trademark owner—a practice known as "cyberpiracy" or "cybersquatting." The Big City Art Museum is an internationally recognized institution that owns the federally registered service mark BCAM. Unfortunately, until this year, the museum made no attempt to secure a domain name registration for bcam.com, bcam.net, or bcam.org. Museum administrators learn that an individual unrelated to the institution has registered the bcam.com domain name and is offering to sell this domain name registration to the institution for $10,000.

- Parties who have used the trademark of a direct competitor in their domain names. The Metropolis Computer Museum decides to develop an independent Web site to satisfy an increasing demand for items offered though its retail and mail order operations. The institution registers the domain name cybernotion.net. Shortly after the site is posted and sales are moving at a brisk pace, the institution receives a cease and desist letter from a specialty mail order retailer that holds a federal trademark registration for the mark CYBERNOTION for use in connection with computer-related gift and novelty items such as mouse pads.

- Parties who have used another's trademark in a domain name in connection with noncompeting goods. Modular Office Design Associates, Inc., in California and the Museum of Digital Art in New York both use the trademark MODA in the physical marketplace without creating any confusion among the public regarding the source of their respective goods and services. However, in the online environment confusion can arise if one party operates under the moda.org domain name and the other party chooses to operate under the moda.com name.

Courts and the bodies responsible for administering the domain name system are struggling to develop consistent, unified, and equitable approaches that reconcile the competing interests of trademark owners and domain name registrants. Both the law and the administrative procedures available to resolve such disputes are evolving and will certainly continue to do so for some time.

Currently, trademark owners (including museums) confronted with objectionable domain names registered by third parties have available two basic means of protecting and enforcing their trademark rights. A museum owning a federal trademark registration may be able to stop another party from registering and/or using a domain name that incorporates the museum's mark by availing itself of the domain name dispute procedure offered by NSI (see "NSI Domain Name Dispute Procedures"). A museum without a federal trademark registration, or one that wants to do more than simply stop the unauthorized use (for example, receive a monetary recovery) may pursue relief in court. Litigation, however, is not without significant costs and uncertainties. This is particularly true in the Internet context, given the evolving state of the law and the difficulties of applying traditional trademark concepts and principles to the online environment.

NSI Domain Name Dispute Procedures

Current NSI System

Although alternative mechanisms for resolving disputes between trademark owners and domain name registrants are being debated, the only currently available alternative dispute resolution mechanism is NSI's Domain Name Dispute Policy.[77]

Under the NSI policy, the owner of a federal trademark registration on the Principal Register (or on an "equivalent registry" in another country) that believes its rights are being violated by a domain name registration must first notify the domain name owner that use of the domain name "violates the legal rights" of the trademark owner and communicate the factual and legal bases for this belief. If the dispute is not resolved at that point, the trademark owner can request relief from NSI. The trademark owner must give NSI a copy of its notification to the domain name owner along with a certified copy of its trademark registration to initiate a formal challenge.

To defend against such a challenge, a domain name owner must submit to NSI within 30 days a federal or foreign trademark registration certificate that was registered before the date the regis-

trant received notice of the dispute. If a domain name owner cannot provide such a certificate, the domain name is placed on hold and remains unavailable for use by either party until the dispute is resolved.

Can the Big City Art Museum in the example above take advantage of the NSI policy to challenge the cybersquatter's registration of its trademark as a domain name and prevent the objectionable domain name registration from being used or transferred to a third party? Under the current NSI policy, the museum may successfully freeze the objectionable domain name if the institution owns a federal registration for the trademark BCAM.

However, if the registration date of the bcam.com domain name precedes the effective date of the BCAM federal trademark registration (the earlier of the filing date or the first use date), the museum cannot initiate the NSI challenge procedure. The museum's only recourse is to enforce its trademark rights through litigation or to purchase the domain name from the cybersquatter. If the cybersquatter is not using bcam.com in connection with content that may cause confusion with the museum's goods and services, it may be difficult for the museum to prove trademark infringement (although it could possibly succeed on a trademark dilution claim). Nevertheless, the museum may ultimately choose to avoid the considerable expense of pursuing litigation and instead consider a token payment to the domain name registrant to settle the matter.

The NSI policy underscores the importance of obtaining and maintaining federal trademark registrations for both trademark owners and domain name owners since it does not recognize common-law trademark rights as relevant to the domain name dispute process. A trademark owner that obtains a federal registration for its mark will increase the likelihood of successfully freezing a domain name holder who misappropriates that mark, and a good-faith domain name owner who registers its domain name as a trademark will be better able to successfully fend off a challenge by a trademark owner. The policy also demonstrates why it is important for museums to regularly monitor NSI's Internet domain name registry for domain names that may affect their trademark rights.[78]

Proposed ICANN Domain Name Dispute Resolution System

The World Intellectual Property Organization (WIPO) has been given responsibility for advising the Internet Corporation for Assigned Names and Numbers (ICANN) on approaches to domain name dispute resolution and the protection of famous trademarks. ICANN may ultimately develop its own registration policies and rules, including a new dispute resolution system that may differ from that of NSI. In April 1999, WIPO issued a final report outlining its recommendations.[79] Although it is unclear whether any of the proposals in the report will be adopted, they do reflect current thinking on some important issues ICANN will have to address in the near future.

In particular, the WIPO report recommends that domain name registration practices be developed to improve the accuracy and reliability of domain name registrant contact information. This recommendation is intended to facilitate the early resolution of domain name disputes by giving trademark owners the information needed to contact registrants and seek amicable resolution of disputes. Further, the WIPO report recommends that new multijurisdictional dispute resolution procedures, involving meditation and arbitration components, be required by domain name registration agreements. The report recommends, however, that such dispute resolution procedures be limited to cases of "bad faith" or "abusive" registration of domain names that violate trademark rights. The WIPO report also recommends that "famous" marks be given special protection such that no other party may register that exact mark as a domain name. Moreover, WIPO suggests that famous trademark owners be granted a presumption that the registration of a confusingly similar domain name by third parties with no valid claim to the mark at issue will harm the trademark owner's rights in the famous mark.

Legal Remedies

Although NSI may provide limited relief by freezing a domain name that violates a museum's trademark rights, a museum may also seek redress in court to stop the offending conduct and, possibly, obtain monetary relief. Conversely, third parties may also seek legal relief against a museum using a domain name that arguably conflicts with its trademark rights. In light of this latter fact, museums should undertake careful due diligence in selecting and clearing possible domain names, including commissioning a comprehensive trademark availability search for domain names under consideration.[80]

The number of lawsuits between trademark owners and domain name users over the right to register and use Internet domain names has been rising steadily. The challenge for courts addressing these disputes is to apply traditional trademark concepts and doctrine to online activities that may fundamentally alter the scope and nature of trademark rights.

Trademark Infringement and Unfair Competition Claims

From McDonald's Corporation to Playboy Enterprises, Inc., trademark owners have opposed third-party domain name registrations identical to their trademarks in court by alleging trademark infringement and/or unfair competition claims under the federal trademark statute, the Lanham Act.[81] In evaluating such claims, courts have generally employed a traditional "likelihood of confusion" analysis in determining whether use of a particular domain name creates a likelihood of consumer confusion.[82]

If the domain name owner is using the domain name to provide or promote goods and services on the Web site similar to those provided by the trademark owner (as illustrated in the Metropolis Computer Museum example), a standard trademark infringement claim may succeed.[83] If, however, a domain name is being used simply as an e-mail address (and there is no associated Web site) or in connection with goods or services unrelated to those of the trademark owner (as in the Modular Office Design Associates example), a trademark owner may not be able to obtain relief using a trademark infringement or unfair competition theory, because the trademark owner will have difficulty establishing a likelihood of confusion.[84] To date, courts have been hesitant to rule on trademark owners' infringement and unfair competition claims, instead choosing to rely on dilution claims to grant relief.[85]

Federal Dilution Act Litigation

The federal trademark dilution statute provides protection against trademark dilution for "famous" marks, without the need to prove a likelihood of confusion.[86] Congress enacted this legislation in part to stop parties from intentionally registering domain names identical to others' widely recognized trademarks.[87] Given its legislative history, and a more flexible analytical process by which a court may find for a trademark owner, the federal dilution law has become the favored weapon of trademark owners trying to challenge domain name registrants. Nearly all trademark owners in Internet domain name disputes have alleged a dilution claim. Courts have tended to apply the federal dilution statute's "famous" mark requirement expansively, allowing owners of trademarks that are not household names to obtain relief under the law.[88]

Two early cases against defendant Dennis Toeppen quickly established dilution as the theory of choice for dealing with parties who register the famous trademarks of others as Internet domain names without authorization.[89] In most cases,

these cybersquatters seek to extort money from trademark owners in exchange for the domain names corresponding to their trademarks. The *Intermatic* and *Panavision* courts found that the act of registering a domain name with the intention to sell it back to a trademark owner constituted "use in commerce," sufficient to satisfy the requirements under the Federal Dilution Act. Subsequently, when evidence of cybersquatting has been found, U.S. courts have generally found for the trademark owner.[90]

Reverse Domain Name Hijacking

From the domain name owner's perspective, abuse of NSI's Domain Name Dispute Policy (which strongly favors registered trademark owners), coupled with the wide latitude courts have given to dilution claims in domain name cases, has led to what some have called "reverse domain name hijacking." This practice occurs when a trademark owner uses the NSI policy and/or dilution litigation to force a domain name owner to cede its domain name, even if the domain name was lawfully obtained first and is either not used as a trademark or is used as a trademark for unrelated goods or services.

Whether a domain name registrant is a victim of a cybersquatter or is itself a pirate depends on the nature of the domain name owner's intended and actual use of the domain name. Does the domain name reasonably relate to the registrant's legitimate, ongoing business, or was it obtained merely for the express purpose of selling it back to the trademark owner?

One example is the *Prince* case, in which Prince Sports Group, a large sporting goods company and owner of a federal registration for PRINCE, challenged Prince plc, a relatively small computer information services company in the United Kingdom, over the right to the prince.com domain name. Prince plc had obtained prince.com two years earlier.[91] Although Prince Sports withdrew its lawsuit before any court decision, the smaller company had to defend the lawsuit to protect its domain name, which was based on its company name and mark of many years. Some domain name owners have alleged trademark misuse as a defense to reverse domain name hijacking. For the moment, however, this theory appears to be disfavored.[92]

Misuse of Metatags as Trademark Infringement/Dilution

In addition to linking and framing, activities that may implicate both copyright and trademark rights (discussed in the next section), inserting another's well-known trademark into one's metatags (hidden Web page code) may also constitute trademark infringement or dilution.

The success of a museum's Web site depends on the ease with which users can find and access it. Currently, most Web users rely on search engines, which search the World Wide Web and return a list of hyperlinks to sites that the search engine determines are responsive to the user's keyword query. Search engines index and identify sites by referencing keywords in the metatags that are part of the Web site's internal coding. Although these metatags are invisible to users, they are the key link between Web sites and their potential visitors.

In an attempt to increase traffic to their Web sites, some owners use the trade names and trademarks of others in their metatags. Consider again the ASMP example. The president of the *Star Blaster* films fan club, Peter Metha, has created his own Web site on the series. The site includes articles by fan club members and offers related merchandise. To attract the largest number of visitors to his site, Metha has included the trademarks AMSCI and ASMP, both federally registered marks of the American Science Museum and Planetarium, in the metatags. Consequently, searches for the American Science Museum and Planetarium Web site that include the key terms "AMSCI" and "ASMP" also retrieve references to the *Star*

Blaster fan club site. The museum is concerned that visitors may be diverted from its Web site to the *Star Blaster* site and that the public may assume the *Star Blaster* site is somehow associated with, related to, or endorsed by the ASMP.

Analyzing whether Metha's conduct is actionable—as trademark infringement, unfair competition, dilution, or false advertising—requires a review of how courts have recently treated metatag misuse. In 1997, a California district court first addressed the legality of the use of third-party trademarks within metatags.[93] In that case the defendant used Playboy Enterprises' federally registered trademarks PLAYMATE and PLAYBOY as both metatag keywords and components of domain names without authorization. Based on this conduct, the district court found that Playboy was likely to succeed on the merits of its trademark infringement, unfair competition, and dilution claims and issued a preliminary injunction ordering the defendants to cease all use of the plaintiff's registered trademarks within metatags and domain names.

In another recent case, the plaintiff sued a defendant that incorporated the plaintiff's marks in its metatags based on a false advertising claim.[94] In that case, the court preliminarily enjoined the defendant from using its competitor's trademarks within its metatags in order to attract users to its Web site. The court found that the defendant used the plaintiff's trademark within the defendant's Web site metatags to make false claims regarding the relationship between the defendant and the plaintiff.

Despite the apparent trend represented by these cases, not all uses of others' trademarks within metatags are impermissible. In *Playboy Enterprises, Inc. v. Welles*, a former Playboy Playmate of the Year, Terri Welles, placed the marks PLAYBOY and PLAYMATE within metatags on her own Web site.[95] Playboy sued Welles, alleging trademark infringement, dilution, and false designation of origin. However, the court found that Welles' use of Playboy's trademarks did not constitute trademark infringement because the marks were used merely in a descriptive sense and were unlikely to lead Web users to believe her site was endorsed or sponsored by Playboy.[96] This case suggests that the use of trademarks within metatags may be permissible when the marks are used for purposes that are not likely to result in consumer confusion (such as descriptive or fair use).[97] In essence, it appears that the legitimacy of using a particular trademark as metatag will turn on whether the defendant is attempting to increase traffic by deceiving Web users or is using the mark in a purely descriptive sense.

In light of recent case law regarding the use of metatags, it would appear that the American Science Museum and Planetarium may have valid claims against Peter Metha under the theories of unfair competition, trademark infringement, trademark dilution, and/or false advertising. The example illustrates why institutions need to exercise care in creating and monitoring their own Web sites to ensure that no third-party marks are improperly used as metatags. In addition, museums should regularly conduct searches for their trademarks on a variety of search engines to find possible instances of objectionable metatag use by third parties.

Linking and Framing on the Internet

Linking

A unique feature of the World Wide Web is its capacity to provide hypertext links from one Web site to another. Such links are actually embedded electronic addresses that point to another Web location. Put another way, links might be viewed as a network of cross-references or electronic citations. By clicking on a highlighted word or icon with a mouse, visitors can move effortlessly through cyberspace to related sites, whether affiliated or unaffiliated with the linking site. For obvious reasons, such links are sometimes called "outlinks" because the visitor actually exits the Web site originally accessed.

Linking presents museums with unparalleled opportunities to disseminate their rich cultural and scientific resources around the world, expanding and transforming their scope. Through hypertext links, visitors to museum Web sites are empowered to explore a seemingly endless branching network of information related to almost any subject. Cultural materials dispersed among museums throughout the world can be electronically reunited. Teachers in remote classrooms can quickly access educational materials on a number of sites. Hypertext links also offer museums opportunities to reach new markets for their products and services, in the process building brand loyalty and goodwill for the museum. By creating links to other museums and performing arts centers, shops, and restaurants, museums can establish their own "value-added networks," with the promise of increasing cultural tourism in their communities.

Yet linking also presents many legal issues for museums. Even the most basic questions can be tricky. For example, when is permission required before linking to another site? If the link is nothing more than a simple cross-reference, permission is not required. Just as in the print world, there is probably an "implied license" or authorization to create such references on the Internet. But courts tend to construe such implied licenses narrowly. Thus, if a link is something more than a simple reference (such as an implied endorsement or affiliation), a court might be reluctant to find such an implied authorization. Moreover, a posted notice on a linked site could defeat any implied authorization. Links that create a commercial advantage for one site at the expense of another are especially suspect.

As museums explore the commercial advantage of value-added networks, linking issues may arise. Consider the experience of the American Science Museum and Planetarium, which for many years had licensed copyrighted materials—such as maps, photographs, and charts documenting the locations and motions of heavenly bodies—to the Galileo Press for publication in the *Encyclopedia of Astronomy*. Negotiations with the Galileo Press for publication of these materials in the online edition of the encyclopedia recently broke down. Shortly thereafter, Galileo announced the publication of its online edition, promoting subscriptions by describing its extensive links to science museums around the world, including ASMP. Visitors to the Galileo site obtained access to other sites by clicking on an icon in a window clearly identified as "external links." The Galileo links also bypassed ASMP's home page, which contains ASMP's trademarked logo and information on the corporate sponsors of the ASMP Web site. Are the Galileo links lawful?

The answer is not entirely clear. Courts draw a distinction between "surface links," which simply send browsers to the home page of another site, and "deep links," which send the viewer to portions of the site below the home page of the linked site. The most closely watched case has been *Ticketmaster v. Microsoft*.[98] After negotiations between the two companies broke down over commercial arrangements under which Microsoft's *Seattle Sidewalk*, a city guide page, would be linked to Ticketmaster's ticket sales site, Microsoft went forward with the links to the Ticketmaster site. In response, Ticketmaster brought suit, alleging infringement and dilution of its trademarks and unfair competition, legal actions discussed more fully in the previous section. The gist of Ticketmaster's argument was that Microsoft's deep links to its site diluted the value of the advertising on its home page and confused users, who were unaware that they had entered a new site. Microsoft and Ticketmaster finally set-

tled their dispute out of court. Although the terms of the settlement are confidential, it is clear that Microsoft removed many of its deep links to the Ticketmaster site. At the very least, museums, whether serving as the linking or linked site, should be quite skeptical about links that create a commercial advantage for one party at the expense of the other.

Until the law becomes more settled in this area, museums can take some practical steps to manage the problem of unauthorized linking. Notices or licenses posted on the museum's Web site can spell out the terms governing linking to the site. The use of gateway technology, such as passwords, is another possibility, although it may prove too restrictive for most museums. A museum also may consider using trademark legends on every Web page. Finally, a museum may enter into a Web linking agreement, which should spell out clearly the conditions for using the museum's trademark on Web sites operated by other entities.[99]

In general, museums should avoid the use of another's trademark as a hypertext link. Instead, they should use the name of the entity in regular type to avoid suggesting that the museum and the other entity have some kind of business affiliation. When creating a link to another site, the best practice is to link to a home page, permitting the linked site to present important welcome, advertising, and trademark information. Finally, museums should consider the use of disclaimers on their sites to reduce the liability for copyright or trademark infringements on any linked sites.

Framing

Another kind of link is sometimes called an "inline" link. Unlike outlinks, inline links actually "pull in" materials from another site (the target site). Without ever leaving the site originally accessed, the visitor can view materials from the target sites, which are automatically displayed within the window border, or frame, of the linking site. The use of this kind of browsing technology is sometimes called "framing." While framing technology is now widely available in commercial Web browsers, its use under certain circumstances may raise legal issues.

Suppose that an enterprising graduate student creates a Web site called Newton's Observatory. Instead of keeping his eyes in the heavens, this student is focused on the content of hundreds of science museums on the Internet, including ASMP. Without ever leaving Newton's Observatory, the visitor to this site can view an extraordinary range of images and texts on astronomy within a frame that displays the Newton's Observatory logo, Web address, and commercial advertisements. Unfortunately, acknowledgments, credits, and copyright management information from the originating museums are sometimes obscured. Newton's Observatory is supported through advertising revenues, subscription fees to an online magazine, and commissions for referrals to Mississippi.com, an online bookstore. ASMP's director, Kate Goodhart, is upset when she learns that images and text from the museum's world-famous science fiction collection can be accessed through Newton's Observatory sites and viewed in frames that eliminate any reference to the originating source. Are such electronic frames lawful? Again, the answer is not clear.

The first case to challenge the legality of framing was *Washington Post Co. v. TotalNews, Inc.*, which pitted some of the nation's most prominent news media organizations against a small Web development company that operated behind Lulu's taco stand in Gilbert, Arizona.[100] The TotalNews site permits a user to view editorial and news content from hundreds of other Web sites within a border that displays the TotalNews logo, Web address, and commercial advertisements. The plaintiffs argued that TotalNews "openly free rides" on their efforts by "simply lifting . . . content wholesale and selling advertising based on proximity to that content."[101] In June 1997, the parties settled the dispute. Under

the terms of the settlement agreement, TotalNews was permitted to retain conventional outlinks to the news sites subject to revocation on 15 days' notice.[102] Following the legal strategy of the plaintiffs in their dispute with the TotalNews site, ASMP may decide to immediately send a cease and desist letter to the Newton's Observatory site, retaining all other legal options.[103]

ASMP might argue that placing a frame around its images and texts constitutes the creation of an unauthorized derivative work. A "derivative work," as explained in chapter 1, is a work based on one or more preexisting works (such as a poster based on an original work of art) where the underlying work is "recast, transformed or adapted."[104] The better view is that placing a wooden frame around of a work of art does not create a derivative work because the original work is not recast, transformed, or adapted. But what about placing an electronic "frame" around protected material borrowed from another Web site?[105] Again, the answer is not entirely clear. At least one federal district court refused to dismiss a case where the defendant argued that its framing of the content of another Web site was not an infringing derivative work but merely a "lens," which permitted Internet users to view the information placed on the Internet by the target site.[106]

Jurisdiction and the Internet

For a court to exercise authority over particular parties in connection with particular disputes, the court must have jurisdiction. To this end, museums should be aware that their Internet or other electronic activities may be construed as a local presence far away, subjecting them to personal jurisdiction in a foreign forum—nationally or even internationally. By the same token, the electronic activities of an alleged infringer of an institution's copyright or trademark rights may subject the infringer to a lawsuit in a forum that is most advantageous to the institution. Although simply placing material on a Web site and making it available on the Internet might not be enough to subject a party to foreign jurisdiction, in several recent cases courts have exercised jurisdiction over parties whose contacts with the forum were solely electronic.

Personal Jurisdiction Basics

Before an action to vindicate copyright or trademark rights can be maintained by or against a museum, the court in which the action is filed must be able to exercise personal jurisdiction over the infringer. A court will always have personal jurisdiction over a potential defendant in the state where the defendant is domiciled or has a business presence. However, that location may not be the most convenient for the plaintiff. Instead, bringing suit in the plaintiff's own state or in another location may provide certain strategic advantages, as well as reducing potential litigation costs.

To determine whether a court may exercise jurisdiction over an out-of-state defendant, courts in the United States traditionally ask whether the defendant has "purposefully avail[ed] itself of the privilege of conducting activities within the forum State, thereby invoking the benefits and protections of its laws."[107] In essence, the inquiry hinges on how much "contact" the defendant has with the forum state. Generally, the more contact in the state where the plaintiff seeks to bring the case, the more "fair" it will be to require a party to defend itself there.[108]

Personal Jurisdiction and the Internet

In the borderless context of electronic commerce and the Internet, applying the principles of personal jurisdiction is not without its complexities. Courts that have been called upon to address these issues have struggled to develop consistent approaches; however, there is currently much disagreement about how much contact with the forum state is enough to allow the courts of that state to exercise jurisdiction. Despite the currently fluid state of the law, central to the analysis in many of the cases decided to date is whether the offending Web site is active or passive in nature. The more active it is, the more likely the court will exercise jurisdiction.

The least active type of Web site merely allows Internet users to visit and read the information provided on the site. For example, in one recent case involving the Blue Note, a well-known jazz restaurant in New York City, a New York district court declined to exercise jurisdiction over a Missouri jazz club called the Blue Note that had a Web page on the Internet.[109] The district court held, and the appellate court affirmed, that "[c]reating a site . . . may be felt nationwide—or even worldwide—but, without more, it is not an act purposefully directed toward the forum state" in a way that would grant jurisdiction to New York courts.[110]

However, some courts have found the exercise of personal jurisdiction to be reasonable despite the apparently passive nature of the Web site. For example, one Connecticut court held that advertising via the Internet constituted sufficient contacts for the court to exercise jurisdiction in a location where the Internet advertisements could be accessed.[111] In that case the defendant used the domain name inset.com, which allegedly infringed the plaintiff's federally registered trademark. The court found that the defendant's advertising on the Internet—along with its toll-free number, both of which could be accessed on demand in Connecticut—constituted sufficient contacts with Connecticut for the court to exercise jurisdiction.

A slightly more active type of Web site allows the Internet user to exchange information with the proprietor of the site. For example, the user may be able to type in his name and home address for inclusion in a mailing list. Courts have construed this activity as sufficient to grant jurisdiction over the Web site proprietor.[112]

The most active type of site allows the Internet user to conduct business directly with the proprietor of the Web site. For instance, many retailers, including museums, offer online shopping and permit customers to select an item, enter his or her credit card number, and have the item shipped to his or her home. The contractual nature of these activities provides a straightforward basis on which to justify the exercise of jurisdiction over the proprietor of the Web site in states where the consumer, but not necessarily the proprietor, resides. For example, in one Pennsylvania case, the court held that it could assert jurisdiction over a California-based defendant that operated an online news service using the domain name Zippo.com.[113] The court reasoned that because the defendant had contracted with seven Internet access providers in Pennsylvania and provided its news service to approximately 3,000 paying customers in the state, it was "doing business over the Internet" and could have anticipated being sued in Pennsylvania for infringement and dilution of the famous ZIPPO trademark.

However, not all Internet personal jurisdiction decisions have turned on this passive-active Web site dichotomy. One Illinois court recently held that because the tort of trademark infringement will be felt mainly in the state where the plaintiff is a domiciliary or has a business presence, a court can exercise personal jurisdiction over a defendant there, regardless of the amount of Internet contact the defendant has with the state.[114] This decision was partly based on the wide reach of the Illinois long-arm statute and court precedent indicating that "entry" by the defendant into the forum state is not required. This decision departs from the analysis employed by most courts that have addressed Internet personal jurisdiction issues, and it is uncertain whether its rationale will be widely accepted.

International Jurisdiction and the Internet

Sometimes, a foreign defendant is subject to jurisdiction in the United States based on electronic activities alone. For example, a New York district court held an Italian defendant in contempt of an earlier permanent injunction that enjoined it from publishing any matter that infringed Playboy's trademarks.[115] When the defendant established an online adult service in Italy called PLAYMEN that was accessible from the United States, the court rejected the defendant's argument that it was not distributing the images violating the injunction. The court reasoned that because the defendant solicited and serviced users in the United States and invited them to download the infringing images, it had engaged in a process that subjected the company to the jurisdiction of U.S. courts.

As these cases show, the Internet's novelty as a medium and the differing factual circumstances in which cases may arise lead to challenging jurisdictional questions and seemingly inconsistent results. Analysis of these issues is fact-specific, but more and more courts appear willing to assert jurisdiction over foreign defendants based on purely electronic contacts if they are interactive and can be shown to have been directed into a state.

Chapter 4
LICENSING

To nonlawyers and lawyers alike, the licensing of intellectual property is surrounded by a surprising number of hopes, fears, and misunderstandings. Once the arcane specialty of attorneys who worked in the back offices of large firms and corporations, the intellectual property license has emerged as a prominent feature of American life. Tucked into computer cartons and software packages, spread over product packages and inserted into publications, and boldly displayed in videotapes and on Web pages, the intellectual property license has become ubiquitous. Perhaps it was inevitable that intellectual property licenses would give rise to owners' hopes of getting rich quick, users' fears of commercial exploitation, and everyone's misunderstandings about the often dense and mysterious legal terms these agreements contain. As owners and users of intellectual property, museums share these hopes and concerns. This chapter's purpose is to make the intellectual property licensing process a little less mysterious and, therefore, a little more useful to museums.

General Terms and Conditions

To illustrate the general terms and conditions of a licensing agreement, consider the hypothetical experience of the American Heritage Village, an outdoor history museum. Susan Parker, the director, recently selected American Silver Treasury, Inc., to produce and distribute a reproduction of the famous Wentworth Independence Bowl (known as the Independence Bowl), made in 1780 to celebrate American independence by Robert Wentworth, the beloved patriot and renowned silversmith. Because of the bowl's historic importance, Heritage Village reviewed proposals from dozens of firms before selecting American Silver Treasury. The limited-edition

engraved silver bowl, which will sell for approximately $5,000, will bear Heritage Village's federally registered trademarks AMERICAN HERITAGE VILLAGE and AHV, which are well known as designations for fine-quality reproductions and adaptations of objects in the museum's collections. Each Independence Bowl will be sold with a copyrighted brochure, *Robert Wentworth: Craftsman and Patriot*, which contains biographical and historical information.

Licensed Property Defined

At the outset, Heritage Village (the licensor) must evaluate carefully what intellectual property rights it will need to license to Silver Treasury (the licensee) to permit the firm to perform under the contract. The terms and conditions of licensing agreements vary significantly depending on the type of intellectual property being licensed and the relationship of the parties. However, all intellectual property licenses—copyright, trademark, patent, and trade secret—should identify and define precisely the intellectual property rights being licensed. To take just one example, a trademark license must carefully define the types of goods and/or services permitted to be sold under the mark being licensed. In the copyright area, the license should unambiguously state which rights in copyright's bundle of rights (reproduction, adaptation, distribution, public performance, public display, and digital audio transmission) are being granted.

The licensed intellectual property rights may be described in the text of the license or in a schedule that is attached and incorporated by reference into the binding obligations of the agreement. The licensed property may be defined in the text of the agreement, either in the license grant clause or in a separate provision. In any case, the intellectual property being licensed should be described in exacting detail, including registration numbers and dates, a full description of the property, and illustrations, when appropriate.

License Grant

Once the intellectual property rights are clearly defined, the license grant clause conveys to the licensee the right to use the intellectual property. The best practice is to use present tense in the license grant. In the Heritage Village example, the language of the license grant might read: "Licensor hereby grants an exclusive, nontransferable license to use the licensor's federally registered trademarks AMERICAN HERITAGE VILLAGE and AHV solely in connection with the manufacture, distribution, and sale of the Independence Bowl, subject to the terms and conditions set forth in this agreement." A separate copyright grant clause might provide: "Licensor hereby grants to Licensee the nonexclusive, royalty-free license to reproduce and distribute the copyrighted Wentworth brochure solely in connection with the Licensee's manufacture, distribution, and sale of the Independence Bowl pursuant to this agreement." To prevent a licensee from arguing later that additional rights were implicitly granted, many licenses also include a provision stating that the licensor reserves all rights not explicitly licensed. Such a provision might state: "All other rights not expressly granted hereunder are reserved by Licensor."

Suppose that American Silver Treasury later decides to sell a large production overrun of the Wentworth brochure to Merchant Mart, Inc., for distribution through its national discount retail chain independent of the sale of the licensed products. This use of the brochure by Silver Treasury is beyond the scope of the copyright license grant, which clearly limits the distribution of the brochure for use in connection with the production, promotion, and sale of the Independence Bowl. If the parties are otherwise unable to come

to an amiable resolution, Heritage Village might take advantage of the agreement's dispute resolution clause to resolve the matter without resorting to litigation (see "Dispute Resolution," later in this chapter).

Scope of License

Heritage Village's license grant restricted Silver Treasury to the following activities: manufacturing, distributing, and selling the Independence Bowl under the Heritage Village marks, and reproducing and distributing the Wentworth brochure in connection with these efforts. There are, however, a number of ways to narrow further the scope of the license. In particular, many licenses include provisions addressing exclusivity, territory, and permissible uses under the agreement.

Exclusivity

Intellectual property licenses may be granted on an exclusive or a nonexclusive basis. Under an exclusive license, the licensee has the sole right to use or exploit the intellectual property. The parties to an exclusive license must determine whether the licensor itself is excluded from exploiting the intellectual property during the term of the license. If so, such exclusion should be expressly stated in the license. Under a nonexclusive license, the licensee may have to share the right(s) with others, including perhaps the licensor and other licensees. From a business perspective, a museum's decision to grant an exclusive license is an important one, reflecting not only the museum's licensing strategy but also its relative strength in the license negotiations. In Heritage Village's case, selecting Silver Treasury as its exclusive licensee made good business sense to Heritage Village because of the special silversmithing capabilities of this firm. Moreover, given Silver Treasury's small size and limited production capabilities, it likely would have been unable and unwilling to make the necessary investment to meet the museum's demanding production standards if not for the exclusive distribution arrangement.

The decision to grant an exclusive license is also significant from a legal perspective because, as noted in chapter 1, exclusive licenses are regarded under copyright law as a "transfer of ownership" (albeit a limited one) and, therefore, must be in writing signed by the owner of the copyright. Moreover, exclusive licensees also can sue for infringements of the licensed intellectual property right.

Territory

A license should contain a clear statement of its geographic limits, if any, with respect to the specific intellectual property rights at issue. Obviously, a grant of worldwide rights is the broadest from a territorial standpoint. But, for purposes of licensing, the world can be divided and subdivided into any number of units, including continents, countries, states, cities, or regions. For example, Heritage Village might agree that Silver Treasury would have exclusive rights to distribute and sell the Independence Bowl in North America, while retaining the right to name other distributors outside this territory.

To take another example, suppose that a museum in Florence, Italy, collaborates with a museum in the United States to organize a traveling exhibition with venues in major European and U.S. cities. The organizing institutions agree to contribute major works to the show and to "cross-license" all necessary copyrights and trademarks in connection with the merchandising of any exhibition-related products, services, or publications. If the U.S. and Italian museums agree to share revenues from such merchandising activities, the parties may decide to divide the revenues according to territory, with the Italian museum entitled to all revenues generated during the European tour and all corresponding proceeds from sales in the United States to go to the U.S. partner. The parties also should address territorial limitations, if any, for merchandising after the end of the traveling exhibition.

Permissible Uses

Limitations on uses under a license are critical in controlling intellectual property rights. Use limitations may be tailored to meet any need the parties deem important. The nature of the limitation will vary widely depending on the type of license, which may run the gamut from pure intellectual property licenses, through audiovisual production agreements, to end-user licenses. To take just one example, a museum licensing images of original works of art in its collections to an institution of higher education may prohibit the use of images for commercial, fund-raising, and other noneducational uses.

As custodians of rich visual and documentary resources, museums increasingly are involved in the development of "new media" products for distribution through traditional or electronic channels of commerce. In such projects, use limitations are often expressed for specific media formats. For example, suppose that in 1985 the fictitious Harbinger Museum and Sculpture Garden was given *Snow Birds*, an original sculptural work, along with written permission from the sculptor, Rocky Miller, to reproduce, adapt, and distribute images of the work in "any manner, medium, or form." Over the years, the museum has relied on that license to make and sell posters, prints, and postcards of images of the popular work. The Harbinger would now like to create and distribute a commercial multimedia work that incorporates a digital image of *Snow Birds*. The museum's attorneys believe that the language of the 1985 license permits such a use, but the lawyers for the Miller estate take the opposite position. Who has the better view?

The Harbinger is facing an increasingly common legal problem in the digital age: When may a copyright licensee exploit a licensed work through new and later-developed technologies? The courts do not offer a uniform approach to answering this question. Under one approach, a license of rights in a given medium includes only such uses as fall within the "unambiguous core uses" of the given medium.[1] Under this view, for example, a 1939 license granting "motion picture" rights would not include distribution through subsequently developed technologies such as videocassettes.[2]

Under a second approach, and probably the better and more widely followed view, "a licensee may properly pursue any uses that may reasonably fall within the medium as described in the license."[3] Applying "neutral principles of contract interpretation" (favoring neither licensor nor licensee), a court following this approach would analyze whether the new technology was foreseeable at the time the parties entered the agreement.[4] If so, it would be covered by the license. Under this test, for instance, a 1988 grant of "worldwide motion picture and television rights" was held to cover home videocassette distribution in 1990 because the new technology was foreseeable at the time of contracting.[5] Following this approach, the production of multimedia audiovisual works by the Harbinger Museum is likely covered under the broad license that the artist granted to the museum because multimedia audiovisual technology was probably foreseeable in 1985 when the license was granted. Conversely, absent contractual language to the contrary, uses that were unknown and unforeseeable at the time of contracting will generally be held outside the scope of the grant.[6] Accordingly, if parties intend a license to cover all uses of a work in any existing or future format or medium, they should include specific language clarifying their intent, such as: "Licensor grants to Licensee the right to exploit the work by any means or methods whatsoever now known or later developed."

Looking ahead, a museum negotiating an intellectual property licensing agreement must assume the Internet is not just foreseeable, it is ubiquitous. Thus, licenses negotiated and drafted today should explicitly address whether "electronic publication rights" or "electronic rights" are included in the grant. A license grant that does not expressly exclude such electronic rights in all likelihood would be interpreted by a court as including such rights. As a matter of good drafting practice, the license should clearly state the specific copyright interest being transferred, describing the authorized medium, format, or technology rather than relying on such vague terms as "electronic rights." Of course, granting or refusing to grant electronic publication rights will affect compensation arrangements, which are discussed in greater detail later in this chapter. Suppose that the publisher of a leading encyclopedia of American history requests permission to reproduce photographs in the Heritage Village collections. For obvious reasons, reproduction rights for the print and electronic versions of the encyclopedia are generally more valuable than those for the print version alone.

"New use" issues also arise for museums in connection with electronic publication projects that involve a preexisting collective work, such as a periodical issue, anthology, or encyclopedia. A collective work, as described in chapter 1, consists of several contributions—each constituting a separate and independent work—assembled into a collective whole that is eligible for a separate compilation copyright. The compilation copyright protects the selection, coordination, and arrangement of independent works. In a typical collective work, the authors of the individual works retain the copyright in their own works, and the party assembling the works generally holds the copyright in the collective work. Copyright law further provides that, in the absence of an express transfer of copyright, the creators of collective works are "presumed to have acquired only the privilege of reproducing and distributing the contribution as part of that particular collective work, any revision of that collective work, and any later collective work in the same series."[7]

Heritage Village, for example, wants to republish an anthology of historical papers entitled *Everyday Life in America: 1820–1920* in electronic media, including online and CD-ROM products. The publication resulted from a symposium the museum sponsored several years ago. First, Heritage Village would need to consider whether its original agreements with the symposium participants permitted electronic use. Assume that, before the symposium, the museum obtained the participants' permission to publish their papers, but the contributors retained the copyrights in their individual works. Heritage Village holds the copyright in the collective work.

Must the museum now obtain the contributors' permission before publishing the collective work in electronic format? Under copyright law, Heritage Village, in the absence of an express transfer of copyright from the contributors, is presumed to have acquired the privilege of reproducing and distributing "any revision of that collective work." It seems clear that the republication of a single essay would not be a "revision of that work."[8] Nor would Heritage Village's privilege extend to publishing a new collective work, for example, in which the selection and arrangement of the papers differed from the original anthology. But what about publishing the identical anthology in electronic format? The answer to that question has been the subject of intense debate.

In a case closely watched by the copyright community, a group of freelance writers sued the New York Times Co., Newsday Inc., Time Inc., and the Atlantic Monthly for republishing the writers' articles in electronic format. In *Tasini v. New York Times*, the writers argued, among other things, that the publisher's "privilege" of reproducing and distributing revisions of their collective works should be treated like any nonexclusive, nontransferable license.[9] Viewed in this way, the writers claimed that the defendant-publishers did not have the right to authorize the use of their works in electronic products. The court was not persuaded by the writers' argument, ruling that the publishers' privilege to revise a collective work included republication of the work online and in

CD-ROM format. However, the judge cautioned that the publisher's privilege only extended to publications that preserved the original selection or arrangement of the earlier collective work.

Under the holding in *Tasini*, a museum could republish in electronic format (including online use) collective works that are the same as the original collective work, a revision of the original collective work, or a later collective work in the same series, even in the absence of any express transfer of copyright. This holding may be significant to many museums in light of their strong information dissemination mandate. On the other hand, museums should exercise the privilege only with great care in light of the rapidly evolving nature of this area of the law and given the well-established academic conventions governing the republication of protected individual works. In the example above, Heritage Village has a fairly strong argument that the republication of *Everyday Life in America: 1820–1920* in electronic format is a permissible revision of that collective work, provided that the selection and arrangement of the original contributions remain the same as the original. Nonetheless, for the reasons set forth above, requesting permission from the contributors to republish the anthology in electronic format is probably the prudent course of action.

License Limitations

Limitations on Use

The license grant is usually a short, concise statement of the rights conveyed. More substantive restrictions on the licensee's ability to exercise the rights granted are ordinarily set forth in a separate provision. In the Heritage Village example, the license grant merely stated that Silver Treasury's use of the licensed property was confined to the manufacture, distribution, and sale of the Independence Bowl and the reproduction and distribution of the Wentworth brochure. More detailed use limitations—including extensive quality control standards for the manufacturing of the

Independence Bowl, as well as standards and procedures for the review and preapproval of advertising and promotional materials—would more appropriately belong in a separate section. Such use limitations are particularly critical to ensure the integrity of the Heritage Village trademark rights. As explained in chapter 2 and discussed further later in this chapter, failure to adequately control or monitor the use of a mark can result in loss of trademark rights. To this end, therefore, Heritage Village might have required curatorial approval of plans, drawings, computer-assisted design files, photographs, and molds at various specified times during the development and manufacturing of the Independence Bowl.

Heritage Village also would set forth detailed instructions on the placement and use of the AMERICAN HISTORY VILLAGE and AHV trademarks, not only on the final product but also on all advertisements, brochures, stationery, and other promotional materials created or distributed in connection with the Independence Bowl. In addition, Heritage Village would likely require review and preapproval rights with respect to all advertising or promotional materials incorporating the museum's marks. Heritage Village also may want to include a clause that expressly prohibits Silver Treasury from using in connection with this or any other project other marks owned by the museum, thereby foreclosing the argument that an implied license was granted to use such marks. Similarly, Heritage Village could provide in this section detailed specifications regarding the color, cropping, and placement of any images provided by Heritage Village to be included in the Wentworth brochure, again including opportunities for approval by the curators.

Limitations on Sublicenses and Assignments

Most intellectual property licenses contain a provision prohibiting or limiting a licensee's right to assign the agreement or sublicense the rights (or obligations) under the license. The purpose of such a clause is to ensure that third parties not

bound by the terms of the license do not use the licensed rights without a waiver provision or the prior written approval of the licensor. The Heritage Village example illustrates the reason for such a provision. In light of Silver Treasury's unique capabilities, and given the extensive quality-control specifications set forth in the license, Heritage Village wants the assurance that only Silver Treasury will use the rights and perform the obligations under the agreement. If Silver Treasury were permitted to assign its obligations without limitation, it might assign the project to a shoddy silversmith who creates low-quality bowls. As a result, Heritage Village's valuable marks would be used in connection with goods manufactured below its quality-control standards. This use, as explained in chapter 2, could subject the marks to challenge.

To prevent this situation, Heritage Village may simply decide that an absolute prohibition on assignments and sublicensing is necessary to achieve its goals under the license. Of course, the museum would always be free to waive its own prohibition if it later decided to do so. As an alternative, the museum may decide to limit Silver Treasury from sublicensing its rights and obligations or assigning the agreement, subject to a condition that the museum, at its sole discretion, must approve in writing the selection of any sublicensees or assignees. This requirement could be qualified further by providing that the museum's approval "shall not unreasonably be withheld." (Other possible approaches are to the third-party problem are explored in "Audiovisual Production Agreements" later in this chapter.) If assignment or sublicensing is permitted, the licensor should require that the assignee or sublicensee explicitly agree to be bound by all terms of the original agreement.

Ownership of Intellectual Property

Many intellectual property licenses contain a standard provision requiring the licensee to acknowledge the licensor's ownership of the rights being transferred. Such provisions are especially important in trademark licenses because multiple claims of ownership of a given mark can invalidate the protection afforded to a mark by undermining the single source–identifying function of the mark. Accordingly, it is good drafting practice for the licensor to require the licensee to acknowledge that the licensor is the "owner of the mark and of all the goodwill associated with the mark" and that the licensee "will not take any action inconsistent with" such ownership rights. It is also common to require the licensee to acknowledge that "all use of the mark and any goodwill associated with the mark shall inure to the benefit of the licensor."

In contrast, separate ownership of the various interests comprising the copyright, or joint ownership of these interests, does not necessarily threaten the validity of these interests and is in fact explicitly contemplated under the Copyright Act.[10] For instance, a typical ownership provision in a license to use a database might provide: "The XYZ database is protected as a collective work and/or compilation under U.S. copyright law, and the Licensee hereby acknowledges the Licensor is the sole and exclusive owner of such rights." Most licensees would have little difficulty in agreeing to such a clause, for it protects the value added by the database compiler (the selection, coordination, and arrangement of the materials). But when the licensee is permitted to create certain new works "based on" the information in the database, called derivative works, ownership clauses can become more contentious. As discussed more fully in chapter 1, such derivative works may be eligible for a separate copyright if the originality standard is satisfied. To control ownership in any derivative works, the licensor may seek an assignment of any derivative work copyrights while the licensee will resist making such an assignment.

Intellectual Property Rights Notices

The accurate display of authorship and ownership information, which has always been important to museums, is becoming even more significant in the digital age.[11] For a museum, the display of such information is consistent with its purpose to provide the public with accurate information about the identity of the creator and the title of the work. It is also important for a museum to assure the public that the products and services offered in the marketplace under its marks conform to its high standards. Such notices also protect the museum by putting the public on notice as to the ownership of the intellectual property rights embodied in the product or service. Finally, intellectual property notices indicate how to contact the museum for further rights information.

For all these reasons, intellectual property notice obligations are generally addressed in intellectual property licenses. For example, in connection with the Wentworth brochure, Heritage Village probably will include detailed requirements regarding the language and format for all attributions and acknowledgments in the brochure, including crediting the author, the photographer, the museum, or the donor. Heritage Village also will likely require Silver Treasury to include in the Wentworth brochure, as well as other promotional and advertising materials, an explicit acknowledgment that the AMERICAN HERITAGE VILLAGE and AHV marks are the federally registered marks of Heritage Village.

Term, Renewal, and Termination

How should Heritage Village determine the length of its licensing arrangement with Silver Treasury? Under what circumstances might either party decide to end the relationship earlier than initially contemplated? Should Heritage Village provide for the renewal of the license, and, if so, on what terms? What, if any, are the obligations of Heritage Village and Silver Treasury after the termination of the agreement? Well-drafted term, renewal, and termination provisions will answer such questions unambiguously.

Term

The parties to an intellectual property agreement are generally free to establish the duration of their business relationship. The term may be only a few months, or run for the entire duration of the intellectual property right at issue. Whatever the term, it should be stated explicitly in the license as a specified date or a period of time following the effective date of the agreement. In the Heritage Village agreement, the parties might agree on the following clause: "This Agreement shall extend from the effective date for an initial period ending December 31, 2004, unless terminated sooner in accordance with the procedures set forth below." The effective date may be keyed to the date that the parties execute the agreement or to another date of the parties' choosing.

As an important element of an intellectual property license, the duration of an agreement is open to negotiation. Licensors usually prefer shorter terms that permit them to pursue other business opportunities as they arise and to remain flexible regarding the selection of licensees. On the other hand, a licensor should not overlook the advantages of a long-term licensing arrangement, which may provide a reliable source of high-quality products over many years and help establish brand loyalty among consumers. Many licensees prefer longer terms over which to spread their start-up costs and initial investments and to lock in marketing rights. In the Heritage Village example, one way to address both parties' preferences would be for Heritage Village to offer Silver Treasury an initial limited-term license subject to a number of renewal options.

Renewal

Renewal provisions range from very simple to very complex. Many intellectual property licenses provide for automatic renewal under the same terms and conditions, subject to the right of either party to terminate by giving notice. For example, a license might provide: "This agreement shall be renewed automatically each year unless either party receives notice of nonrenewal at least thirty (30) days prior to the end of the current term." More complex renewal provisions may be needed in product development, manufacturing, and distribution agreements. For example, Heritage Village may want to consider a renewal option that could be exercised by the licensee only if it satisfactorily performed under the agreement and met certain defined sales levels for the Independence Bowl.

Termination

Suppose that Heritage Village and Silver Treasury agree to an initial three-year term. Nonetheless, the parties may want to specify in the agreement specific conditions (and procedures) that will trigger the early termination of the agreement. Termination can be "for cause" or "without cause." A standard termination for cause provision may terminate the agreement for serious breaches by a party, usually referred to as breaches of a "material term or condition of the agreement." The parties also may specify which breaches will be regarded as material. For example, the failure to pay royalties in a timely manner, the failure to maintain quality controls, and the breach of an intellectual property representation or warranty (described later in this chapter) are generally regarded as material breaches.

Termination for cause provisions usually specify procedures and time frames for notifying the breaching party. Depending on the nature of the breach, the breaching party may be given the opportunity to "cure" the breach to avoid early termination of the agreement. A sample termination for cause provision is: "Either party can terminate this agreement in the event of a material breach of this agreement by the other party that is not cured within thirty (30) days after the receipt of written notice thereof."

By contrast, under a termination without cause provision, either party may end the agreement for any reason, or no reason at all, provided that adequate notice is given to the other party. Such a clause gives the parties an easy, no-penalty exit from a business arrangement that is not working out or is unproductive. A termination without cause provision generally does not provide for an opportunity to cure because there is no breach; the point of the provision is to permit the parties to change their minds. A sample termination without cause provision is: "This agreement is subject to termination by either party upon at least thirty (30) days notice to the other party."

Termination Obligations

An intellectual property license should also set forth what obligations, if any, remain in effect after the termination of the agreement. The principal purpose of post-termination provisions is to protect the intellectual property of the licensor and prevent its unauthorized use. The first obligation usually imposed upon a licensee is to cease and desist from using the intellectual property covered by the agreement. In copyright licenses, it is not uncommon to require the licensee to certify that any copies of the licensed work have been deleted from any electronic storage media or destroyed. Similarly, a trademark licensor may require the return or certification of destruction of all products or other materials bearing the licensed mark to prevent such products from entering the marketplace without authorization. The cease and desist requirement is especially important to trademark owners because, as noted previously, products manufactured outside the quality control provisions of the licensing agreement place the trademark owner at risk of losing its rights in the mark. In some cases, the trademark owner may permit the licensee to sell off inventory on hand at the time of termination, provided that the merchandise was produced under the quality controls of the license.

Compensation

The parties to an intellectual property license—from the most basic permission to the most complex joint venture—have wide latitude in structuring compensation arrangements tailored to the particular transaction. Indeed, a copyright or trademark owner is not obligated to receive any compensation in exchange for the use of the licensed rights. Many trademark and copyright licenses, outside such categories as product licensing, are granted on a "royalty-free" basis. Suppose that Heritage Village decides to grant a royalty-free license to independent filmmaker Craig Taylor to use copyrighted materials in connection with the making of a documentary film for public television. Structuring the transaction as a royalty-free transaction made sense to Heritage Village's director, Susan Parker, because it not only advances the museum's educational mission but also increases its visibility, possibly resulting in increased visitation and membership. However, if Taylor were then to request permission to use the same materials in a companion book to the film—to be priced at $59.95, heavily promoted, and distributed through a national retail book chain—Parker probably would reach a different conclusion, and the parties would have to renegotiate and/or modify the terms of the prior license. Under such circumstances, she would likely decide that the museum should receive reasonable licensing fees for the use of its works. Taken together, Parker's decisions also seemed prudent to the board of trustees, who were mindful of both the museum's educational mandate and the real need to increase earned income to sustain museum operations.

In determining an appropriate compensation arrangement with Taylor, Heritage Village may choose from various formats, including a lump-sum payment on signing the license; periodic royalty payments (monthly, quarterly, or yearly) calculated as a percentage of the licensee's sales or income; minimum guarantees; and advance payments. Heritage Village also should address in advance the number of complimentary copies Taylor should provide.

Compensation provisions should also be buttressed by record-keeping and audit requirements. For example, it is very common to require the licensee to keep complete and accurate records of all transactions involving the licensed property and financial records documenting royalty payment calculations. Such records may be subject to an audit provision, which generally permits the licensor to inspect the books of the licensee upon reasonable advance notice. Some audit clauses set forth detailed provisions governing the time, place, procedures, and frequency of audits.

On the basis of its recent experience in licensing, Susan Parker has asked the curators to work with the chief business officer to develop some guidelines for licensing museum intellectual property. She was particularly interested in factors that the museum might take into consideration in setting fees under certain licenses. In response to her request, the staff came up with the following nonexhaustive list: the status of the licensee (commercial or nonprofit); the purpose of the use (for-profit, education, research, or scholarship); the licensee's potential sales or income derived from the use of the licensed property; the nature of the end-user community (general public, students); the territorial scope of the license (worldwide, national, or local); the nature of the media or technology at issue (print, electronic, online, or broadcast), and staff time and other museum resources needed to make the licensed resources available.

Representations and Warranties

In a typical transaction involving tangible property—such as the sale of a wristwatch—the buyer may want assurances from the manufacturer that the product will keep time accurately under certain conditions. Such assurances that goods or services will perform as promised are known in the law as "representations and warranties." In

transactions involving the licensing of intangible property like copyrights and trademarks, representations and warranties are different and more complex. The inherent nature of intellectual property sometimes makes it difficult for owners of such rights to be absolutely certain that they own all the rights being transferred. Thus, there is the risk that the license will interfere with or infringe the rights of others claiming an ownership interest. To avoid becoming entangled in lawsuits with third parties, licensees often require representations and warranties from licensors that will permit their "quiet enjoyment" of the licensed property. The breach of such representations and warranties may result in the early termination of the agreement and may require the breaching party to cover any damages suffered by the non-breaching party as a result of the breach.

Under a typical representation and warranty provision, the licensor promises that he is the sole and exclusive owner of the intellectual property rights, that he has the authority to grant the license, and that the transfer of rights will not violate the rights of any third persons. Suppose that Heritage Village entered into an audiovisual development agreement with the XYZ Company to produce a video biography of Robert Wentworth under which the museum agreed to provide XYZ with certain materials, including texts and photographs. The XYZ Company insisted that the agreement include the following provision: "Licensor represents and warrants that the materials made available under the terms of the agreement do not infringe any copyright, trademark, patent, trade secret, or any other personal or proprietary right of any third person." In a copyright license, the licensor also may be required to guarantee that the work is original and not previously published.

Indemnification

An indemnification provision is a legal mechanism that shifts the risk of liability from one party to another for the payment of costs, expenses (including legal fees), and damages arising from the breach of any express representation and warranty. However, the coverage afforded by an indemnification provision is often limited to costs and damages arising from breach of representations and warranties regarding intellectual property. To continue the above example, the agreement might include the following indemnification provision: "Licensor shall defend, indemnify, and hold harmless XYZ Company against any and all claims by third persons that the materials infringe any copyright, trademark, patent, trade secret, or other personal or proprietary right of any third persons, arising from any use of the licensed materials." If it later turns out that Heritage Village, despite its best efforts to confirm its ownership of the transferred rights, does not own the copyrights or trademarks, it will be financially responsible for any damages that the XYZ Company may suffer as a result of the museum's breach of its representation and warranty.

Dispute Resolution

Recall from earlier in this chapter the scenario in which American Silver Treasury sold a production overrun of the Wentworth brochure to Merchant Mart, Inc., for distribution through its national discount retail chain. The transaction seems to be a clear violation of the licensing agreement and a violation of the museum's copyright and trademark rights. How will the parties resolve this dispute? This task would be made much easier if the parties agreed in advance on a dispute resolution procedure. A standard dispute clause might provide: "Licensor and licensee shall make good-faith efforts to resolve any questions concerning the interpretation of the agreement or disputes arising out of or connected with the agreement." Under such a provision, Heritage Village and Silver Treasury would be required to at least attempt to resolve their dispute amicably (for example, by the payment of a retroactive licensing fee to the museum). However, if its attempt failed, Heritage Village might find itself entangled in costly and lengthy copyright and trademark infringement litigation.

To avoid this outcome, many intellectual property licenses include an alternative dispute resolution (ADR) provision, which either recommends or mandates a procedure such as arbitration. In arbitration, a neutral third party (the arbitrator) decides the dispute through a hearing in which both parties have an opportunity to present their case. The parties may agree in advance to be bound by the decision of the arbitrator (binding arbitration) or not to be so bound (nonbinding arbitration). Under a nonbinding arbitration clause, the parties may eventually wind up in court if one or both of them are unsatisfied with the arbitrator's decision. Accordingly, if the parties genuinely want to avoid litigation, they should select a binding arbitration clause, such as: "Questions or disputes that the parties are unable to resolve themselves shall be submitted to arbitration in accordance with the rules for commercial arbitration of the American Arbitration Association (AAA) pertaining at the time. The decision of the arbitrators shall be final and binding upon the parties, and judgment upon the award rendered by the arbitrators may be entered in any court having jurisdiction thereof." The parties also are free to select other arbitration rules, to specify the location of the arbitration, and to allocate the costs for the arbitration between the parties.

Governing Law

If Heritage Village and Silver Treasury opted for nonbinding arbitration that did not resolve their dispute, they could very well find themselves going to court. But which court? And what law? Because the dispute would involve the issue of whether Silver Treasury infringed Heritage Village's copyright, the lawsuit would have to be filed in federal court. Which federal court would depend on other considerations as well, including what state has a relationship to either the parties or the subject matter of the claim.

In this dispute, as in many disputes arising under intellectual property licenses, a key question is whether there has been a material breach of the contract. To answer this question, a judge may be required to interpret the terms and conditions of the license, which is a matter of state contract law rather than federal copyright law. That brings us full circle: Where will the lawsuit be filed (the "choice of forum" question), and what law will govern the interpretation of the license (the "choice of law" question)? The attorneys for Heritage Village, which is located in and organized under the laws of the State of North Anglia, prefer that the lawsuit be filed in their home state and that the license be interpreted under North Anglian law. The attorneys for Silver Treasury, which is located in and organized under the laws of the State of West Anglia, take the opposite position. Who wins?

Fortunately, Heritage Village and Silver Treasury agreed to decide these questions in advance by including the following provision: "The validity and interpretation of this agreement and the rights and obligations of the parties hereunder shall be governed by the laws and adjudicated exclusively by the federal and state courts located in the State of Cornucopia." This provision includes both a choice of law and a choice of forum provision. The parties also are free to select a neutral state, as they did here, rather than specifying the licensor's or licensee's state for choice of law or choice of forum purposes. Some states may not uphold a choice of law or choice of forum clause when the state chosen has no relationship whatsoever to the transaction.

Enforcement

Heritage Village should determine in advance whether Silver Treasury will have any obligation or right to enforce the intellectual property rights being licensed. The general rule is that only the owner or an exclusive licensee of a copyright or trademark may sue for infringement. Nonexclusive licensees generally do not have enforcement rights even if the agreement is silent on this matter. Nonetheless, if a licensor does not want to permit its licensees, whether exclusive or nonexclusive, to exercise any rights of enforcement, it is good practice to so state in the license. There are, however, certain advantages to a licensor permitting (or requiring) exclusive licensees to enforce the licensor's intellectual property rights. For example, some of the burden and costs of enforcing intellectual property rights are shifted under the license. Many licensors retain the initial right to bring an infringement action, while permitting the licensee the option of bringing suit should the licensor choose not to pursue the alleged infringer. Of course, the parties should determine in advance who would be entitled to recovery under such circumstances. Even if Heritage Village decides not to grant enforcement rights to Silver Treasury, it should still enlist Silver Treasury's assistance in policing the market for infringers and require it to provide prompt notice of any apparent infringements.

Copyright Licenses

To illustrate some of the special rules that generally apply to the licensing of copyrighted materials, and to introduce some of the licensing practices in specific copyright industries, consider the hypothetical case of the American Decorative Arts Museum (ADAM). As part of its millennium celebration, ADAM plans to produce a multimedia program, *American Sampler: Decorative Arts in America, 1800–2000*. In producing the audiovisual work, the curators plan to draw deeply on ADAM's unsurpassed collections of American ceramics, silver, textiles, furniture, and furnishings, installed in more than 100 magnificent period rooms.

To make their subject come alive, the curators would like to use a broad range of content, including textual materials, photographs, musical works, and sound recordings. Many of these materials are in the public domain and available for use without the need to pay fees or request permission. For materials that remain under copyright protection, ADAM's curators understand that a certain amount of copying of protected works is permitted under the fair use doctrine for purposes such as criticism, comment, teaching, scholarship, and research. The use of other materials, the staff recognizes, will require identifying the owner of the copyright and obtaining a license either from the owner or a collective rights agency representing the owner. Let's see how ADAM should approach this daunting task.

Copyright License Requirements

The U.S. Copyright Act imposes certain formal requirements on obtaining a license, which differ depending on the nature of the license. Any license that transfers ownership of a copyright, or any right within copyright's bundle of rights, must be in writing and signed by the copyright owner.[12] Under the Copyright Act, an exclusive licensing arrangement is regarded as a transfer of ownership; therefore, a written document signed by the copyright owner is required. However, a nonexclusive license is expressly excluded from the definition of transfer of ownership under the Copyright Act. As a result, nonexclusive licenses are enforceable even if not in writing.

Suppose that, during a collecting trip, an ADAM curator requested permission to use a photograph of a beautiful Amish diamond quilt in the multimedia program. In response, the photographer gave the "two thumbs up" sign. Can the museum rely on such conduct for permission? On a number of occasions, the courts have enforced an "implied license" in which a person's words or conduct indicate an intent to grant permission to use a copyrighted work.[13] One pitfall, however, is using a work in a manner beyond the scope of the implied license.[14] This curator could not likely go on to use the photograph of the quilt on notecards sold in the museum shop without obtaining permission. Given the obvious problems of proving that a copyright owner intended

to grant permission, the best practice is to reduce any permission to writing, whether the license is exclusive or nonexclusive.

Another fundamental copyright transfer rule, introduced in chapter 1, is that the "[t]ransfer of ownership of any material object . . . does not in itself convey any rights in the copyrighted work embodied in the object" without an agreement.[15] Failure to keep this basic rule in mind could have unfortunate results for a museum, whether acting as licensor or licensee. For example, in *Marshall v. Music Hall Center for the Performing Arts, Inc.*,[16] a photographer donated to the Graystone International Jazz Museum a number of photographs of famous jazz musicians, including Dizzy Gillespie. The museum, in turn, gave the sponsor of the Detroit Jazz Festival permission to use the Gillespie photograph on the cover of the festival program. The museum had no such right to grant because it owned only the material object embodying the creative expression—the photograph—and nothing more. Although the museum fortunately was not named in the lawsuit, the photographer sued the festival sponsor for copyright infringement and won.

Image Licenses

Whether a museum is the licensor or the licensee, the licensing of still images, which, for copyright purposes include photographs and graphic arts, are of central importance. Moving images, which include motion pictures, television, and video, are subject to different licensing requirements. In an image-hungry world, image licensing, sometimes referred to in the commercial sector as the visual content industry, is rapidly expanding, with a growing number of firms beginning to specialize in the electronic delivery of images over the Internet. "Image licensing" is really an umbrella term for a wide range of business and nonprofit activities, including licensing by large stock photography houses, archival photographic collections, collective rights societies representing artists and artists' estates, commercial fine arts image libraries, and museum licensing consortia. The latter include collaborative efforts by museums to build digital libraries with a view to making their collections more widely available.

Given the special importance of image licensing to museums, there are a number of key issues to focus on when granting or receiving an image license. As a licensee, a museum will want to make sure that it obtains the derivative work right (sometimes called the adaptation right) in the image. Without securing this right, a museum would not be permitted to create new works based upon the original work, which would include "recasting, adapting, or transforming" the image, for example, to transform a photograph into a poster.

By contrast, a museum acting as licensor may be reluctant to grant the adaptation right in order to ensure the veracity of the original image, a concern of increasing importance in the digital age. If granting the adaptation right is necessary, the museum may seek to add a limitation or condition to the grant in order to retain control over the work. For example, a museum licensing a compilation of images of artworks from its collections to an institution of higher education may permit limited adaptations such as recolorizing a slide for instructional purposes. However, the museum may require the destruction of the modified images on termination of the license. Under some circumstances, a museum may need to obtain a waiver of moral rights from the artist before permitting any transformation or adaptation of the work (see "Moral Rights," later in this chapter).

Compensation arrangements under an image license vary widely. A museum may offer analog or digital images (at a range of resolutions to be set by the museum) to the public free of charge either through traditional or electronic distribution channels. To borrow a phrase from the visual content industry, the museum would be offering free visual content. Museums were engaged in this approach long before commercial firms recognized its advantages, thereby fulfilling their mandate of disseminating information and, in the process, building loyal audiences for a wide range of cultural products and services. In the electronic environment, such an approach will continue to serve museums well.

On the other hand, if the purpose of an image license is to increase the earned revenues of a museum or to defray the significant costs of digitizing and distributing visual content, there are several possible compensation arrangements. Under a flat admission fee, a museum may provide access to visual content for a set fee. Transaction fees may be used in connection with the use of a specific image. In establishing a fee schedule for such uses, a museum may take into consideration the factors described earlier in this chapter (see "Compensation"). Subscription fees may be appropriate when the licensee regularly provides museum images to the public, such as through a magazine or journal, whether in print or electronic format. Finally, licensing fees permit the unlimited use of museum resources for a specified time, place, or purpose. For example, a museum may choose a licensing fee approach to make a database of visual resources available for use by a regional consortium of colleges and universities. The fee may be based on the number of enrolled students, the number of institutions, or some other measure.

Museums are beginning to form collectives or consortia to build large digital libraries of high-quality images and related multimedia documentation with a view toward making them more widely available in formats and under terms that are tailored to the needs of users. Licensing collectives offer participating museums many benefits. First, the museum reduces the cost of processing individual requests for single images and, in some cases, the cost of clearing and negotiating rights with artists and rights holders. Second, the museum community as a whole benefits by standardizing practices for digitizing and documenting collections. Third, museums gain access to the rich holdings of other museums. This arrangement also offers many benefits for licensees, who will gain single-point access to a library of digital materials for a low annual fee while avoiding the delay and inconvenience of obtaining individual permissions. Image licensing fees may be paid directly to the museum or through licensing collectives, whether organized on a for-profit or nonprofit basis.

The new digital image library consortia build on the experiences of the pioneering Museum Educational Site Licensing (MESL) project. Launched in 1995 by the Getty Information Institute and MUSE Educational Media, this two-year collaboration brought together seven museums and seven universities to develop a test model of licensing digital materials across closed campus networks. At the conclusion of the project, the sponsors and participants created a digital library of approximately 9,000 images that were mounted by each university and used in a variety of ways by faculty and students. Although the MESL participants did not reach a consensus on a "one-size-fits-all-institutions" license, they did succeed in identifying many of the key legal and policy issues.[17]

As the MESL project neared conclusion, two new nonprofit consortia were formed: the Museum Digital Library Collection (MDLC) and the Art Museum Image Consortium (AMICO). MDLC was formed to provide technical and financial assistance for digitizing all types of museum collections. MDLC also plans to manage, store, distribute, and license museum digital resources and related software to educational institutions, libraries, commercial entities, and the public.[18] AMICO, launched by a group of art museums in 1997 to compile and provide increased educational access to a collective digital library of images and related documentation of works in their collections, has begun to offer its digital library to institutions of higher education, schools (K-12), and libraries.[19]

Music Licenses

Suppose that there was broad agreement among the American Decorative Arts Museum's curators that period music should be an integral part of the *American Sampler* project, but there was no consensus on the best approach for doing so. Some curators wanted to use musical compositions, either in the public domain or subject to copyright, and hire musicians to re-record the works for the project. In fact, some of the musical compositions could be found in the collections of ADAM's library. Other curators felt that the use of prerecorded music would be more economical. Given the different types of music, and the variety of ways to obtain musical content, the curators anticipated that some copyright licenses would be required. But what type of licenses, from whom, and for how much?

At the outset, ADAM's curators should be aware that there are two separate copyrights to keep in mind. First, a composer of a musical composition (or his or her assignee) owns the copyright in the musical composition itself (for example, lyrics and music of a song) that is fixed in a tangible medium of expression (for example, sheet music, an audiotape, or a compact disc). The owner of the copyright in a musical composition has all of the exclusive rights of copyright, including the rights to record, adapt, and publicly perform the work.

Second, once a musical composition is recorded, the resulting sound recording (sometimes referred to as a phonorecord) is eligible for a separate copyright. A sound recording is the work that results from the fixation of sounds, including those that are musical or spoken. The sound recording copyright covers the creative expression added by the record producer, such as the musical arrangement or the mixing of sounds. The sounds may be fixed in any format, including discs, tapes, or other media. However, the sounds accompanying an audiovisual work are specifically excluded from the definition of a sound recording.

From a licensing perspective, the key point is that the owner of the copyright in a musical composition generally cannot grant permission to reproduce a particular recording of a work, unless he or she also holds the rights in the sound recording in the work. Conversely, the owner of the copyright in the sound recording cannot authorize the copying of the underlying musical work. Because two copyrights are involved, two separate licenses are generally required. Suppose that ADAM curators want to use Jesse Jones' classic song, *Yankee Doodle Rag*, performed by the Back Bay Fiddlers and recorded by Triangle Records, Inc., in the *American Sampler* program. The museum will need to obtain licenses from both Jesse Jones (or his estate, or his music publisher if he assigned his rights to it) as the owner of the copyright in the underlying musical composition and from Triangle Records, Inc., as the owner of the copyright in the sound recording. Licenses from record companies, known as "master licenses," are generally not easy to obtain. ADAM probably will not need to obtain permission from or pay fees to the performers, Back Bay Fiddlers, because they probably do not own any copyright interests in the musical composition or sound recording. Usually, the creative contribution of musicians and other performers is rewarded in the United States under a separate labor contract rather than through the copyright system. However, to continue the example, Triangle Records' contract with the Back Bay Fiddlers may require the company to obtain their permission before granting a master license to ADAM.

Like the owners of copyrights in other categories of protected works, the owner of copyright in a musical work (whether an individual composer or a music publisher acting on his or her behalf) is free to enter into a wide range of licensing arrangements. However, a special rule applies to the licensing of musical works. Under the copyright law, once a musical work has been distributed to the public in the United States in the form of a sound recording, any other person may obtain a license to make and publicly distribute another sound recording of the work. Such licenses are known as "compulsory licenses" because the copyright owner's permission is not required (although payment of royalties set by law is required).

ADAM will not need to worry about a compulsory license for the *American Sampler* project for two reasons. First, the museum is not recording its own version of the song. Second, a compulsory license applies only to the making of sound recordings and does not cover music that accompanies a motion picture (a soundtrack) or an audiovisual work such as the *American Sampler* multimedia program. For such uses, a separate synchronization license, which permits the reproduction and distribution of music in synchronization with audiovisual works, is required. Although a synchronization license may seem like the closest fit to ADAM's needs, many music publishers are beginning to grant multimedia licenses, which address intellectual property issues across a range of creative expression. Just to complete this suite of music licenses, there is also a mechanical license, which permits the reproduction and distribution of music in the form of records, tapes, audiocassettes, and audio compact discs, collectively referred to in the Copyright Act as "phonorecords." Mechanical licenses are not, however, required for the production of multimedia works because multimedia works are not included in the Copyright Act's definition of phonorecord.

Where should ADAM begin? The museum may obtain music licenses directly from the composer or the music publisher authorized to promote and license the composer's works. Many composers use the Harry Fox Agency, Inc., which was established by the National Music Publishers Association, to serve as their licensing agent to grant sound recording, synchronization, mechanical, and multimedia licenses.[20]

Suppose that ADAM hires the Back Bay Fiddlers to perform Jesse Jones' *Yankee Doodle Rag* and other classic American musical works at a large reception following the launching of the *American Sampler* project. Such a public performance of original musical works does not fall within the limited scope of the synchronization or multi-media licenses. Under such circumstances, ADAM would need to obtain a public performance license. There are two types of public performance licenses: dramatic (covering works that combine music, action, and plot, such as an opera) and nondramatic (all other public performances of musical works). The American Society of Composers, Authors, and Publishers (ASCAP), Broadcast Music, Inc. (BMI), and the Society of European Stage Authors and Composers (SESAC) [21] are the principal performing rights societies authorized to grant nondramatic public performance licenses. Under a blanket license from ASCAP, BMI, or SESAC, and subject to the payment of annual licensing fees, a museum would be permitted to make unlimited use of any musical work in the society's catalogue for nondramatic performance purposes.

Suppose that a museum merely transmitted background music through radios or televisions located in a museum restaurant or exhibition gallery. Under copyright law's "home style" exemption to the public performance license requirement, the museum would not always be required to obtain a public performance license. In 1998, Congress expanded the scope of this exemption. However, whether the exemption applies will depend on the nature of the museum activity, space, and technology. Specifically, there is an exemption for non-food-service or nondrinking establishments that have less than 2,000 square feet, or, if larger than 2,000 square feet, that use only six speakers or four televisions with screens smaller than 55 inches. Food-service and drinking establishments qualify for an exemption only if they are no larger than 3,750 square feet and use no more than six speakers or four televisions with screens smaller than 55 inches.

Audiovisual Production Agreements

Suppose that ADAM decided to enter into an audiovisual production agreement with High Tech Industries, Inc., instead of producing the *American Sampler* multimedia program on its own. Audiovisual production agreements are really hybrid agreements, combining elements of copyright, trademark, and other intellectual property licenses with general contractual provisions that would govern the production of any material object, from an exhibit case to a CD-ROM. It may be helpful to think about audiovisual production agreements as covering two distinct elements of the final product: the material object embodying the work and the expressive content contained in the work. General contract principles govern the former, while intellectual property principles govern the latter. Audiovisual development agreements also may include software licenses, discussed briefly later in this chapter.

Most museums are familiar with general commercial law and good contracting practice. However, a brief review of some of the clauses that ADAM should include in its audiovisual production agreement with High Tech may be helpful. At the beginning of the agreement, the subject matter of the contract should be identified clearly. What specific audiovisual product(s) will be covered—films, videotapes, audiotapes, CD-ROMs, DVDs, interactive works? Will the audiovisual product include computer software that controls such things as image sequences, animation, or interaction? Will ADAM have any approval rights, such as the right to approve the writer, lead programmer, director of photography, film editor, composer, or production manager? ADAM should establish the list of deliverables under the contract and the basic production and programming schedules for the project.

All of the production obligations of High Tech should be clearly set forth in the agreement. ADAM should consider clauses requiring the company to furnish the script and other material elements of the work; a list of cast members, producer, director, and writer; functional specifications upon which the software will be based; and a list of computer programmers.

Unless in the public domain, the use of preexisting creative materials in *American Sampler*, such as text, photographs, graphics, and music, may require copyright licenses. An obvious source for such materials is the museum itself. However, ADAM should not assume that it owns the copyright in all objects in its collections. Take, for example, the famous Hanover Mills Textile Collection, which contains original textile designs from the Civil War period through 1985, when Hanover Mills, a U.S. manufacturing plant, closed its doors because of fierce overseas competition. Although the gift was quite generous and of great historical importance, Hanover Mills retained all copyright rights in the textile designs for its own licensing program. Although ADAM's limited use of selected designs from this collection in the *American Sampler* multimedia program may be covered under the fair use doctrine, under the circumstances it may be prudent to obtain a license from the company. Even if the museum already has a license to reproduce works in its collection, the license grant may not include use in new formats. The museum should review its documentation carefully and consider the new use analysis explained earlier in this chapter.

Intellectual property ownership provisions are critical elements of audiovisual production agreements. ADAM should obtain ownership of the *American Sampler* multimedia program, along with all of the elements of this audiovisual work, including any literary, dramatic, musical, software, and other components. ADAM may require High Tech to acknowledge that the museum owns all intellectual property rights in the final product and that the company has "no right, title, or interest" in the audiovisual work or any of its elements. ADAM should further require that each

copy of *American Sampler* bear a copyright notice identifying the museum as the copyright owner.

The precise legal mechanism under which ADAM will obtain ownership of *American Sampler* is through appropriate work made for hire and assignment provisions (see chapter 1). Specifically, the production agreement should contain a provision clearly stating that *American Sampler* and all its elements are works made for hire or specially ordered or commissioned works, as the case may be. Merely labeling a work as a work made for hire may not be the end of the matter, for a judge is free to review a wide range of factors to determine the copyright status of a work. What if a court later determines that *American Sampler* or any of its elements is not a work made for hire? As an additional safeguard, ADAM should require the following provision: "In the event that *American Sampler*, or any part thereof, is found not to be a 'work made for hire,' High Tech hereby transfers and assigns to ADAM any and all right, title, or interest in *American Sampler* or any part thereof." If ADAM permits High Tech to use subcontractors in the creation of *American Sampler*, it should require that the company obtain from each subcontractor a written agreement assigning to the museum all rights to any parts or elements of *American Sampler* held by the respective subcontractor.

An additional concern museums must consider when creating multimedia works is right of publicity issues. For example, suppose that ADAM incorporated a photograph of Andrew Anthony, one of the great designers of the century, into a photomontage for use on the packaging of *American Sampler*. Such use may implicate the right of publicity, an individual's right to commercially exploit his or her name or likeness, discussed more fully in appendix E. In determining whether ADAM needs to obtain permission from Anthony (or his estate), the first issue is whether the proposed use is commercial. In this case, the requirement appears to be satisfied because product packaging is generally regarded as part of marketing, and, therefore, commercial in nature. The answer might be different if the same image were used in connection with the commentary on Anthony's works within the audiovisual work. The second consideration is whether the person whose likeness or name is being used is alive. Many states consider the right of publicity to be a personal right that expires when the individual dies. However, a few states consider the right of publicity a property right, which the individual's heirs or assigns may exercise.

Software Licenses

From basic word processing software, to computer-assisted exhibition design, to collection management programs, museums operate on a sophisticated technological base that is transforming almost every aspect of museum work. How does a museum obtain intellectual property rights in software? The answer for basic, off-the-shelf software is simple; such software is usually sold under a shrink-wrap license, discussed more fully later in this chapter (see "Electronic and Web Licenses"). For now, it is enough to say that the terms of such licenses are nonnegotiable. If the museum does not agree to them, the only remedy is to return the product, get a refund, and purchase a different product.

More complex considerations arise when a museum hires a software developer to create customized software, either as a freestanding program or part of a larger project such as an interactive exhibition or an audiovisual work. Under such circumstances, the terms of the license are fully negotiable. Because these programs are critical to various aspects of museum operations, the museum should approach such license negotiations in a manner that will achieve the most favorable outcome. From a technical perspective, the museum should be prepared to set forth its program requirements in exacting detail. From a legal perspective, a principal objective is to obtain ownership of the copyright in the software itself.

Most software developers are independent contractors, unless the museum hires the developer as an employee. (The rules for determining whether a person is an employee or an independent contractor are explained in chapter 1.) For copyright ownership purposes, the key point is that the copyright in software created by an independent contractor belongs to the independent contractor, unless the museum takes steps to obtain copyright ownership. The usual method is to include an assignment provision in the contract with the software developer. A typical assignment provision is: "Contractor hereby irrevocably assigns, conveys, and otherwise transfers to [name of assignee] all rights, title, and interest worldwide in and to [name of software product] and all proprietary rights therein, including any and all copyrights, patents, and trade secret rights." If the developer cannot or will not assign the copyright, the mu-seum should at least obtain an exclusive license to use the software developed under the contract. For software created as part of an audiovisual work or motion picture, the museum can obtain ownership in the copyright by entering into a special kind of work made for hire arrangement for certain "specially ordered or commissioned works." In the *American Sampler* example, ADAM required that any software created under subcontract to High Tech for use in the museum project would be created as a specially ordered or commissioned work with all intellectual property rights assigned to the museum.

Termination of Copyright Transfers

An often-overlooked rule in the copyright law permits a copyright owner to terminate or revoke a copyright grant during a five-year period beginning 35 years from the date of the original grant. This statutory reversionary right, which may not be waived or contracted away, is designed to protect the economic interests of individual artists and authors (and their heirs) by effectively giving them a second chance to license or assign their works. Consistent with this rationale, the termination right does not apply to works made for hire. Any provision in a licensing agreement or contract that attempts to diminish this reversionary right will be ruled null and void by a court. However, unless or until the creator or his or her heirs exercise the termination right, a copyright license or transfer will continue for the remainder of the copyright term. As a practical matter, most copyright licenses will have expired under their own terms long before 35 years from the date of the original grant. Should this reversionary right become relevant under a particular license, detailed rules governing this option, including important notice provisions, are set forth in chapter 1.

From a licensing perspective, the termination right presents a number of potentially important considerations. Assume, for example, that the Herb Baxter Design Collection was donated to ADAM in 1990 by the designer, along with a letter signed by him licensing all copyright rights in the works to the museum on an exclusive basis. If the designer dies in 2000, under current rules, ADAM's copyrights would extend to 2070 (life of the author plus 70 years). In 2010, ADAM enters into a 25-year publishing agreement with the Big Apple Publishing Company to publish a catalogue of the collection. Suppose that in 2016 the designer's widow, who owns the termination right, notifies ADAM of her desire to terminate her late husband's copyright grant to the museum in 2026 (36 years after the date of the initial grant). What are the licensing implications of the widow's decision? Moreover, how might the parties have structured their licensing arrangements in anticipation of such a decision? Under current copyright law, the widow's exercise of the termination right was perfectly lawful even though it will adversely affect ADAM's arrangement with Big Apple.

After providing proper notice to ADAM, the termination date may be anytime during the 36th through the 40th year from the date of the original transfer. On the date of termination of the

rights (2026, but not sooner), the widow may enter into new licensing arrangements to exploit the copyrights in her late husband's designs. For example, she may decide to negotiate a new, more lucrative licensing agreement with the Pineapple Publishing Company for the publication of her husband's designs. However, there is one exception to this rule. Immediately upon giving notice to ADAM, the widow may renegotiate her late husband's exclusive license with the museum. Given ADAM's obligation to license these works to Big Apple until 2035, it would certainly be beneficial for ADAM to continue to have licensed rights in the designs. For obvious reasons the payment of royalties on catalogue sales will be an important negotiating issue for the widow and ADAM. As a technical matter, any renegotiated royalties will not be effective until termination in 2026. However, there is nothing to stop the museum from offering higher royalties before that time to improve its negotiating position.

Moral Rights

Effective June 1, 1991, U.S. copyright law recognized an artist's limited right of attribution, right of integrity, and right to prevent the destruction of copies of certain works of art under the Visual Artists Rights Act of 1990 (sometimes referred to as "VARA rights"). As noted in chapter 1, VARA rights cannot be transferred but can be waived in part through a written document signed by the artist that clearly identifies the uses to which the waiver applies. Blanket waivers are not permitted.

Suppose that ADAM owns an important Karen Harding still photograph created for exhibition purposes, which it obtained from a commercial gallery along with a document transferring the copyright. The photograph is a "work of visual art" under VARA. Suppose further that ADAM would like to modify the work slightly for use in the *American Sampler* project. Even though ADAM owns the copyright in the photograph, it will need to obtain a written waiver signed by Harding identifying the particular use to which the waiver applies. Similarly, if ADAM provides the Harding photograph to High Tech under its audiovisual production agreement, the museum may be required to represent and warrant that the particular use will not violate the moral rights of any third person. Absent a written waiver from Harding, ADAM should not sign any agreement that includes such a representation and warranty. Within a licensing agreement, a waiver of VARA rights may be incorporated into the intellectual property rights ownership provision or in a free-standing clause.

Recording and Searching Copyright Licenses

Documents transferring copyright interests, including exclusive and nonexclusive licenses, may be recorded with the U.S. Copyright Office. For a licensee, the principal advantage of recording such a transfer document is to help resolve subsequent conflicting transfers of the same rights. A museum also can conduct a search of Copyright Office transfer records as part of its due diligence (investigation obligation) of a potential licensor, providing additional comfort (over and above any representation and warranty) that the licensor is the true and exclusive owner of the rights being transferred.

Despite these advantages, however, several factors limit the usefulness of Copyright Office investigations. First, copyright owners are not required to register works or record transfer documents at the Copyright Office. Second, the Copyright Office does not maintain lists of works by subject or works that are in the public domain. Third, there have been numerous changes in copyright law in the United States over the last 20 years.

Trademark Licenses

The Heritage Village example discussed in this chapter illustrates how crucial trademark licensing can be to a successful museum merchandising program. Careful licensing is especially important for reproductions from the collections, because this activity leads the public to rely on the museum's trademark or logo not only as a source identifier, but more broadly as a symbol of fidelity to the original. But trademark licensing is not confined to the sale of adaptations and reproductions. Today, museums are effectively using marks that identify and distinguish their products and services from others in the marketplace in wide range of applications, including affinity credit card programs, publishing ventures, and electronic commerce on the Internet. In addition to the issues common to all intellectual property licenses, museums should be aware of some special concerns in the trademark area, including the need to maintain adequate quality controls, recordation requirements, and certain unique terms and conditions.

Formal Requirements

Unlike the U.S. Copyright Act, which requires that certain copyright licenses be in writing, the federal trademark law (the Lanham Act) has no such formal requirements for trademark licenses. However, trademark law imposes a substantive requirement on trademark owners that is reflected in the well-drafted trademark license—quality control obligations. A trademark indicates to consumers that a single source controls the quality of the good or service being offered in the marketplace under the mark. Quality control provisions in licensing agreements ensure a fundamental trademark principle: that the goods or services sold under a mark are manufactured or provided under circumstances that will result in the quality the public has come to associate with goods or service sold under that mark.

A number of important legal consequences flow from the central role that consistent product quality plays in trademark law. Perhaps the most significant is the notion of trademark abandonment. If a trademark owner permits a licensee to use the trademark in connection with goods and services of inconsistent quality, the value of the mark as a source identifier is seriously eroded. Over time, the mark may lose all of its value as a source identifier, leaving the trademark owner exposed to claims that the mark has been abandoned. For good reason, then, the slightly pejorative term "naked licensing" sometimes refers to the practice of granting trademark licenses without quality control provisions.

Well-drafted trademark licenses must contain adequate quality control provisions. What constitutes "adequate" provisions depends on a range of factors, including the type of license, the nature of goods or services sold under the licensed mark, and the relationship of the licensor and licensee. The American Heritage Village example illustrates this point. One would anticipate a fairly extensive set of quality control provisions given the unique nature of underlying product (the Independence Bowl), the value of the AMERICAN HERITAGE VILLAGE and AHV marks, and the new relationship of licensor and licensee. In this case, the provisions will probably take the form of substantive instructions about Heritage Village's manufacturing requirements and other standards, such as packing and shipping instructions. The ultimate goal, however, is to ensure that the Independence Bowl is of the same high quality as the other products marketed under the museum's trademark.

At the other end of the continuum, most affiliation or sponsorship agreements may require less extensive and detailed control provisions. Suppose, for example, that the American Heritage Village granted permission to the State Association of Garden Clubs to use its trademark in a brochure advertising an association fund-raising event that the museum has agreed to sponsor.

Under these circumstances, the museum may simply require that its mark be faithfully reproduced and used in an aesthetically pleasing manner. These provisions could be accomplished in a letter to the association (to be countersigned and returned to the museum), stating that permission to use the AMERICAN HERITAGE VILLAGE mark in the brochure is granted solely for the purpose of identifying the museum as a sponsor of the particular event. The letter could further state that any use of the mark suggesting the museum's association or affiliation with the association for other purposes or for other events is prohibited without the prior written approval of the museum. Heritage Village should clearly identify the format of the mark that is approved for use in the brochure, attaching an illustration or photograph. Finally, the museum should require that it approve the proposed brochure in advance of publication.

Affinity card agreements represent another, if highly specialized, type of trademark licensing arrangement. Under such an arrangement, a museum may permit a credit card company or bank to use its trademark on or in connection with a credit card. In return, the museum may receive a royalty based on the total number of cards issued and/or a percentage of each dollar cardholders charge to the card. The bank or credit card company may also be granted a limited copyright license to use certain materials that the museum prepares to promote the card and disseminate information regarding the museum's programs. In turn, the museum will also probably obtain a license from the company or bank to use its logos in museum materials acknowledging the support of its affinity card partner. As with all trademark licenses, a museum entering into an affinity card arrangement must ensure that adequate quality control provisions for the use of the institution's marks are in place. In addition, the museum should be particularly sensitive to protecting itself against any claim of liability for cardholder debts by expressly providing in the agreement that the museum is in no way involved in the debtor-creditor relationship between the credit card company or card-issuing bank and their cardholders.

Electronic and Web Licenses

One of the significant public policy issues in the digital age is whether contract law will replace copyright law in the protection of digital content after distribution. On one side of the debate stand those who see a continued, vital role for copyright law in the increasingly commercial landscape of the Internet. Advocates for the inherent balance of copyright view with dismay the prospect of ubiquitous, "vendor-centric" licenses, which threaten to displace the traditional copyright balance in the digital environment. With some alarm, these commentators warn that such licenses may be used to enforce restrictions that deny or weaken some fundamental copyright principles, such as fair use and the public domain, that ensure the delicate balance is maintained between the public interest and the rights of copyright owners.

On the other side of the debate are those who view copyright as a useful set of supplementary rules for the marketplace. These freedom-of-contract theorists see copyright as providing a remedy for those rare instances when free markets do not operate efficiently or fail altogether. Although the proponents of freedom of contract agree that copyright law is a useful mechanism to prevent others from taking a free ride on the investment of the copyright owner, they also believe that where parties freely enter into a contract involving intellectual property, such as a software license, its terms should be enforced. While this debate probably will never be resolved to the satisfaction of both sides, it takes on added importance in the online environment. Consider the implications for Heritage Village.

In connection with an exhibition of the same title, Heritage Village recently published an interactive, educational multimedia program entitled *Profiles in Patriotism: 1765 to 1865*. The work is a compendium of patriotic stories, commentary, and biographical materials, with a long introductory essay on American values by Professor John Mills. Although many of these materials are in the public domain, Heritage Village owns a compilation copyright in the book and separate copyrights in several of the individual essays it contains. The museum sells the teacher's edition of the book in its shop at a lower rate than the commercially distributed edition. However, in order to gain access to the teacher's edition, teachers must agree to the terms of a shrink-wrap license, which includes a prominently displayed educational use limitation in the package insert.

Dan Scanner obtained a copy of the teacher's edition of *Profiles in Patriotism* and, notwithstanding the license terms, uploaded the entire program (text and images) to his *Peter Pan's Lost Boys* site, where the contents were available for downloading by subscribers. Heritage Village wrote to Scanner, explaining the goals and resources of the museum's educational and publications programs and asking him to remove the materials. Scanner responded, explaining that "information wants to be free" and that the terms of the museum's license were unenforceable.

Heritage Village does have legal recourse. While the enforceability of shrink-wrap licenses for software (a close cousin of the more recent click-wrap license) was in doubt for a number of years, in *ProCD, Inc. v. Zeidenberg*, an influential appeals court held that such contracts were fully enforceable.[22] In this case, ProCD marketed a CD-ROM called *Select Phone*, which featured a version of its database containing listings and information from more than 3,000 telephone directories, along with search and retrieval software. ProCD marketed its product to commercial and consumer users, charging consumers a much lower price than it charged commercial users. Defendant Zeidenberg purchased the consumer version of the product, which contained a shrink-wrap license agreement on the outside of the product packaging, encoded in the CD-ROM, reproduced in hard copy in the manual, and on the screen whenever the user ran the software. Zeidenberg violated the use restriction by making the unprotected data from the product available on the Internet from the Web site of his corporation, Silken Mountain Web Services, Inc. ProCD sued Zeidenberg and Silken Mountain Web Services for breach of the shrink-wrap license and other violations. Like Scanner, Zeidenberg argued that ProCD's shrink-wrap license was enforceable.

The trial court agreed with Zeidenberg, but the case was reversed on appeal. The appellate court opinion noted the "policy implications" of making "boilerplate contracts" unenforceable in our modern society, opining that standard-format contracts are "economically efficient" as a convenient mechanism to reduce the transaction costs involved in everyday purchases. In "real life," the court noted, the consumer often pays for goods or services before the detailed terms are communicated to them. For example, consumers often buy boxed goods with warranty disclaimers tucked inside or over-the-counter drugs with critically important information set forth in package inserts. Similarly, the court noted that intellectual property licenses are routinely enforced in day-to-day commerce. Video rental stores often limit the use of rental to home viewing, and law students access the LEXIS/NEXIS® database free of charge under a license restricting such use to educational purposes only.

The modern trend in case law seems to favor the enforceability of shrink-wrap and click-wrap licenses. Moreover, legislation currently under consideration may buttress the enforceability of these contracts by eliminating the traditional writing requirement. The Uniform Computer Information Transactions Act (UCITA) (previously proposed as the new article 2B under the Uniform Commercial Code) provides that the terms of a standard form license are binding if the user has an opportunity to review the terms of the license (either before or immediately after initial use of the product) and manifests assent to these terms by conduct.[23] Most recently, in *Hotmail Corporation v. Van$Money Pie, Inc.*, a federal district court in California found that persons were bound by the "terms of service" posted on a Web site as a consequence of clicking on an "I agree" button.[24]

Museums can take a number of practical steps to ensure the enforceability of licenses on their Web sites. First, the rules for use of the site, if any, should be clearly visible to all visitors. On its home page, the museum should make it clear what visitors can and cannot do with the materials posted to the site. Terms and conditions that are buried or inaccessible are less likely to be enforced. Second, if the museum intends the visitor to be contractually bound to a particular term or condition, the best practice is to have the visitor affirmatively click on an "I agree" button (even though it may not be strictly required). A visitor should not be permitted to gain access to a product or service offered for sale on the museum's Web site until assent to the terms and conditions is indicated. Finally, the use of copyright and trademark symbols throughout the Web site will alert visitors that the museum considers certain materials to be proprietary and may preclude the successful assertion of the innocent infringement defense.

Chapter 5
INTERNATIONAL ISSUES

Not too long ago, the world's museums operated in relative isolation from one another. True enough, museums had a long history of borrowing and lending objects across national borders. During the 1970s, Americans went in droves to see popular international exhibitions such as *Archaeological Finds from the People's Republic of China* and *Treasures of Tutankhamun*. International blockbusters aside, the daily rhythm of museum work was very much domestic in scale. Legal questions—much less international legal questions—were not the stuff of everyday museum life. Did the United States maintain copyright relations with China or Egypt? How could a museum protect an exhibition catalogue distributed in Europe? What about those "knock-offs" of museum merchandise (rumored to have been made in Taiwan) being sold on the front steps of the museum? Could anything be done about offshore trademark piracy? Such questions, however important, still had a remote, exotic feel.

That comfortable world is gone, a casualty of the information age and the globalization of world markets. As an illustration, consider a recent hectic day at the Cosmopolitan Museum of Art. The director is thinking about sending an exhibition to Neverland but is wary about intellectual property protection there. The Cosmopolitan's curator of 20th-century art would like to send an annotated list of recent U.S. market prices for contemporary art to his colleagues in Europia but has some questions about protection of nonoriginal databases there. The museum's webmaster has just learned that an offshore Web site operated from the Pirate Islands is encouraging subscribers in the United States to download copyrighted and trademarked Cosmopolitan materials. Finally, the Cosmopolitan's director of merchandising would like to learn more about trademark protection in

the Crown Republic, where he is considering entering into a licensing agreement to manufacture and distribute a new line of soft sculpture merchandise. When museum activities extend beyond U.S. borders, what are the risks, the protections, and the rules?

The answers to these questions will involve the museum's attorneys and, increasingly, outside domestic and foreign counsel. In their daily work, however, museum professionals can do much to protect museum intellectual property and reduce the risk of liability in an increasingly global market.[1] Although each international activity or transaction presents unique issues, almost all involve finding the answers to three fundamental questions. First, in what countries does the museum seek protection? Second, what protection is available under that country's national intellectual property laws? Third, what treaty provisions may provide protection or facilitate obtaining intellectual property rights in the absence of or as a supplement to local laws? The museum should have answers to all of these questions *before* entering into any international activity or transaction, whether sending a traveling exhibition abroad, publishing an exhibition catalogue in a foreign country, or authorizing a foreign business to make or sell trademarked merchandise. The purpose of this chapter is to alert museums to the international dimension of intellectual property protection and suggest a general framework for approaching transnational problems.

Suppose that the Cosmopolitan Museum of Art is considering worldwide circulation of *The Family of Mankind*, one of the most popular exhibitions ever mounted by a museum in the United States. In connection with the world tour, which includes venues in both the developed and developing world, the museum will distribute a catalogue for the exhibition (in print and CD-ROM formats) and a line of exhibition-related merchandise bearing the museum's distinctive logo and U.S. trademark. While the Cosmopolitan anticipates a very favorable response to the exhibition throughout the world, the museum is especially interested in promotion and marketing efforts in the European Community and the Pacific Rim, where it has recently opened branch museum stores.

The International Treaty System

Museums often wonder how they can obtain "international copyright" or "international trademark" protection for their works, products, or services. The quick answer in both cases is: There is no such thing. If the museum is looking for a single copyright or trademark, subject to a unified body of international law, that will protect the museum's works, services, and products abroad and is enforceable in foreign courts, it does not exist. The building blocks of international protection turn out to be national legal systems linked through an increasingly intricate network of bilateral and multilateral agreements.

Territorial Limitations

Intellectual property rights are entirely the creatures of national laws. Sovereign nations enact laws that govern the granting, protecting, and enforcement of intellectual property within their borders. Courts and administrative agencies generally confine enforcement of intellectual property rights to conduct occurring within their own borders, or occasionally to conduct occurring outside of the state's borders that affects conduct or property rights within those borders.

An "undisputed axiom" of U.S. copyright law, according to one of the leading commentators, is that it has no application to extraterritorial infringements.[2] Similarly, trademark rights are established, maintained, and enforced within the territory of the United States. For example, in the United States, trademark rights are acquired through use of the mark in U.S. commerce. In most cases, to enforce such rights actual use of the mark must have occurred in the United States. Use abroad does not confer trademark rights in the United States. Courts in this country have long held that remedies under U.S. trademark law should not be given extraterritorial effect to reach "foreign citizens acting under presumably valid trademarks in a foreign country."[3]

Of course, even under a strict territorial approach, courts sometimes struggle to find ways to stretch national boundaries to provide remedies for its citizens for infringing conduct abroad. In the area of copyright, for example, judges have found a number of ways to "domesticate" foreign infringing conduct. All of the following patterns have been held to fall within the territorial boundaries of U.S. copyright protection: (1) conduct that begins in the United States (such as an unauthorized reproduction) and is completed outside the United States (such as an unauthorized master copy created in the United States with further manufacturing outside); (2) infringing conduct that commences outside the United States and is completed inside the United States; (3) infringing conduct that occurs within the United States and related unauthorized conduct outside the United States (such as unauthorized reproduction causing unauthorized distribution or display abroad); and (4) infringing conduct inside the United States, with recovery of lost profits outside the United States.[4]

The strict territorial boundaries of U.S. trademark law also have proven to be somewhat more fluid than one might have imagined. More than in the area of copyrights, courts have shown willingness to apply U.S. federal trademark law to reach allegedly infringing conduct that occurs outside the United States if necessary to prevent harm to U.S. commerce. In general, the courts will consider the following factors in determining whether to give federal trademark law extraterritorial effect:

(1) the effect of the defendant's activities on U.S. commerce, (2) the citizenship of the defendant, and (3) the existence of a conflict with the foreign trademark law.[5] Nonetheless, courts may be reluctant to apply U.S. trademark law to foreign activities because of the political sensitivities involved. Therefore, as with copyrights, the extraterritorial application of U.S. law provides an uncertain basis for the protection of intellectual property rights abroad.

As a result of the 1991 Supreme Court decision involving the application of U.S. civil rights laws abroad, the territorial principle in U.S. law has been given new life.[6] According to the Supreme Court, U.S. courts must presume "that legislation of Congress, unless a contrary intent appears, is meant to apply only within the territorial boundaries of the United States."[7] To overcome this presumption, the party claiming extraterritorial application of U.S. law must show "the affirmative intention of the Congress clearly expressed."[8] Ironically, as U.S. citizens begin to explore the nongeographic space of the Internet, territoriality remains the organizing principle of U.S. law.

In a case involving a licensing dispute over the animated Beatles film *Yellow Submarine*, a federal appeals court in California also found no need to navigate beyond U.S. territorial waters.[9] Noting the longstanding and "undisputed axiom" that U.S. copyright laws have no application in extraterritorial infringement, the court held that the mere authorization within the United States of acts of infringement overseas does not violate U.S. copyright law. Not all federal courts agree. A court in Tennessee not only reached the opposite legal conclusion but also lectured the California appeals court for ignoring the "economic reality" of modern electronic piracy.[10] The court stated: "[P]iracy has changed since the Barbary days. Today, the raider need not grab the bounty with his own hands; he need only transmit his go-ahead by wire or telefax to start the presses in a distant land."[11]

The federal court in Tennessee was raising an important question (even though the extraterritorial application of U.S. law did not provide a very satisfying answer). Copyright and trademark infringement claims increasingly arise out of transmissions over the Internet. These networks are indifferent to national boundaries, but copyright and trademark law is inherently territorial. How will U.S.-based museums pursue infringement claims before foreign courts? How will courts assert their authority to resolve disputes involving multiple distant parties? What law will apply to infringements on the Internet: the law of the nation where the transmission originated, the law of the state where the transmission was received, or, perhaps, the law of some intermediate point, such as the location of the Internet service provider where the infringement may have occurred?

The answers to these questions are unclear. In the near term, national courts are beginning to develop a body of case law in response. For example, as discussed more fully in chapter 3, U.S. courts are more likely to take "personal jurisdiction" over the parties to an Internet-based dispute when the Web site is "active" (such as actively soliciting business in its territory) rather than "passive" (such as merely posting information about the museum). As a rule of thumb, a court is unlikely to take jurisdiction over an Internet-related dispute unless there is a substantial connection between the parties or an activity within the court's jurisdiction. To continue the earlier example, a U.S. court might take jurisdiction over a dispute involving a Web site operator located in the Pirate Islands if protected museum digital assets are being downloaded without the museum's permission by subscribers located within the United States. Thus, underlying territorial principles will likely play a continuing role in the development of Internet law. In the long term, nations will need to revise and enter into new international agreements to address differences between legal systems in regulating Internet conduct. The next section explains the organizing principles of the international system.

International Treaty Structure

The system of international treaties for the protection of intellectual property began to emerge during the 19th century. The classical international intellectual property system had three major goals: (1) to eliminate or simplify the formalities in national intellectual property laws, (2) to act as counterweight to the natural tendency of nations to accord foreign works weaker protection, or no protection at all, and (3) to reduce the trade-distorting effects of differences in national laws. Today, a number of international intellectual property and international trade agreements link the vast majority of nations into a more or less cohesive network that provides the means to protect, under their own national laws, the creative works produced by the authors and artists of other nations.

In broad outline, the modern treaty structure is built on the foundation of two 19th-century agreements. The Paris Convention for the Protection of Industrial Property of 1883[12] provided a basis for the international protection of patents and trademarks, while the Berne Convention for the Protection of Literary and Artistic Works of 1886[13] provided a framework for the international protection of copyrights. The Universal Copyright Convention (UCC),[14] adopted in 1955, provided a multilateral agreement for nations that did not belong to the Berne Union. In response to changes in technology and in the marketplace, the Berne Convention has undergone five revisions and two additions since 1886. Most recently, the Berne Convention was updated for the digital age by the adoption of the World Intellectual Property Organization (WIPO) Copyright Treaty[15] by the Diplomatic Conference at Geneva on December 20, 1996.

In many countries the creative contributions of performers, producers of phonograms, and broadcasting organizations are not eligible for full copyright protection because they are not deemed "original works of authorship." Instead, such contributions are accorded somewhat weaker protection under national "neighboring rights" laws. The leading international neighboring rights treaty is the Rome Convention for the Protection of Performers, Producers of Phonograms, and Broadcasting Organizations.[16] The United States, which protects sound recordings under copyright, does not belong to the Rome Convention. Sound recordings are the subject of another treaty, the Convention for the Protection of Producers of Phonograms against Unauthorized Duplication of Their Phonograms (the Geneva Convention),[17] which is aimed at fighting record and tape piracy around the world. The United States is a member of the Geneva Convention.

The framework for the international protection of trademarks and service marks has undergone a similar process of growth and change. Building on the foundation of the Paris Convention, the recent Trademark Law Treaty makes it easier to protect trademarks and service marks around the world and streamlines the process under which applicants can register goods and services internationally.[18] Although the United States is not a member, the Madrid Protocol provides a convenient mechanism for applicants to file for registration of marks in all its member countries by filing an international application in one signatory country.[19]

Recent international trade agreements provide an important overlay to these treaties. In April 1994, the United States and other countries, from Algeria to Zimbabwe, signed a historic agreement to slash tariffs on goods and services and to establish a World Trade Organization (WTO) as part of the Uruguay Round of the General Agreement on Tariffs and Trade (GATT).[20] At the time, few museums took note of the historic agreement.

However, some of the GATT-WTO treaty provisions and related obligations of the United States have had a profound effect on the operations of U.S. museums. The Trade-Related Aspects of Intellectual Property Rights agreement (TRIPS),[21] one of three agreements that form the basis of the WTO, requires almost every important country in the world to enact into national law relatively high levels of intellectual property protection. Even more significantly, the TRIPS agreement obligates member countries to provide remedies and procedures under their domestic laws to ensure that intellectual property rights can be effectively enforced not only by their own nationals but also by foreign copyright owners.[22]

Enhanced protection and improved enforcement of intellectual property rights around the world come with a domestic price tag: The United States became obligated to protect pre-existing works from other countries that are party to the agreement. As discussed more fully in chapter 1, under the Uruguay Round Agreements Act (URAA),[23] the United States amended U.S. copyright law to restore copyrights in foreign works that had fallen into the public domain in the United States because of failure to comply with U.S. copyright formalities.

Intellectual property protection also has been significantly strengthened through regional trading arrangements. The Treaty of Rome, which established the European Community, provides a foundation for the protection of the full range of intellectual property rights, including copyrights, trademarks, and patents in the community.[24] Over the years, a "supranational" body of community intellectual property case law has developed as a result of decisions of the Court of Justice. In addition, the European Commission has undertaken an ambitious program to harmonize the copyright laws of member states and has introduced the European Community Trademark, which provides a means to obtain trademark protection in 15 European countries by filing only one application. The community's intellectual property program is based on a series of "directives" issued by the commission, which require member states to conform some aspect of their national laws to community-wide standards.

Paralleling the development of a free-trade area in Europe, the North American Free Trade Agreement (NAFTA)[25] created a free-trade area for the North American market. The intellectual property provisions include copyrights, trademarks, and patents. (NAFTA includes a number of provisions from the prior Canada–United States Free Trade Agreement, including provisions governing cultural industries.) The agreement requires Canada, Mexico, and the United States to apply the substantive provisions of the leading international treaties discussed above and supplements these conventions. With respect to copyrights, NAFTA requires protection of computer software as literary works and databases as compilations. In the area of trademarks, NAFTA sets forth the basic rights that each government must grant with important provisions governing "use" requirements for maintaining protection, the licensing of trademark rights, and the transfer of royalties between countries.

International Treaty Law Principles

A defining characteristic of sovereign nations is the capacity to negotiate and enter into legally binding agreements with other nations. A country that plays a role in negotiating the treaty consents to be bound by its terms by signing and "ratifying" the agreement. States that do not originally negotiate and sign the agreement may later "accede" to the agreement. The date that a treaty "comes into force" may be set forth in the agreement and is usually conditioned on a minimum number of states signing the agreement. For example, the recent WIPO copyright treaties will come into effect only after ratification by 30 countries.

Once a nation ratifies a treaty, it is bound under principles of international law to perform its obligations in good faith and not to frustrate the purpose of the treaty. The terms of a treaty may be amended, invalidated, or terminated by the parties. For example, the Berne Convention has been revised five times since 1886, with each successive revision resulting in additions to the scope and nature of protection provided authors. Although the latest Berne text is the only one available to new members, Berne members adhering to earlier texts are not required to ratify later texts. In effect, there are five separate convention texts. As illustrated by the following example, this point is of more than academic interest.

In evaluating the extent of copyright protection available in each foreign venue for *The Family of Mankind* exhibition, the Cosmopolitan's attorneys should inquire about the particular treaty text to which the country adheres. Assume that the exhibition is scheduled for Italy, a country where copyright protection and enforcement have sometimes lagged behind modern standards. Indeed, the latest Berne text that Italy adheres to is the 1887 Paris text (although it also adheres to the 1957 Geneva text of the UCC). To take another example, the latest Berne text to which Greece adheres is the Paris 1920 text. Italy and Greece, of course, are members of the WTO. Doesn't their WTO membership require these countries under the TRIPS agreement to offer high levels of protection? In theory, yes, but not all WTO members are meeting their TRIPS implementation deadlines.

Once a treaty becomes binding, it must be implemented in national law. International agreements become part of domestic law in essentially two ways: self-execution and legislation. A treaty is said to be "self-executing" if its obligations automatically become part of the law of the land. The provisions of a self-executing treaty are directly enforceable in a nation's courts even without the enactment of domestic implementing legislation. In such cases, the treaty obligations are sometimes

said to have "direct effect." For example, the provisions of the Berne Convention are directly enforceable in the courts of the Federal Republic of Germany. By contrast, when the United States signs an international intellectual property agreement, its provisions generally do not become part of U.S. law until Congress enacts implementing legislation. For example, a foreign artist could not use Article 6bis of the Berne Convention (which generally covers moral rights) as the basis to sue a U.S. museum to withdraw his or her work that is part of a current exhibition. The provisions of the Berne Convention are not directly enforceable in U.S. courts without U.S. implementing legislation. Although U.S. copyright law recognizes certain moral rights of artists and authors, the right to withdraw a work on public display is not one of them.

When the United States became a member of the Berne Convention, for example, the obligations of the treaty were made part of U.S. law through the Berne Implementation Act of 1988.[26] More recently, the WIPO copyright treaties were implemented under the Digital Millennium Copyright Act of 1998.[27] Largely because U.S. law already contains high standards of protection, the United States generally has taken a minimalist approach to implementation, amending U.S. law only to the extent necessary to comply with treaty obligations. Because trade agreements like the GATT and WTO agreements contain diverse obligations, it is a little more difficult to generalize about the nature of their implementation. Although the TRIPS agreement was implemented in the United States through the URAA, in most countries the copyright and trademark provisions were self-executing.

International Organizations

Several international organizations play leading roles in the negotiation and administration of the world's principal intellectual property treaties. Of these, the World Intellectual Property Organization (WIPO), a specialized agency of the United

Nations, is perhaps the most important.[28] WIPO administers the world's leading intellectual property agreements, including the Paris Convention, the Berne Convention, the Trademark Law Treaty, and the Madrid Protocol. To be more precise, WIPO administers numerous "unions," each composed of many states that have agreed to adhere to individual agreements and to establish a permanent entity that would survive the entrances and exits from these conventions by individual states. The United Nations Educational, Scientific, and Cultural Organization (UNESCO) administers the UCC and collaborates with WIPO in the administration of the International Convention for the Protection of Performers, Producers of Phonograms, and Broadcasting Organizations (the Rome Convention).[29] More recently, the WTO assumed the important role of administering the TRIPS agreement, including the settlement of certain intellectual property-related trade disputes.[30]

International Copyright Protection

While the United States emerged in the last decade as world leader in the movement for increased international copyright protection, it came to this position only after a long and painful transition. During the 19th century, the United States was essentially isolationist in its approach to copyright matters. In 1790, Congress extended copyright protection to works published and authored by United States citizens, flatly rejecting the policy of extending protection to foreign authors. That remained U.S. international copyright policy for almost 100 years. As former register of copyrights Barbara Ringer put it: "Until the Second World War the United States had little to take pride in its international copyright relations; in fact, it had a great deal to be ashamed of."[31]

By the beginning of the 20th century, pressure to reform this isolationist position began to mount. However, the United States still was not ready to join the Berne Convention, largely because of its unwillingness to give up the formalities of U.S. copyright law. Instead, the United States entered into a number of bilateral agreements, which generally granted reciprocal copyright protection to foreign authors. Immediately after World War II, the United States entered into its first multilateral copyright agreement, the UCC, which (unlike Berne) permitted member countries to require compliance with procedural formalities. Recently, however, the UCC was gradually eclipsed by the Berne Convention, which offered a wider membership and more extensive protection. In 1989, more than 100 years after its initial adoption, the United States joined the Berne Convention. From an initial membership of 10 in 1886, the Berne Union has grown into an association of more than 120 nations.

Highlights of the Berne Convention

To ground this overview of the Berne Convention, consider the hypothetical example posed at the beginning of the chapter: the proposed world tour of *The Family of Mankind*. First, the Cosmopolitan Museum of Art should determine the extent of domestic copyright protection in each country and region where publication, exhibition, and product distribution are planned. This step is necessary before any publication abroad, which itself may determine the copyright status of the work. Next, the museum should determine whether the United States maintains copyright relations with the country or region where protection is sought.[32] Other multilateral and bilateral agreements may be applicable. For example, the Cosmopolitan may wish to think twice before sending the exhibition to Afghanistan, a country with which the United States currently does not have copyright relations. Assuming that copyright relations exist, the museum may be able to obtain protection in that country by complying with the terms of the relevant treaty. However, even if it is unable to take advantage of a treaty, protection may still be available under the country's domestic copyright laws.

The Berne Convention, like most other international intellectual property treaties, operates on two fundamental principles: minimum standards and national treatment. Under the minimum standards principle, member countries agree to extend certain minimum levels of protection to all works within the scope of the treaty. For example, the Berne general term of protection is the life of the author plus 50 years. All Berne members have agreed to enact into national law a copyright term that at least meets this standard. As explained in chapter 1, the United States and nations of the European Union exceed this standard by extending protection for the life of the author plus 70 years.

Special Berne minimum terms apply to cinematographic works (50 years after the work is made available to the public, or, if it is not made public, 50 years after creation). Anonymous and pseudonymous works are protected for 50 years after the work is lawfully made available to the public. As an exception to the general term, Berne requires that photographic works and works of applied art receive a minimum protection of 25 years from their creation. As a rule of thumb, and for reasons discussed more fully below, foreign copyright duration rules may apply to the works of non-U.S. nationals included in the *Family of Mankind* exhibition and related materials when distributed abroad.

Under the national treatment principle, a Berne member country must extend the same treatment to the works of nationals of other Berne Union members as it extends to the works of its own authors. The Berne Convention does not require its members to conform every aspect of their national laws to an international standard. Berne members agree only to treat nationals of other member countries like their own citizens for purposes of copyright. Accordingly, when considering the level of protection available under foreign law, the point of departure is always the national law of the country where protection is sought, which includes its treaty obligations.

Consider the example of the Museum of Man, located in Datlandia, and its neighbor, Ozlandia. Both Datlandia and Ozlandia are members of the Berne Union and have similar copyright laws. However, Datlandia extends copyright protection to nonoriginal databases while Ozlandia does not. If the Datlandian Museum of Man distributes its nonoriginal database in Ozlandia, what copyright protection should it anticipate under the national treatment principle? Ozlandia would be obligated to extend only the same protection it accords its own nationals—none. However, there is nothing in the Berne Convention that would prevent Ozlandia from providing foreign database compilers greater protection than it accords its own nationals.

There are a number of exceptions to the national treatment principle. One of the longstanding Berne exceptions is known as the "rule of the shorter term." Under this rule, a country where copyright protection is sought is only required to protect foreign works as long as they would be protected in their country of origin unless the law of the protecting country provides otherwise. Now that the United States has adopted a copyright term of life of the author plus 70 years, the Cosmopolitan Museum should have little difficulty under the rule of the shorter term in protecting the *Family of Mankind* exhibition and related works in any country during its world tour. However, this somewhat antique rule still applies under certain circumstances.

To illustrate the point, consider the case of the Museum of Photography, located in the Far Away Islands. The museum would like to distribute its publication, *Photographic Treasures of the Far Away Islands*, in Artlandia, a prosperous neighboring country. Artlandia grants a term of life of the author plus 50 years for photographic works, while the Far Away Islands only protects photographic works for 25 years from the date of creation. The Museum of Photography should not rely on the national treatment as guarantee that some of the photographs will not enter the public domain in Artlandia. Under the rule of the shorter term, which is an exception to the national treatment principle, Artlandia is obligated to grant only 25 years of the protection, the copyright term in the Far Away Islands. Thus, some of the photographic works from the Far Away Islands could fall into the public domain in Artlandia, even though comparable domestic works are still under protection in Artlandia. Luckily, however, Artlandian law "provides otherwise," and the photographs will be accorded the full term of protection available for domestic works in Artlandia—life of the author plus 50 years.

How can museums secure protection under the Berne Convention? Like protection under U.S. copyright law, protection under the laws of Berne members arises automatically. There are no formalities, no need to file a registration application with the national copyright office, place a copyright notice on the work, or notify WIPO. However, to qualify for protection under the convention each work must satisfy at least one of the convention's two independent criteria: (1) the nationality or residence of the creator and (2) the place of publication of the work. These criteria are sometimes called "points of attachment."

The general rule is that the published and unpublished works of nationals or residents of Berne member countries are eligible for protection under the terms of the treaty in all other Berne Union countries. For example, on March 1, 1989 (the date of U.S. adherence to the treaty), works by U.S. nationals became eligible for protection in all Berne Union members. Likewise, the works of nationals and residents of other Berne Union countries automatically became eligible for protection under U.S. law.

Under the Berne Convention, a work is published when it is made available to the public in sufficient numbers to satisfy the demand for the work, considering the nature of the work. Like the definition of publication under U.S. law, the performance, broadcast, or exhibition of a work generally would not constitute a publication. While the Berne definition of publication does not specify a means of production (such as printing), it does require the distribution (or offering for sale) of material objects rather than mere display or communication to the public. For eligibility purposes, the Berne Convention treats publication in any Berne Union country within 30 days of first publication anywhere as equivalent to first publication in a Berne member country.[33]

To return to the *Family of Mankind* example, the Cosmopolitan has two bases for claiming copyright protection in other Berne Union countries. First, after March 1, 1989, the *Family of Mankind* catalogue and CD-ROM were automatically protected in all other Berne Union countries because of the nationality and residence of its creator, the Cosmopolitan Museum. Second, assuming the catalogue and CD-ROM were published in the United States after March 1, 1989, or at any time in a Berne country, they will be protected in all other Berne countries. Moreover, by 1999 more than 134 countries agreed to abide by the Berne Convention when they signed the GATT-WTO Agreements.

What about the converse—the protection of works of foreign creators in the United States? The works of foreign creators are protected under a number of other bases in the United States. The rule for protection of the unpublished works of foreign authors is straightforward. All such works are protected in the United States from the moment of creation without regard to the nationality or domicile of the author.[34] For published works of foreign authors, there are four bases of protection in addition to the Berne Convention.[35] First, one or more of the authors is a national or domiciliary of the United States or a country with which the United States has copyright relations (or is stateless person). Second, the work is first published in the United States or in a country that is party to the UCC no earlier than September 15, 1955. Third, the work is published by the United Nations or any of its specialized agencies or by the Organization of American States. Fourth, the work is covered by a presidential proclamation extending protection to works originating in a specific country. Under these broad principles, and given the fact that the United States belongs to Berne, the UCC, and WTO, it is difficult to imagine that any foreign contributor to the *Family of Mankind* exhibition would not be protected under U.S. law.

Another cornerstone of the Berne Convention is its prohibition against "formalities." Specifically, article 5(2) states that the "enjoyment of [the] rights [of authorship] shall not be subject to any formalities."[36] While most countries long ago dispensed with copyright formalities (such as copyright notice or registration requirements), the United States was required to amend its copyright law in order to fulfill this Berne obligation. Effective March 1, 1989, the United States abolished the mandatory copyright notice. However, the U.S. notice requirement remained in effect for works that predated U.S. adherence to Berne. The provisions of U.S. law governing the "cure" of earlier defective notices (for works distributed in the United States between January 1, 1978, and March 1, 1989) also remained in effect.[37] At the time it joined Berne, the United States also eliminated the registration requirement as a prerequisite for bringing an infringement suit involving works whose country of origin is a member of the Berne Union other than the United States.

To illustrate the effect of U.S. adherence to Berne, consider the prior experience of the Cosmopolitan Museum of Art. A best-selling merchandise line in the museum shop is the Carlos Della Tore giftware collection, which is based on original artwork that had fallen into the public domain during the 1940s for failure to comply with U.S. copyright requirements. The Cosmopolitan had no obligation to obtain a license from the Della

Tore estate when the United States eliminated its copyright notice requirement on March 1, 1989. The notice requirement remained in effect for works that predated U.S. adherence to the Berne Convention. The copyrights in the Della Tore works may have been automatically restored on January 1, 1996, as a result of the URAA, which is discussed more fully in chapter 1. However, the Cosmopolitan may be able to take advantage of the URAA's special provisions for reliance parties and derivative works.

The subject matter protected under the Berne Convention is very similar to the categories of works protected under U.S. law. All members of the Berne Union have agreed to extend protection to any original work of authorship "in the literary, scientific and artistic domain, whatever may be the mode or form of its expression."[38] A broad range of creative works fall under this definition, including books, pamphlets, and other writings; dramatic and dramatico-musical works; musical compositions; cinematographic works; drawings; paintings; architecture; sculpture; engravings and lithographic works; and photographic works.[39] The Berne Convention also requires member countries to protect derivative works and collections of literary and artistic works. The recent WIPO copyright treaties explicitly recognize that computer programs are covered by the Berne Convention. Under these modern international standards for copyrightable subject matter, the Cosmopolitan should be able to protect abroad a variety of works related to the *Family of Mankind* exhibition, from the exhibition catalogue to brochures. Because Berne establishes a floor (minimum standards), not a ceiling, for the protection of copyright by its members, other countries may grant additional rights to creators, including rights that are not recognized in the United States.

The Berne Convention expressly excludes from protection "news of the day" or "miscellaneous facts having the character of mere items of press information."[40] The treaty also distinguishes between unprotectable facts and protectable original expressions containing "sufficient intellectual effort for them to be considered as literary or artistic works."[41] Protection of a governmental or other official's works is made optional for each member state, as is the protection of industrial designs. WIPO is currently working to clarify the status of nonoriginal databases and multimedia works. As noted earlier, the creative contributions of performers, producers, and broadcasting organizations are not protected under the Berne Convention. Instead, such contributions may qualify for somewhat weaker protection under "neighboring rights" laws under the Rome Convention.

The Berne Convention requires member countries to protect certain exclusive rights. In some ways, Berne's bundle of exclusive economic rights—including the rights of reproduction, public recitation, and public performance (which includes broadcasting)—is quite similar to the rights enumerated in U.S. copyright law. Berne lists the right of translation separately and provides for a number of exceptions to the right for developing countries. In other ways, the U.S. panoply of rights is stated more comprehensively, with the rights of distribution and public display separately listed. The recent WIPO copyright treaties update Berne by recognizing a broad right of public distribution and a broad right of "communication to the public" that includes the Internet.[42] In implementing the WIPO copyright treaties, the United States took the position that these rights already exist under current U.S. law.

In addition to Berne's list of exclusive economic rights, article 6bis of the convention requires its members to recognize the "moral right" of authors. Here, the precise treaty language is important: "Independently of the author's economic rights, and even after the transfer of the said rights, the author shall have the right to claim authorship of the work and to object to any distortion, mutilation, or other modification of, or other derogatory action in relation to, the said work, which would be prejudicial to his honor or reputation."[43] For many museums, institutions that may serve as intermediaries between living creators and the public, the commands of article 6bis—at once precise and open-ended—resonate with great importance. Article 6bis speaks to the "spiritual" side of the economic relationship between the museum and the creative community that is established through copyright law. But what legal obligations do these words actually impose on U.S. museums?

To answer this question, it is necessary to take a step backward and briefly comment on moral rights within national laws. Under foreign copyright laws, most notably in Europe and civil law countries, protection may extend to a broader range of rights said to be "personal" to the author or artist.[44] While subject to numerous and subtle variations, a suite of moral rights in foreign national law may include: the right to control the first publication of a work (the "right of publication"); the right to receive credit for authorship (the "right of attribution" or "paternity"); the right to remain anonymous or to use a pseudonym; the right to object to a distortion, mutilation, or other modification of the work (the "right of integrity"); and the right to withdraw a work from circulation (the "right of recall").

Of these, the United States became obligated to protect only the author's rights of attribution and integrity, in a manner more limited than in European nations, when it joined Berne in 1989. For many years, the conventional wisdom was that moral rights were alien to American law. Nonetheless, an ad hoc working group of private-sector and government attorneys revisited the issue and concluded that although U.S. law did not expressly grant the moral rights set forth in article 6bis, "the totality of U.S. law" did provide protection for the limited rights of attribution and integrity sufficient to comply with article 6bis.[45]

That conclusion was based on a broad reading of the derivative work right in the Copyright Act, section 43(a) of the Lanham Act (discussed more fully below), and various state laws protecting the noneconomic interests of artists. With the enactment of the Visual Artists Rights Act of 1990 (VARA),[46] which is discussed more fully in chapter 1, the attribution and integrity rights of U.S. artists and authors were strengthened, although the scope of protection remained much more limited under U.S. law than under its foreign counterparts. However, consistent with U.S. copyright-based industries' longstanding antipathy to moral rights, the United States successfully insisted on an exception to article 6bis in the WTO and NAFTA agreements.

Although moral rights are not transferable or waivable under the copyright law of France (and nations that follow the French model), there is nothing in article 6bis that compels this result. French law states: "The author shall enjoy the right to respect for his name, his authorship, and his work. This right shall be attached to his person. It shall be perpetual, inalienable, and imprescriptible."[47] However, consistent with Berne's silence on issues related to copyright ownership and transfer, the treaty does not proscribe rules for the transfer of moral rights. Under the laws of many nations, moral rights are not transferable, although they may be waived. In 1996, the U.S. Copyright Office issued a report on the waiver provision in VARA, concluding that no change in U.S. law was required at this time because of the relatively low frequency of waivers and relatively modest impact of the provision on artists' bargaining position.[48]

Berne members also may impose limitations on the exclusive rights of owners. For example, a Berne member may require a compulsory license for broadcasting and public communication rights, subject to a duty to pay fair compensation. There are also narrow limitations on the rights of public performance. Finally, the Berne Convention contains a provision limiting the reproduction right for purposes that are roughly parallel to the U.S. doctrine of fair use. In general, a Berne member may permit reproduction of works "in certain special cases" where reproduction neither conflicts with the "normal exploitation of the work" nor "unreasonably prejudices the legitimate interests of the author."[49] While the U.S. fair use doctrine applies in "special cases," its foreign law counterparts tend to be more tailored to achieve specific policy purposes.

For example, the U.S. doctrine of fair use is much broader than the Canadian notion of "fair dealing." Suppose that the Cosmopolitan failed to obtain permission to reproduce a protected work in the CD-ROM version of the exhibition catalogue. Nonetheless, the museum decided to go forward with publishing the CD-ROM because it believed that its use was a fair use under U.S. law. However, when the product is distributed in Canada, the reproduction may be challenged under the narrower Canadian notion of fair dealing. For this reason, and in light of the reach of Internet activities, reliance on fair use as a defense to infringement becomes especially tricky.

It is also important to note areas not covered by international copyright conventions. Significantly, neither the Berne nor UCC conventions govern issues of copyright ownership and transfer. Instead, these matters are left to national laws. Accordingly, when the Cosmopolitan Museum enters into transactions involving copyright ownership or transfer in any of the foreign venues for *The Family of Mankind* (such as a licensing agreement for the local production of an exhibition poster), it should consult domestic and/or foreign counsel with a sound knowledge of the law and commercial practices of the country.

In general, the copyright laws of most foreign countries, unlike those of the United States, favor the individual creator over the employer with respect to questions of initial ownership. Counsel from countries that follow the continental tradition of copyright protection may be quite insistent that their law does not contain the analog of the U.S. work-made-for-hire doctrine that governs works created by employees within the scope of their employment. Indeed, few countries have anything similar to U.S. rules that govern "specially commissioned works." It is best to identify early in the negotiation process copyright ownership and transfer issues that may arise in specific collaborative arrangements. For example, copyright ownership and transfer issues should be addressed specifically for the coauthorship of joint works and the production of audiovisual works, where foreign rules may differ significantly from U.S. law. If needed, the museum should obtain a copyright assignment.

European Union

In the area of copyright, the European Commission has issued directives covering computer software, rental rights, copyright term, and databases. Of these, the European Union Directive on the Legal Protection of Databases, which required implementation by member states on January 1, 1998, is perhaps the most controversial.[50] Under the directive, full copyright protection is available for "original" databases that are the "author's own intellectual creations." More significantly, the directive also provides for *sui generis* protection (that is, unrelated to copyright) against "unfair extraction" and "reutilization" of the whole or a substantial part of nonoriginal databases. Thus, the very kind of database denied protection under the U.S. Supreme Court's decision, *Feist Publications, Inc. v. Rural Telephone Service, Inc.*,[51] would be accorded some protection under the European Union's (EU) database directive. Such protection lasts for 15 years, and the period is "reset" every time there is a substantial change in the content of the database.

The directive has important implications for U.S. museums and educational institutions. First, U.S. researchers and scholars may find it more difficult to obtain access to nonoriginal European databases (although most EU members recognize a fair use exception for research, education, and scholarship). Second, and more important, U.S. museums and educational institutions may have difficulty gaining protection under the directive for nonoriginal databases. To qualify for such protection, the organization must be an EU national or resident, or an entity incorporated or having its principal place of business in the EU. Few U.S. museums will qualify under these conditions. To return to the example in the beginning of the chapter, the list of recent U.S. market prices for works of contemporary art compiled by the Cosmopolitan Museum's curator of 20th-century art will not be eligible for *sui generis* protection in the European Community.

Alternatively, the EU may extend *sui generis* protection to U.S. nonoriginal databases on the basis of an agreement with the United States under which similar EU databases would be given comparable protection in the United States, the so-called "reciprocity" requirement. However, since the *Feist* decision, a legislative solution to protecting nonoriginal databases in the United States has been elusive. Nonetheless, legislation reintroduced early in 1999 would provide protection against the misappropriation of "collections of information" in the United States.[52] Unlike earlier proposed U.S. database legislation, the current proposal adds a fair use provision that exempts "individual acts of use" or "extraction of information" for educational, scientific, or research purposes.

International Trademark Protection

Establishing and enforcing trademark rights beyond the borders of the United States has historically been of concern only to a limited number of institutions, including those few museums with established branches in other countries, international merchandising programs, or international traveling exhibition programs. However, in an era of global electronic communications and commerce, international trademark issues have become increasingly relevant to every institution regardless of its size or scope. Emerging technologies enable museums to reach new audiences and new markets almost instantaneously. The capacity of electronic technology to expand a museum's exposure worldwide presents significant challenges in terms of protecting the integrity of the museum's marks in the global marketplace. The degree to which trademarks relating to services provided through the Internet may be protected internationally remains unclear. Every museum that uses the power of digital technologies to reach and expand its audience should be familiar with the general contours of international trademark rights and protection and are advised to pay attention to fast-moving developments in this area.

International trademark law, however, is an exceedingly complex subject that defies simple explanation. As noted in the beginning of the chapter, the principle of the "territoriality" of trademarks—the notion that "trademark rights exist in each country solely according to that country's statutory scheme"[53]—is a unifying theme. It is important to recognize that, with limited exceptions, there is currently no centralized mechanism for securing or enforcing trademark rights internationally. Instead, U.S. trademark owners seeking to protect their marks outside the United States must rely on the law, registration procedures, and standards of individual nations, all differing considerably and offering varying degrees of protection.[54] To the extent there is an "international" law of trademark, it can most fairly be characterized as a patchwork of discrete national regimes. This mosaic of systems is overlaid with numerous global, regional, and bilateral treaties that harmonize the national laws of member states by imposing minimum standards of protection and, in some instances, a certain degree of reciprocity.

U.S. and International Trademark Laws Distinguished

As explained in chapter 2, trademark rights in the United States are acquired through use of the mark in commerce, not by mere registration of the mark. In most instances, actual use of the mark must have occurred in the United States to enforce such rights. Priority of trademark use in this country depends solely on priority of use in the United States, not on priority of use anywhere in the world. In other words, a museum that has been using a trademark in this country has rights to the trademark superior to those of an entity that has been using that same mark in another country and that now wishes to use it in the United States.

Consider the Cosmopolitan Museum of Art example. In addition to its highly regarded collections and exhibition program, the Cosmopolitan is also well known for its model retail and mail order operations, through which the museum offers a variety of consumer products. The museum has an international reputation, and merchandise bearing the distinctive CMA mark is highly prized throughout the world, although the Cosmopolitan's marketing efforts are limited to the United States. The museum learns that an enterprising citizen of Datlandia has filed with the U.S. Patent and Trademark Office an application for the federal registration of the CMA mark for use in connection with various household products either identical to or highly related to those covered by the Cosmopolitan's federal registration. Even if the Datlandian entrepreneur's use of the CMA mark in Datlandia predates the museum's date of first use in the United States, the museum can successfully challenge the registration and use by this party in the United States.

Conversely, a U.S. museum wishing to do business or enforce its trademark rights abroad may not rely solely on use and registration of marks in the United States to assert its rights in other countries; it must comply with the requirements of other countries' trademark systems. However, in contrast to U.S. trademark law, which recognizes common-law trademark rights based on use of a given mark without state or federal registration, most countries grant exclusive rights based on registration alone. In such countries, therefore, priority is given to the party who is first to register the mark, not the first to use the mark. Moreover, registration in such countries may not require any proof that the mark is being used in that country or anywhere else. The advantage of this approach is that it allows a trademark owner first to secure rights in a given mark and then, knowing those rights are secure, develop a marketing plan for its goods and services. The disadvantage of such a system is that it allows illegitimate enterprises to register marks they do not own, either to pass themselves off as the mark's actual owner or to sell the registration to the owner for financial gain.

To illustrate this principle, consider again the Cosmopolitan example. The demand for products bearing the CMA mark is extremely high in the Pacific Rim island nation of the Crown Republic. The museum develops a plan to expand its retail operations by entering into licensing agreements with certain parties to sell products bearing the museum's distinctive logo in various retail outlets in Lotipac, capital of the Crown Republic. Museum administrators contact their U.S. trademark counsel, who discovers that the CMA mark has been registered by the Datlandian entrepreneur in multiple international classes with the Crown Republic Trademark Office.

Even without actual use of the CMA mark in the Crown Republic, assuming priority in this island nation is based on registration, the enterprising Datlandian likely has superior rights to the mark and may present a obstacle to the Cosmopolitan Museum's plans. However, limited protection may be available to challenge this type of practice under certain international agreements, particularly if a "well-known" mark is involved, as discussed in greater detail later in this chapter.

Trademark law in the United States and trademark regimes of other countries can be distinguished in other important respects. Of principal significance to museums is the fact that several countries do not recognize service mark use (in contrast to trademark use) and, thus, do not provide for registration of service marks; other countries have only recently commenced the practice of service mark registration. In addition, some countries do not allow the filing of multiclass applications, but instead require a separate application for each separate class of goods and services that the mark is being used to identify.

A recently ratified international treaty known as the Trademark Law Treaty, however, requires member states to register service marks and extend equivalent protection to service marks as they do to trademarks.[55] The Trademark Law Treaty also requires member states to permit applicants to file a single application covering goods and services in multiple classes.[56] These practices may be of particular relevance to museums that are interested in using their marks in connection with a variety of products and services, perhaps in connection with broad international merchandising efforts. The extension of service mark protection is also of obvious significance to museums, as the provision of educational services (rather than the sale of goods) is a principal activity of most institutions.

International Trademark Registration: Process and Procedure

The first step in seeking trademark registrations outside the United States is to designate the countries or regions in which protection is sought. Generally, obtaining registrations in other countries can be a relatively expensive endeavor, approximately two or three times the cost of obtaining a registration for the same mark in the United States. Therefore, an institution may wish to consider obtaining foreign trademark registrations only for its most valuable marks in countries where the museum currently has or reasonably anticipates having a significant, relatively long-term presence.

With respect to registration of marks in Europe, however, it may be possible to reduce the cost of obtaining several individual country registrations by filing a "multicountry" application to register the mark as a European Community Trademark (CTM). The CTM system, described in greater detail below, provides a means for a museum to protect its marks in 15 European countries by filing a single application.

Where appropriate—to take advantage of certain procedural benefits provided under the Paris Convention, the principal treaty governing the international protection of trademarks—a museum may wish to consider filing corresponding foreign applications whenever it files applications for federal registration with the U.S. Patent and Trademark Office (PTO). One of the primary purposes of the Paris Convention is to ensure that member states afford the same trademark protection to nationals of other member states as they afford their own nationals. The Paris Convention does not create an international mechanism for trademark registration, nor does it provide a vehicle for securing an "international" trademark registration. It does, however, promote some degree of uniformity by providing for the application of domestic laws of member countries in a nondiscriminatory way.[57]

One of the chief benefits of the Paris Convention is that it provides for a six-month right of priority once a trademark owner files its first application in a member country. For a U.S. applicant, the right of priority is measured from the date on which it files an application to register a mark in the United States. Once the U.S. application is filed, any additional applications filed in member countries will receive the same filing date as the U.S. application, provided they are filed within six months of the U.S. filing date.

For example, suppose the Cosmopolitan Museum files an application with the PTO on June 1 for the federal registration of the mark THE FAMILY OF MANKIND for use in connection with educational services, interactive CD-ROM products, and assorted printed material, including posters and catalogues. Pursuant to the Paris Convention, the Cosmopolitan may file applications to register the same mark in other Paris Convention member countries until December 1, and all of the applications filed in these foreign countries will receive the benefit of the June 1 filing date for priority purposes. It is important for a institution to obtain the earliest possible filing date because in most foreign jurisdictions, when there are two applicants for the same mark, the applicant with the earlier filing date will be able to prevent the other applicant from achieving registration (and thus acquiring rights in the mark). If the Cosmopolitan does not file applications in other Paris Convention countries within six months of the U.S. filing date, however, it is not necessarily precluded from registering its mark in those countries in the future. Rather, the institution merely loses the benefit of relying on the filing date of the earlier-filed U.S. application.

Role of U.S. and Foreign Counsel in International Trademark Registration and Prosecution

U.S. trademark counsel can provide valuable assistance in estimating and analyzing the costs and benefits of seeking registrations for the institution's marks in particular countries. For those institutions with well-developed international marketing and merchandising operations, U.S. trademark counsel can also play a indispensable role in helping the museum coordinate and develop a broader international trademark enforcement and protection strategy.

In most instances, however, the principal responsibility for foreign trademark prosecution and enforcement is most effectively handled by local foreign counsel familiar with the relevant markets and the subtleties of the applicable law. Although reliance on local trademark counsel may add to the cost of registering the institution's marks in other countries, engaging local counsel early in the process is often indispensable. They are in the best position to assess the registrability of a given mark, and they have intimate knowledge of the application form, requirements, and processes in their countries. Moreover, in many countries applications for trademark registration must be filed by local counsel or agents.

Choosing Trademarks for International Use

A museum contemplating expanding its activities into overseas markets should confirm that the marks it intends to use internationally are registrable and marketable outside the United States. Generally, to be registrable, a trademark must meet the relevant country's minimum standards of protectability and must not conflict with other parties' established trademark rights. As in the United States, such standards might include a minimum level of distinctiveness as well as prohibitions against the registration of morally offensive or scandalous matter.[58] In addition, some countries may prohibit the registration of marks incorporating colors, arbitrary combinations of letters, or slogans or marks consisting of shapes of goods, product containers, or other unusual indicators of origin (such as sounds, smells, or moving images).

It is also advisable to consider potential negative connotations that may be associated with particular words or phrases in a mark or with colors comprising trade dress; consulting local trademark counsel with respect to this matter may be useful. A mark that sounds interesting or is easy to pronounce in English may not exhibit the same attributes in a non-English-speaking culture. Local counsel familiar with a country's languages and culture can assist with determining whether the use of a given mark might have unforeseen consequences. Perhaps the most striking example of the harm that can occur if a mark's conformity with local language and customs is not considered is the well-known case of the Nova automobile.

In that instance, General Motors failed to anticipate the effect of a mark that translates as "no go" in Spanish on the sale of automobiles in Spanish-speaking countries.

Depending on the mark, a museum seeking foreign registration of its marks should also consider commissioning an international search of prior registrations and pending applications in all the countries in which it anticipates using its marks. For a newly adopted or proposed mark, a comprehensive international search may help avoid the expense and inconvenience of either having to change the mark after it has been introduced or defend against a challenge by a prior registrant of an arguably confusingly similar mark in the country where the museum seeks registration. Searches can be conducted through local counsel in the country where registration is sought or, in some instances, through a U.S. commercial trademark search service such as Thomson & Thomson, which can access trademark registry databases of foreign jurisdictions.

Museums should note that clearance searches might not reveal all potential obstacles to trademark registration in the country searched. Indeed, because the standard for likelihood of confusion varies from country to country, marks that would be confusingly similar in one country may not be in another. Moreover, because the cost of foreign clearance searches may be quite high in some instances, the institution may consider moving forward with an application without first conducting a search, particularly when it has long-standing use of the mark in the United States and/or the mark has considerable recognition or renown outside the United States.

Choosing International Classes and Other Application Formalities

WIPO has developed a model international goods and services classification structure (see appendix C), which is discussed in greater detail in chapter 2.[59] While many countries adhere to the general outline of this structure, they are free to require, as does the United States, that trademark applicants be more specific as to the exact nature of goods and services being provided within each class. In addition, as mentioned above, some countries require a separate trademark application for each class of goods or services in which the mark is being used. This fact can make the foreign registration process particularly expensive for a museum that uses its marks in connection with a wide variety of goods and services, from educational services to retail merchandise. Moreover, in some countries local laws make it difficult to prevent others from registering the same mark in connection with goods or services in classes not included in the museum's applications. For defensive purposes, therefore, it may be necessary to register a mark not only in classes in which use will be made but also in classes where actual use by the institution is unlikely.

Some countries require the satisfaction of a series of formalities either during the application process or, in many instances, before an application can be filed. For example, some may require that the museum submit certified copies of its U.S. application or registration for the mark (if any), notarized powers of attorney, or other legalized documents. These requirements can add considerably to the time and expense associated with filing a foreign trademark application. Timing may be particularly important if the museum plans to exercise its right of priority under the Paris Convention by filing foreign applications during the six-month priority window. Despite the current wide variation in administrative requirements from country to country, there is a general trend toward normalization and standardization of application and registration requirements. The Trademark Law Treaty represents a significant effort in this regard and is designed to eliminate some of the administrative formalities that make trademark registration in certain countries an extremely expensive and time-consuming endeavor.

Timing of Registration Process and Renewal and Maintenance Requirements

Registration of marks in other countries can take anywhere from a few months to several years, depending on the logistics of the registration process and the nature of the mark being registered. For example, in some countries, the registration process does not involve any substantive review of the information contained in the application and, therefore, registration takes place fairly quickly. In many of these countries, however, local law makes it fairly easy for third-party owners of prior registrations to challenge arguably similar newly registered marks. Other countries have quite complex substantive registration procedures and may subject applications to even more rigorous review than is conducted in the United States.

Once registered, a mark is given a registration date that, depending on the basis of the application and/or the procedures of a given country, (1) may reflect the date the application was actually filed, (2) may represent an arbitrary date occurring some time after the actual filing of the application, or (3) may, if filed on the basis of a prior application in another country pursuant to the Paris Convention, correspond to the filing date of the earlier filed application. Although use of a mark is not typically required to achieve registration in many countries throughout the world, most countries do have provisions in their trademark laws that render marks vulnerable to third-party challenge if the mark is not used in the respective country within a certain period of time (for example, within five years of registration).

Every country has its own maintenance and renewal requirements. Renewal intervals can range anywhere from 7 to 20 years. Registration dates and renewal deadlines should be monitored carefully by museum personnel. U.S. counsel and/or foreign counsel may be of assistance in providing reminders as renewal or other maintenance deadlines approach.

Multinational Trademark Regimes

Although international trademark rights are governed by the doctrine of "territoriality" and generally arise as a function of the law of particular nations, the globalization of markets has led both to increased harmonization of trademark standards and practices through international treaties and to efforts to develop independent, multinational trademark registration and protection systems. The European Union Community Trademark and Madrid Protocol systems represent two of these latter efforts and may provide U.S. institutions, particularly those with established business operations in Europe, with useful mechanisms for securing and enforcing trademark rights in the nations that adhere to these systems.

European Union Community Trademark System

For museums with operations or a significant presence in Europe, the European Union Community trademark (CTM) registration system may provide a cost-effective and efficient mechanism to secure multinational trademark registration and achieve broad protection of the institution's trademarks in European Union (EU) countries.[60] The CTM system has many advantages for institutions that are active throughout Europe because it provides protection in all EU countries. However, obtaining a CTM registration may cost approximately two to three times as much as registering a mark in a single EU country and therefore may only be appropriate in limited circumstances.

The CTM system permits trademark owners to file one application and obtain one registration that grants the trademark owner rights in all 15 EU nations (Austria, Belgium, Denmark, Finland, France, Germany, Greece, Ireland, Italy, Luxembourg, the Netherlands, Portugal, Spain, Sweden, and the United Kingdom). The CTM does not abolish the country-specific trademark systems of member nations but provides an alternative approach for applicants wishing to protect their marks throughout the EU. Another important feature of this system is that an applicant need not have used the mark, registered it, or previously applied for its registration anywhere.

Because nationals of the Paris Convention countries are eligible to register their trademarks as CTMs, any U.S. museum may apply for and obtain a CTM registration. In addition, a museum may claim priority under the Paris Convention for a CTM application filed within six months of a U.S. application to register the same mark. Moreover, museums that already hold national registrations in EU countries may convert these existing registrations into CTMs and will have priority under the CTM system to use their marks in connection with the same goods and services listed in the national registrations.

Madrid Protocol

The Madrid Protocol is another mechanism for obtaining multinational trademark protection. This independent international trademark registration treaty, administered by WIPO, supplements an earlier international trademark treaty known as the Madrid Agreement. The Madrid Protocol was signed by 27 countries; as of May 1999, however, only nine countries (not including the United States) have ratified it.[61] Accordingly, the vast majority of U.S. museums are not eligible to file applications under the Madrid Protocol. However, the system may be available to certain U.S. institutions that qualify as "domiciliary" of a member country or have what is termed an "effective trading establishment" in a member country.[62] Unfortunately, what constitutes an "effective trading establishment" under the Madrid Protocol is unclear, as there currently are no guidelines for interpreting these criteria and no decisional law on the subject. However, an institution with an established branch in a member country would in all likelihood be able to avail itself of the provisions of the Madrid Protocol.

The Madrid Protocol permits trademark owners to obtain trademark rights in other countries through a single filing in their home country's trademark office. Under this system, the international application filed in the applicant's home country is passed along to WIPO, which files an application for registration of the mark in all member countries designated by the applicant. Applications are examined by WIPO only for compliance with formal requirements, with more substantive examination occurring in each country designated by the applicant. In this regard, each individual country application is treated as if it had been filed in that country independently. Individual countries have 18 months in which to decide whether to refuse to register the trademark. Any objections of trademark owners with potentially conflicting national rights must be voiced at the national level after the mark is published for opposition.

Because the Madrid Protocol functions as a bundle of national applications and not as a unitary system like the CTM system, use in one country is not adequate to establish use in others for the purpose of maintaining trademark protection. Similarly, a judgment of infringement in one country is not enforceable in another and would have to be relitigated in each country at considerable expense.

International Trademark Enforcement

Only museums with significant international operations are likely to dedicate the resources necessary to establish and maintain a portfolio of international trademark registrations. However, in an era when more and more museums are utilizing global electronic media to reach the public, international considerations are becoming increasingly relevant regardless of a museum's scope and size. The absence of geographic boundaries in electronic communication, although of limitless benefit in many respects, may be difficult to reconcile with an international trademark system based on independent national trademark laws.

The global exposure a museum receives through its Web site may reinforce its existing international renown or quickly create it. Such exposure does not necessarily translate to global trademark goodwill or, more significantly, universal protection for the institution's Internet-borne marks. In fact, because most nations grant trademark rights on a first-to-register as opposed to a first-to-use basis, use of global electronic media to increase a museum's domestic or international exposure may jeopardize the integrity of the institution's trademarks unless this effort is preceded by a costly and time-consuming international trademark registration campaign.[63]

This does not mean that U.S. museums are completely powerless to enforce their trademark rights without corresponding trademark registrations in foreign countries. Indeed, for the vast majority of museums, which do not need to implement a preventive international registration strategy or have the resources to implement one, certain mechanisms are available to protect the institution's marks abroad. Chief among these is the "famous" or "well-known" marks doctrine, explained in the next section, under which a trademark or service mark is given protection in a particular nation if it satisfies a requisite level of renown, even though the mark is not actually used or registered in that country. A museum, therefore, should take steps to monitor objectionable third-party use of its marks beyond U.S. borders by either commissioning an international watching service (available through commercial search companies) or engaging in informal regular in-house monitoring of the Internet.[64]

Protection of Well-Known Marks under the Paris Convention

The Paris Convention requires its member nations to afford "well-known" trademarks certain protections from infringement even where the mark is not actually used or registered in a given nation.[65] The Paris Convention provides for protection against use by another of a well-known trademark in connection with identical or similar goods when such use is likely to create confusion as to the source of the goods. It also requires member states to refuse trademark applications and/or cancel registrations for marks that are confusingly similar to a well-known mark. Thus, under certain circumstances, a museum may rely on the well-known marks doctrine if an unauthorized third party uses or files an application to register the museum's mark in a foreign jurisdiction and the museum would not otherwise have any form of recourse against that third party.

The Paris Convention is not self-executing; member countries must enact their own legislation implementing the convention's provisions related to well-known marks. In practice, this has led to a lack of uniformity in the laws of the member states, as each nation has a slightly different interpretation of its obligations under the convention. For example, the Paris Convention does not require that a mark be "used" in a country in order to be well known there, although many nations have imposed a use requirement. In addition, because the Paris Convention lacks provisions defining the audience to which the mark must be well known, there is considerable variation among nations as to what constitutes a well-known mark. As a rule, however, an institution's mark may become known in another nation not only through use (for example, through traveling exhibitions or merchandising efforts) but also through indirect means, including advertising in internationally distributed media (print or electronic), discussion of the museum's programs and collections in local media, or information from returning travelers who visited the museum while in the United States.

It is important to note that the Paris Convention's protection of well-known marks applies to trademarks but not service marks. There is, however, a general trend toward broadening the scope of protection to service marks through other treaty mechanisms, as described in the next section. Therefore, because museums primarily offer serv-

ices rather than goods, the protection afforded by the Paris Convention's well-known marks provision may be of limited value to institutions that do not have corresponding merchandising programs. Moreover, even if a mark is well known in a particular jurisdiction, the Paris Convention requires member countries to prohibit unauthorized use of the same marks only in connection with "identical or similar" goods, so that all unauthorized uses of a mark may not be preventable.

International Trademark Enforcement through GATT

The GATT Trade-Related Aspects of Intellectual Property agreement (TRIPS), introduced in the beginning of this chapter, is a comprehensive multilateral agreement on intellectual property designed to establish minimum standards of protection for all aspects of intellectual property, including trademarks.[66] TRIPS is of particular relevance to U.S. museums because it extends the protection afforded to well-known marks under the Paris Convention in significant ways. Most important, TRIPS extends protection to well-known service marks, so all well-known museum marks (not just trademarks) fall within the scope of protection. In contrast to the Paris Convention, which protects well-known trademarks only with respect to identical or similar goods, TRIPS prevents unauthorized use of a well-known mark on dissimilar goods or services if such use would cause potential purchasers to associate these goods or services with the owner of the well-known mark.[67] TRIPS also more clearly defines a "well-known" trademark as well-known to the relevant sector of the public, not necessarily to the general public. This feature may be especially important to museums with marks that may have considerable renown within a particular field, specialty, or discipline but are not necessarily recognized by the broader public.

TRIPS is likely to provide wider geographic protection for well-known marks than the Paris Convention because the number of TRIPS member countries (134 as of May 1999) may ultimately far exceed the number of Paris Convention countries (154 as of May 1999). TRIPS member countries must also provide for criminal sanctions for willful trademark counterfeiting, and such sanctions must include imprisonment or monetary fines sufficient to deter counterfeiters.

Pan-American Convention

The Pan-American Convention, established in 1929, offers another basis for international enforcement of a museum's trademarks.[68] Its member states are Columbia, Cuba, Guatemala, Haiti, Honduras, Nicaragua, Panama, Peru, the United States, and Uruguay. The convention permits U.S. trademark owners to oppose the registration of an "interfering" trademark in another member country if the party seeking registration of the trademark is acting in "bad faith." To demonstrate such bad faith, the U.S. trademark owner must establish that the party seeking registration had knowledge of the trademark owner's use of the mark in connection with the same goods. Under the terms of the Pan-American Convention, the trademark owner is required to bring an enforcement action through local counsel in the country where the unauthorized registration is being challenged.

Enforcing Rights through Bilateral Treaties

Museums may also enforce their trademark rights through bilateral treaties that provide for the reciprocal treatment of trademark rights. The United States has entered into such treaties with Ethiopia, Germany, Greece, Ireland, Israel, Italy, Japan, and Taiwan. The language and the scope of protection offered by these treaties differ. Moreover, because many trademark treaties are not self-executing, a museum will need to verify with the assistance of counsel whether the relevant country has enacted legislation that grants trademark owners private rights of action to enforce its rights.

Appendix A

GUIDANCE ON TRADEMARK AVAILABILITY SEARCHES

Preliminary Trademark Searches

Preliminary searches, whether conducted by outside trademark counsel or in-house by museum personnel, generally involve a review of computerized Patent and Trademark Office (PTO) trademark records. Several companies offer searchable databases of PTO records. LEXIS-NEXIS,® for instance, offers the CCH Trademark Research Corporation's federal trademark library in its "FEDTM" file, located in the LEXIS/NEXIS TRDMRK LIBRARY. WESTLAW® offers the comparable Thomson & Thomson TRADEMARKSCAN® database in its TRDMRK library.

Other online database providers, such as Dialog Information Services, Inc. (www.dialogweb.com) and CORSEARCH®, Inc. (www.corsearch.com), offer their subscribers access to searchable PTO records databases (either online or in CD-ROM form). In addition to subscription fees, the cost of the preliminary search may vary depending on the amount of time spent and the amount of material (if any) printed as a result. Typically, the search report provides mark-specific entries listing information including: (1) the relevant mark; (2) the description of goods and services covered by the application or registration; (3) the status of the application or registration (i.e., pending, abandoned, canceled, or registered); (4) the date of first use of the mark, if applicable; and (5) the name and address of the application or registration owner and the name and address of the filing correspondent, if applicable.

For organizations that do not subscribe to a database service, MicroPatent's online trademark search service, TRADEMARKWEB®, offers a convenient and economical means of conducting occasional preliminary searches (www.micropat.com). The PTO also makes available the federal trademark database in a searchable form (www.uspto.gov). While the PTO database is available at no cost, it does not include abandoned applications and canceled or expired registrations. Moreover, this database may be of limited use for broad searches designed to identify certain variations of the mark in question, and it may not be updated as frequently as its commercially available counterparts.

Regardless of which database is used, it is important to recognize that the PTO application processing system prevents these databases from being absolutely current. Close attention should be paid to the database's dates of coverage, and the museum should consider conducting a follow-up search to confirm that the chosen mark remains clear before actually beginning use of a mark or filing an application.

State Trademark Searches

In addition to searches of the PTO register, searches may be conducted of the corresponding state trademark registries. Most commercial trademark database providers also offer searchable state trademark databases.

Internet Searching

Another important component of the preliminary search process is a general Internet search. This search may reveal common-law use of a mark that would not otherwise be indicated if the search were limited to PTO records alone. By entering a proposed mark or variations of the mark in the search field on multiple search engines, the search should identify each instance where the relevant term appears on the Web pages indexed by that search engine.

Full Availability Searches

After the preliminary search is conducted and no conflicting marks are identified, it is ordinarily advisable to commission a more comprehensive "full search." Under certain circumstances, particularly when the museum has or should have some reason to suspect that conflicting marks exist, the failure to conduct a full search may be considered as evidence of willful trademark infringement, leading to increased damages in an infringement action. Full search reports can be commissioned from national trademark search firms, including Thomson & Thomson, CCH Trademark Research Corporation, and CORSEARCH. These full search reports offer exhaustive information typically compiled from databases of federal trademark applications and registrations; state trademark registrations; common-law trademarks from numerous sources; state corporate and fictitious name registrations; and Internet domain name registrations.

The full search is considered the most cost-effective means of assessing the potential risks to the use and/or registration of a given mark. A museum may choose to commission the full search without conducting a preliminary search; however, it is often more cost-effective to clear the mark initially though the preliminary search process. Generally, the cost ranges from $300 to $500 per mark, depending on how quickly the report must be generated and, in some instances, the breadth of the goods and services covered by the report.

Design Searches

A museum may be interested in seeking protection for a mark that consists wholly or partly of a design component. Design marks present unique challenges that are handled comprehensively and reliably by commercial trademark search firms.

Private Investigations

In certain cases, a preliminary search of PTO records or a full search may identify an entity that appears to be using a mark, but the exact nature and scope of that use are unclear. It may be advisable to retain a trademark investigation firm to obtain more information that will determine whether a potential conflict does in fact exist. The cost of such an investigation depends on its scope. Some firms charge a flat rate of approximately $300 to $600 per entity investigated, and others charge on an hourly basis. The cost may be a small price to pay to learn whether a particular reference represents a significant risk to the museum's plans for a certain mark.

Appendix B

FEDERAL TRADEMARK/SERVICE MARK APPLICATION

DECLARATION

The undersigned being hereby warned that willful false statements and the like so made are punishable by fine or imprisonment, or both, under 18 U.S.C. 1001, and that such willful false statements may jeopardize the validity of the application or any resulting registration, declares that he/she is properly authorized to execute this application on behalf of the applicant; he/she believes the applicant to be the owner of the trademark/service mark sought to be registered, or if the application is being filed under 15 U.S.C. 1051(b), he/she believes the applicant to be entitled to use such mark in commerce; to the best of his/her knowledge and belief no other person, firm, corporation, or association has the right to use the above identified mark in commerce, either in the identical form thereof or in such near resemblance thereto as to be likely, when used on or in connection with the goods/services of such other person, to cause confusion, or to cause mistake, or to deceive; and that all statements made of his/her own knowledge are true and that all statements made on information and belief are believed to be true.

DATE   SIGNATURE

TELEPHONE NUMBER   PRINT OR TYPE NAME AND POSITION

INSTRUCTIONS AND INFORMATION FOR APPLICANT

TO RECEIVE A FILING DATE, THE APPLICATION MUST BE COMPLETED AND SIGNED BY THE APPLICANT AND SUBMITTED ALONG WITH:

1. The prescribed **FEE ($245.00)** for each class of goods/services listed in the application;
2. A **DRAWING PAGE** displaying the mark in conformance with 37 CFR 2.52;
3. If the application is based on use of the mark in commerce, **THREE (3) SPECIMENS** (evidence) of the mark as used in commerce for each class of goods/services listed in the application. All three specimens may be the same. Examples of good specimens include: (a) labels showing the mark which are placed on the goods; (b) photographs of the mark as it appears on the goods, (c) brochures or advertisements showing the mark as used in connection with the services.
4. An **APPLICATION WITH DECLARATION** (this form) - The application must be signed in order for the application to receive a filing date. Only the following persons may sign the declaration, depending on the applicant's legal entity: (a) the individual applicant; (b) an officer of the corporate applicant; (c) one general partner of a partnership applicant; (d) all joint applicants.

SEND APPLICATION FORM, DRAWING PAGE, FEE, AND SPECIMENS (IF APPROPRIATE) TO.

Assistant Commissioner for Trademarks
Box New App/Fee
2900 Crystal Drive
Arlington, VA 22202-3513

Additional information concerning the requirements for filing an application is available in a booklet entitled **Basic Facts About Registering a Trademark,** which may be obtained by writing to the above address or by calling: (703) 308-HELP.

TRADEMARK/SERVICE MARK APPLICATION, PRINCIPAL REGISTER, WITH DECLARATION	MARK (Word(s) and/or Design)	CLASS NO. (If known)

TO THE ASSISTANT COMMISSIONER FOR TRADEMARKS:

APPLICANT'S NAME:

APPLICANT'S MAILING ADDRESS:

(Display address exactly as it should appear on registration)

APPLICANT'S ENTITY TYPE: (**Check one** and supply requested information)

	Individual - Citizen of (Country):
	Partnership - State where organized (Country, if appropriate): _____ Names and Citizenship (Country) of General Partners: _____
	Corporation - State (Country, if appropriate) of Incorporation:
	Other (Specify Nature of Entity and Domicile):

GOODS AND/OR SERVICES:

Applicant requests registration of the trademark/service mark shown in the accompanying drawing in the United States Patent and Trademark Office on the Principal Register established by the Act of July 5, 1946 (15 U.S.C. 1051 et. seq., as amended) for the following goods/services (**SPECIFIC GOODS AND/OR SERVICES MUST BE INSERTED HERE**):

_____
_____
_____
_____

BASIS FOR APPLICATION: (Check boxes which apply, **but never both the first AND second boxes,** and supply requested information related to each box checked.)

[ ]	Applicant is using the mark in commerce on or in connection with the above identified goods/services. (15 U.S.C. 1051(a), as amended.) Three specimens showing the mark as used in commerce are submitted with this application. • Date of first use of the mark in commerce which the U.S. Congress may regulate (for example, interstate or between the U.S. and a foreign country): _____ • Specify the type of commerce: _____ (for example, interstate or between the U.S. and a specified foreign country) • Date of first use anywhere (the same as or before use in commerce date): _____ • Specify manner or mode of use of mark on or in connection with the goods/services: _____ (for example, trademark is applied to labels, service mark is used in advertisements)
[ ]	Applicant has a bona fide intention to use the mark in commerce on or in connection with the above identified goods/services. (15 U.S.C. 1051(b), as amended.) • Specify intended manner or mode of use of mark on or in connection with the goods/services: _____ (for example, trademark will be applied to labels, service mark will be used in advertisements)
[ ]	Applicant has a bona fide intention to use the mark in commerce on or in connection with the above identified goods/services, and asserts a claim of priority based upon a foreign application in accordance with 15 U.S.C. 1126(d), as amended. • Country of foreign filing: _____ • Date of foreign filing: _____
[ ]	Applicant has a bona fide intention to use the mark in commerce on or in connection with the above identified goods/services and, accompanying this application, submits a certification or certified copy of a foreign registration in accordance with 15 U.S.C 1126(e), as amended. • Country of registration: _____ • Registration number: _____

NOTE: Declaration, on Reverse Side, MUST be Signed

PTO Form 1478 (REV 6/96)   U.S. DEPARTMENT OF COMMERCE/Patent and Trademark Office
OMB No. 0651-0009 (Exp. 06/30/98) There is no requirement to respond to this collection of information unless a currently valid OMB Number is displayed.

This form is found on the following Web site: www.uspto.gov/web/forms/index.html

Click on: PTO/TM/1478

Appendix C
INTERNATIONAL SCHEDULE OF CLASSES OF GOODS AND SERVICES

1. Chemicals used in industry, science & photography, as well as in agriculture, horticulture & forestry; unprocessed artificial resins, unprocessed plastics; manures; fire extinguishing compositions; tempering & soldering preparations; chemical substances for preserving foodstuffs; tanning substances; adhesives used in industry.

2. Paints, varnishes, lacquers; preservatives against rust & against deterioration of wood; colorants; mordants; raw natural resins; metals in foil and powder form for painters, decorators, printers & artists.

3. Bleaching preparations & other substances for laundry use; cleaning, polishing, scouring & abrasive preparations; soaps; perfumery, essential oils, cosmetics, hair lotions; dentifrices.

4. Industrial oils & greases; lubricants; dust absorbing, wetting & binding compositions; fuels (including motor spirit) and illuminants; candles, wicks.

5. Pharmaceutical, veterinary & sanitary preparations; dietetic substances adapted for medical use, food for babies; plasters, materials for dressings; material for stopping teeth, dental wax; disinfectants; preparations for destroying vermin; fungicides, herbicides.

6. Common metals & their alloys; metal building materials; transportable buildings of metal; materials of metal for railway tracks; non-electric cables & wires of common metal; ironmongery, small items of metal hardware; pipes & tubes of metal; safes; goods of common metal not included in other classes; ores.

7. Machines and machine tools; motors & engines (except for land vehicles); machine coupling & transmission components (except for land vehicles); agricultural implements other than hand operated; incubators for eggs.

8. Hand tools & implements (hand operated); cutlery; side arms; razors.

9. Scientific, nautical, surveying, electric, photographic, cinematographic, optical, weighing, measuring, signaling, checking (supervision), life-saving & teaching apparatus & instruments; apparatus for recording, transmission or reproduction of sound or images; magnetic data carriers, recording discs; automatic vending machines & mechanisms for coin-operated apparatus; cash registers, calculating machines, data processing equipment & computers; fire-extinguishing apparatus.

10. Surgical, medical, dental & veterinary apparatus & instruments, artificial limbs, eyes & teeth; orthopedic articles; suture materials.

11. Apparatus for lighting, heating, steam generating, cooking, refrigerating, drying, ventilating, water supply & sanitary purposes.

12. Vehicles; apparatus for locomotion by land, air or water.

13. Firearms; ammunition & projectiles; explosives; fireworks.

14. Precious metals & their alloys & goods in precious metals or coated therewith, not included in other classes; jewelry, precious stones; horological & chronometric instruments.

15. Musical instruments.

16. Paper, cardboard & goods made from these materials, not included in other classes; printed matter; book binding material; photographs; stationery; adhesives for stationery or household purposes; artists' materials; paint brushes; typewriters and office requisites (except furniture); instructional and teaching material (except apparatus); plastic materials for packaging (not included in other classes); playing cards; printers' type; printing blocks.

17. Rubber, gutta-percha, gum, asbestos, mica & goods made from these materials & not included in other classes; plastics in extruded form for use in manufacture; packing, stopping & insulating materials; flexible pipes, not of metal.

18. Leather & imitations of leather, & goods made of these materials & not included in other classes; animal skins, hides; trunks & traveling bags; umbrellas, parasols & walking sticks; whips, harness & saddlery.

19. Building materials (non-metallic); non-metallic rigid pipes for building; asphalt, pitch & bitumen; non-metallic transportable buildings; monuments, not of metal.

20. Furniture, mirrors, picture frames; goods (not included in other classes) of wood, cork, reed, cane, wicker, horn, bone, ivory, whalebone, shell, amber, mother-of-pearl, meerschaum & substitutes for all these materials, or of plastics.

21. Household or kitchen utensils & containers (not of precious metal or coated therewith); combs & sponges; brushes (except paint brushes); brush-making materials; articles for cleaning purposes; steelwool; unworked or semi-worked glass (except glass used in building); glassware, porcelain & earthenware not included in other classes.

22. Ropes, string, nets, tents, awnings, tarpaulins, sails, sacks & bags (not included in other classes); padding & stuffing materials (except of rubber or plastics); raw fibrous textile materials.

23. Yarns & threads, for textile use.

24. Textiles & textile goods, not included in other classes; bed & table covers.

25. Clothing, footwear, headgear.

26. Lace & embroidery, ribbons & braid; buttons, hooks & eyes, pins & needles; artificial flowers.

27. Carpets, rugs, mats & matting, linoleum & other materials for covering existing floors; wall hangings (non-textile).

28. Games & playthings; gymnastic & sporting articles not included in other classes; decorations for Christmas trees.

29. Meat, fish, poultry & game; meat extracts; preserved, dried & cooked fruits & vegetables; jellies, jams, fruit sauces; eggs, milk & milk products; edible oils & fats.

30. Coffee, tea, cocoa, sugar, rice, tapioca, sago, artificial coffee; flour & preparations made from cereals, bread, pastry & confectionery, ices; honey, treacle; yeast, baking powder; salt, mustard; vinegar, sauces (condiments); spices; ice.

31. Agricultural, horticultural & forestry products & grains not included in other classes; living animals; fresh fruits & vegetables; seeds, natural plants & flowers; foodstuffs for animals, malt.

32. Beers; mineral & aerated waters & other non-alcoholic drinks; fruit drinks & fruit juices; syrups & other preparations for making beverages.

33. Alcoholic beverages (except beers).

34. Tobacco; smokers' articles; matches.

35. Advertising; business management; business administration; office functions.

36. Insurance; financial affairs; monetary affairs; real estate affairs.

37. Building construction; repair; installation services.

38. Telecommunications.

39. Transport; packaging & storage of goods; travel arrangement.

40. Treatment of materials.

41. Education; providing of training; entertainment; sporting & cultural activities.

42. Providing of food & drink; temporary accommodation; medical, hygienic & beauty care; veterinary & agricultural services; legal services; scientific & industrial research; computer programming; services that cannot be placed in other classes.

Appendix D

COMPONENTS OF THE APPLICATION FOR FEDERAL TRADEMARK REGISTRATION

For most trademarks, completing the application for federal registration is relatively straight-forward. For organizations that wish to file an application without the assistance of counsel, the U.S. Patent and Trademark Office (PTO) Web site includes detailed instructions and numerous sample application forms (www.uspto.gov/teas/e-TEAS/index.html). See appendix B for the PTO's standard trademark/service mark application with declaration. The PTO Web site also contains sample application forms for collective marks and certification marks.

Basic Forms

The requisite components of an application for federal registration vary depending on the basis for applying to register the mark.

Registration of Trademarks Already in Use

1. A completed application form which must be verified and signed by the authorized individuals or corporate officers[1]

2. A drawing of the mark that conforms to PTO rules[2]

3. Three specimens per class showing use of the mark in connection with the goods or services listed in the application[3]

4. Statement of the dates of first use of the mark[4]

5. If counsel is filing on behalf of the applicant, a power of attorney granting the counsel authority to complete trademark registration process

6. Application fee per class (currently $245)[5]

ITU Applications

The information and documents contained in an application based on the intention to use a mark (an "ITU" application) are similar to those required for a use-based application, with two notable differences: (1) Specimens and first use dates are not submitted, and (2) a statement attesting to the applicant's bona fide intent to use the mark in commerce must be included.[6]

Description of Goods and/or Services

The application must include a description of the goods and/or services to be offered under the mark.[7] This description is a critical component of the application because it establishes the scope of the applicant's rights in the relevant mark. The goods and/or services should be described in clear and concise language using terms reflecting common commercial usage.

All goods and services fall within one of the 42 categories specified in the International Schedule of Classes of Goods and Services (appendix C).[8] The applicant should include in the description the appropriate classification of the subject matter covered in the application, although the applicant is not required to provide the classification. The PTO Web site includes a searchable database for determining the appropriate international classification: (www.uspto.gov/web/offices/tac/doc/gsmanual).

The description of goods and/or services cannot be amended after the application has been filed to add products or services not within the scope of those originally identified.[9] For example, an application for the registration of a mark covering "museum services in Class 41" cannot later be amended to include "retail services in Class 42." Instead, a new and separate application must be filed covering the additional goods and/or services.

The following list includes representative descriptions contained in current federal registrations for several well-known museum marks:

Class 16 Goods (paper goods, including printed matter, artists' materials, instructional and teaching materials)

- A registration for MUSEUM STORE for "assorted sized art prints and posters accompanied by various mats and assembled frames, comprising a total package of framed and/or matted prints" in Class 16[10]
- A federal registration for SALVADOR DALI MUSEUM for "non-fiction art books, catalogues, postcards, bookmarks, bumper stickers, calendars, and shopping bags" in Class 16[11]

Class 18 Goods (leather and goods made of leather not included in other classes; traveling bags; umbrellas, etc.)

- A federal registration for the METROPOLITAN MUSEUM OF ART for "tote-bags; umbrellas" in Class 18[12]

Class 25 Goods (clothing, footwear, and headgear)

- A federal registration for the METROPOLITAN MUSEUM OF ART for "t-shirts, bow ties, cummerbunds, and vests" in Class 25[13]

Class 41 Services (educational services, including providing training; entertainment; sporting and cultural activities)

- A federal registration for the J. PAUL GETTY MUSEUM for "museum and educational services, namely, operating a museum; providing guided tours and exhibitions; development and preservation of art; conducting lectures and seminars in the fields of the arts and humanities; publication of books,[14] newsletters, and pamphlets in the fields of the arts and humanities" in Class 41

- A federal registration for CREATIVE DISCOVERY MUSEUM for "educational and entertainment services in the nature of a children's museum; educational services, namely conducting workshops, classes, and seminars pertaining to children's education in the subjects of music, art, and the sciences; arranging and conducting art exhibitions; publication of books and newsletters; conducting entertainment exhibitions in the nature of film presentations, plays, and puppet shows" in Class 41[15]

Class 42 Services (providing food and drink and any other services that cannot be placed in other classes, including general retail, catalogue, or mail-order services)

- A federal registration for SOLOMON R. GUGGENHEIM MUSEUM for "retail store services featuring jewelry, watches, clothing, toys, games, and printed matter such as publications, calendars, posters, notecards and the like; association services, namely promoting the interests of patrons and members of the museum"; "restaurant services"; and "lending and rental of photographs and transparencies," all in Class 42[16]
- A federal registration for SMITHSONIAN ONLINE for "computer online services, namely access to a computer database of digital museum images and other educational materials related thereto" in Class 42.[17]

Drawing Page

Every application must include a drawing page that complies with PTO requirements.[18] The drawing page must include the applicant's name, address, and a description of the goods and/or services specified in the application. For use-based applications, the drawing page must also include the date of first use of the mark and the date of first use in commerce.[19] For applicants applying to register word marks with no stylization or design elements, the mark is simply typed in capital letters at the bottom of the drawing page.

Drawing pages for design and/or stylized marks require detailed pen-and-ink drawings representing the marks. The form of these representations must comply with detailed PTO rules regarding size, coloration, and other features.[20] It is critical that the mark represented on the drawing page be consistent with the mark shown on the specimens supporting the application. Any differences in appearance between the mark as represented on the drawing page and the mark as actually used in commerce may result in the rejection of the application or serve as a basis for potential future challenge by third parties.[21]

Specimens of Use

The application for federal registration must include three specimens of the mark as actually used in connection with the goods and/or services identified in the application.[22] The specimens must be actual samples showing how the mark is being used in commerce. Moreover, the mark shown in the specimens must be *identical* to the mark as shown in the application; even a slight variation may be grounds for refusal.

Trademark Specimens

For a mark used on goods, acceptable specimens include tags, labels, containers, point-of-sale displays, or photographs of the goods showing use of the mark on the goods themselves. Photographs or photocopies of the specimens may be submitted if it is not practicable to submit actual specimens because of the size or cost of the original specimens.[23] Invoices, announcements, order forms, bills of lading, product catalogues, publicity releases, letterhead, and business cards are generally not acceptable specimens of goods.

For instance, a museum seeking a federal registration for the mark JOHN DOE MUSEUM OF ART for use in connection with exhibition catalogues in Class 16 must submit (1) photocopies of a portion of the catalogue using the mark, (2) a label

with the mark, (3) or the catalogue itself as a specimen. The museum cannot use as specimens copies of its publications announcements or mail order catalogue because these do not show the mark used on the goods themselves. The mail order catalogue may, however, show evidence of service mark use (e.g., retail or mail order services).

Service Mark Specimens

If the mark is used to identify services, acceptable specimens include signs, brochures describing the services, and advertisements for the services. Photographs that show the mark in connection with the services or that show the mark either as it is used in the rendering or advertising of the services are also acceptable. The key to service mark specimens is that they must either (1) show the mark and include some clear reference to the type of services rendered under the mark in some form of advertising (e.g., billboard or print ad) or (2) show the mark as it is used in the rendering of the services (e.g., on coffee cups and plates for retail food/restaurant services).[24]

Business cards or blank business letterhead may serve as suitable specimens, but the mark itself must make some reference to the services.[25] For example, blank letterhead showing the mark CITY MUSEUM OF ART may be acceptable for "museums and educational services in Class 41." If, however, the mark sought to be registered is CMA or merely a design element (e.g., a logo based on the facade of the museum building), blank letterhead that does not refer to or show a connection to the relevant services would not be suitable. On the other hand, copies of letters actually written on CMA letterhead that refer to the relevant services offered by the museum may be acceptable (e.g., a letter from the museum director offering a traveling exhibition to other institutions).

Electronic Filing

In addition to the various sample application forms available on its Web site, the PTO has recently developed and implemented a Trademark Electronic Application System (TEAS). TEAS allows an applicant to complete the trademark application form and check it for completeness over the Internet (www.uspto.gov/teas/e-TEAS/ index.html). Applicants can either (1) submit an application directly to the PTO over the Internet or (2) print out the completed application for mailing to the PTO. In either case, the applicant may submit the required drawing page by typing in the mark (if words only) or attaching a scanned image (in the cases of stylized marks or designs). Fee payment options under TEAS include credit card, PTO deposit account, or check.

Initial Action by PTO

In due course—currently approximately 6 to 12 months after an application is filed—a PTO examining attorney will review the application. The mark will be searched for conflicts with marks previously registered on the federal Principal and Supplemental Registers[26] as well as with earlier filed pending federal applications. The examining attorney will also review the application for compliance with other statutory and regulatory requirements. After this initial review, the examining attorney will either approve the mark for publication or issue an Office Action noting matters that the applicant must resolve before the application can move forward.[27] The Office Action may request simple revisions to the application, or it may set forth one or more substantive objections.

Refusal Based on Likelihood of Confusion—Section 2(d)

One of the most common substantive objections to registration arises when a conflict is found with a registered mark. Under this circumstance, the examining attorney will issue an Office Action refusing registration of the applicant's mark based on a likelihood of confusion under section 2(d) of the Trademark Act.[28] If a conflict is found with an earlier-filed pending federal application, the examining attorney cannot issue a refusal under section 2(d) until the pending application is registered.[29] The examining attorney will advise the applicant of the prior pending application and likely will suspend the prosecution of the application until the prior pending application is either registered or abandoned. The suspension period may last for years.

Descriptiveness Refusals—Section 2(e)

The examining attorney may also find that the mark is merely descriptive of the goods and/or services offered in connection with the mark.[30] If the examining attorney considers the mark descriptive, an Office Action will be issued refusing registration based on section 2(e) of the Trademark Act.[31] An applicant may overcome such a refusal by successfully arguing that the mark is not merely descriptive or by making the requisite showing that the mark has "acquired distinctiveness." Under federal trademark law, proof of substantially exclusive and continuous use of a term for five years is presumptive evidence that the term has achieved secondary meaning.[32] In addition, the following factors may be considered as proof of secondary meaning: (1) direct consumer testimony or consumer surveys; (2) amount, manner, and scope of advertising; (3) established place in the relevant market; and (4) amount of sales and number of customers.[33] As a practical matter, the PTO only accepts a showing of less than five years' use of the mark as evidence of secondary meaning where there is overwhelming evidence of advertising expenditures and/or sales revenue or other consumer evidence.

Disclaimers

In certain circumstances, the examining attorney may request a disclaimer of a word component of a mark on the ground that the term conveys a feature of or describes the goods and/or services identified by the mark.[34] If agreed to, a disclaimer is an acknowledgment on the part of an applicant that it does not claim exclusive rights to use the term in question separate and apart from the mark as a whole. In other words, the applicant is merely stating that it is claiming only the whole composite mark as its property and makes no claim to the particular components disclaimed. For instance, the PTO regularly requires museums seeking to register marks that include descriptive terms, such as "museum" or "store," to disclaim their exclusive right to these terms separate from their mark as a whole.[35] Ordinarily, a disclaimer will not significantly affect the applicant's right in the mark as a whole, unless all terms comprising a mark are disclaimed (a situation that could only arise where the mark includes a design element in combination with words).

Other Bases for Refusal

Likelihood of confusion under section 2(d) and descriptiveness under section 2(e) are but two possible grounds for refusal to register a mark. Assuming likelihood of confusion and descriptiveness are not barriers to registration of a particular mark, an applicant's mark may still be refused registration for a variety of other reasons. For example, section 2 of the Trademark Act provides numerous exceptions for marks that either cannot be registered under any circumstances or that may only be registered upon proof of secondary meaning.[36] Marks that cannot be registered under any circumstances include scandalous and immoral marks (e.g., obscene or indecent terms or depictions), deceptive marks, and marks that disparage or falsely suggest a connection with persons (either living or dead), institutions, beliefs, or national symbols. Marks that consist of the United States flag or the coat of arms of any state or foreign country cannot be registered. Marks that consist of a name, portrait, or signature identifying a living individual cannot be registered without that individual's written consent. Finally, marks adopted and used after December 8, 1993, that are deceptively misdescriptive of the geographic origin of the goods and services can no longer be registered.

In addition to setting forth a substantive objection to the application, an Office Action may question the sufficiency of the specimens in the case of a use-based application, or request a revision to the application, such as a clarification of the description of goods and/or services or confirmation of the applicant's corporate status.

A response to the Office Action must be filed within six months from the date it is issued or the application will be deemed abandoned.[37] The complexity of the issue(s) raised by the examining attorney will determine the amount of time it will take to prepare a response and, therefore, the cost of the overall registration process. For institutions that opt to file and prosecute their own trademark applications, the question of whether to seek the advice of counsel in responding to an Office Action will depend on the complexity of the issue raised by the examining attorney and the importance of the mark to the institution.[38]

Appendix E
RIGHTS OF PRIVACY AND PUBLICITY

The rights of privacy and publicity recognize that an individual has certain personal and pecuniary interests in his or her name, voice, picture, likeness, and other identifying characteristics that restrict certain uses of these attributes without the individual's consent. Although privacy and publicity rights are not technically "intellectual property" rights, they are closely related concepts that may be implicated in a wide range of museum activities.

It is critical to understand that rights of privacy and publicity exist separate and apart from copyright and trademark rights. As explained in chapter 1, when a museum acquires an object that features an image or portrayal of a real individual—whether a photograph, painting, film, letter, or manuscript—the institution obtains an ownership interest only in the physical object embodying that image or depiction. If the museum does not hold the copyright in the object, it may be restricted in what it may or may not do with that object. Similarly, even in situations where the institution has acquired the copyright in the object, the work is in the public domain, or a particular use qualifies as a "fair use," the independent rights of privacy and publicity held by individuals depicted or described in such works (or their heirs) may significantly restrict the museum's freedom to use the material as it sees fit.

An Overview of the Rights of Privacy and Publicity

The rights of privacy and publicity vary significantly from state to state. These rights are sometimes provided by statute, by common law, and in some instances by both. In light of the varying nature and scope of these rights, generalizations can only go so far. Applicable state law must be considered whenever issues implicating the rights of privacy and publicity arise. With this caveat in mind, the following section describes the broad contours of publicity and privacy rights, explains how to identify situations in which they may be implicated, and suggests practical considerations for avoiding difficulties in this area.

The Right of Privacy

The right of privacy generally protects persons against unwanted public exposure and any resulting emotional harm.[39] It actually embodies four distinct types of harm: (1) intrusion upon seclusion; (2) public disclosure of private facts; (3) publicly placing another in false light; and (4) appropriation of name or likeness.[40] Injury resulting from these violations is generally measured in terms of the plaintiff's mental or physical distress. Because privacy rights protect an individual's dignity, the rights usually last only for the individual's lifetime.[41]

Of the four privacy interests, the second and fourth types arguably are most relevant to museums.[42] Actionable disclosure of private facts occurs when embarrassing facts concerning the private life of another individual are made public. Such a disclosure will not be actionable unless it is offensive and objectionable to a person of ordinary sensibilities. Moreover, the scope of the right to be free from such disclosure is not the same for all individuals; generally, public figures have more limited rights to protect disclosure than private citizens.

The context in which the images or facts were originally captured factors significantly into the determination of whether disclosure is permissible. If, for instance, an embarrassing photograph is taken in a public place (i.e., where the individual's conduct was open to public view), the person's right to challenge the publication of such a photograph may be limited. In contrast, if an embarrassing image of a person is captured in a private setting (i.e., where the individual has no reason to expect subsequent disclosure), disclosure should only be made with that person's authorization.

An individual's right to be free from public disclosure of private facts is not absolute and stands in tension with the First Amendment rights of others to make disclosures of private facts that are of legitimate concern to the public. This constitutional privilege is not limited to the dissemination of news providing commentary or current affairs. It also extends to "information concerning interesting phases of human activity and embraces all issues about which information is needed or appropriate so that individuals may cope with the exigencies of their period."[43]

For example, consider a science museum that is fortunate to have been given the research notebooks of a prominent living physicist. The physicist assigned the copyright in the notebooks to the institution, which now wants to publish portions of the notes in an upcoming volume dedicated to the physicist's life and work. Intertwined among the physicist's musing on topics of great scientific interest are intimate details of his personal life as well as the private lives of other not-so-well-known individuals. Such details have unquestionable value from a biographical standpoint. Disclosure of these details for scholarly purposes may be defensible (i.e., protected from privacy claims) to the extent that these details can be considered to be of "legitimate public concern." However, perhaps the more critical inquiry is not into the legality of such disclosure, but into the ethical dimensions of releasing sensitive private information about individuals who are not widely known to the public. In many cases, consideration of these ethical components will counsel in favor of nondisclosure, thereby avoiding the necessity of addressing the more difficult and often less clear-cut legal issues involved.

The Right of Publicity

The right of publicity is the right of an individual, especially a public figure or celebrity, to control the commercial value of his name, picture, likeness, or other identifying characteristic and to prevent others from unfairly appropriating that value for commercial gain. The right of publicity is an outgrowth of, and has significant overlap with, the appropriation category of privacy, but is generally viewed as being more in the nature of a property right. In other words, the property interest protected by the right of publicity is the value of an individual's identity, which, if used for advertising or promotional purposes without consent, deprives that individual of compensation to which he or she would otherwise be entitled. Typically, right of publicity claims are made by celebrities who have built up a valuable image, but publicity rights may be available to the famous and nonfamous alike. The more famous a person is, however, the greater the potential commercial value of his or her name, image, or likeness, and the greater his or her right of publicity. By contrast, the more famous a person is, the greater the public interest in his activities, and the lesser his right to limit otherwise actionable invasions of privacy.

In contrast to privacy rights, which generally terminate at death, the right of publicity may survive after death and is considered descendible property in some jurisdictions.[44] There is significant disparity among jurisdictions, however, as to whether the right of publicity is inheritable or whether it dies with the individual. For instance, certain states specify that the right of publicity lasts for a specific number of years after death,[45] and others condition survival of the right beyond death on the requirement that the person to whom the right is tied must have exploited his or her name or likeness during his or her lifetime for commercial gain.[46]

The right of publicity does share similarities with its close cousins, unfair competition and trademark law. Indeed, the unconsented use of a person's name or likeness may often falsely suggest sponsorship or affiliation and may be actionable under state and/or federal unfair competition law.[47] Moreover, as discussed in detail in chapter 2, the names of real individuals, either living or historical, may also develop independent "trademark" significance when used as an identifier of the source of goods and/or services. Again, it is important to remember that the right of publicity is distinct and separate from rights protectable under trademark and unfair competition law, and it may be relied upon by an individual to challenge the use of a name or likeness where there is no risk of public confusion and regardless of whether the individual has made "trademark" use of his or her name or likeness.

The distinction between privacy and publicity is not always clearly delineated by courts and state statutes. For example, New York courts have found claims under each of these two rights to be duplicative, and consequently, all right of publicity claims fall under the New York "privacy" statute.[48] Furthermore, state statutes differ with respect to the scope of protection afforded by these rights, with some narrower than others. For instance, the New York privacy statute protects living persons from the unconsented use of their names, portraits, or pictures "for advertising purposes or for the purposes of trade."[49] California, on the other hand, has a statute that protects privacy and publicity rights of living and deceased persons (for 50 years after death) by forbidding the use of a person's identity without consent "in any manner, on or in products, merchandise, or goods, or for purposes of advertising or selling, or soliciting purchases of, products, merchandise, goods, or services."[50]

Privacy and Publicity: Remedies

There are several remedies available for violation of the rights of privacy and publicity. First, a civil action may be brought to obtain an injunction to halt the unauthorized use. Second, monetary damages may be available. With respect to invasion of privacy, damages can be measured by the plaintiff's mental or physical distress. For an infringement on the right of publicity, damages may be measured by the plaintiff's lost profits and/or the defendant's gains. Finally, if the defendant knew that the use was unauthorized, a court may award exemplary damages in its discretion.

Limitations of the Right of Publicity: Countervailing Considerations

As with the right of privacy, there are inherent tensions between an individual's right of publicity and the First Amendment rights of those who wish to use the names and likenesses of others for their own purposes. For example, there are strong justifications for allowing the use of an individual's name or image to communicate ideas, news, thoughts, and opinions in mediums such as fine art, television documentaries, books, catalogues, film, and exhibitions, even though many of these applications may have some arguable "commercial" aspects. However, if the use of these personal attributes serves the purpose of contributing information to the public debate on political or social issues, or of furthering the free expression of artistic talent that contributes to society's cultural enrichment, then the use will generally be immune from liability for right of publicity violations. As such, the use of the name or likeness of an individual in factual, educational, historical, or archival materials is generally protected, as is the use of a name or likeness in entertainment media, including fictionalizations, novels, parodies, satires, and even unauthorized biographies (although such uses may not be protected from privacy claims if inaccurate, embarrassing, or defamatory). In contrast, when a person's name or image is used principally for commercial or advertising purposes (i.e., on a billboard sign without any accompanying protected expression), it will not be shielded by the First Amendment.

While the foregoing rule is easy to state in the abstract, it is often difficult to apply, particularly in the museum and art context. Consider the case of *Simeonov v. Tiegs*.[51] In 1979, model Cheryl Tiegs agreed to allow sculptor Mihail Simeonov to make an alginate impression of her face, throat, and a small portion of her upper chest to demonstrate that the impression substance would be safe for use on an elephant that was to be molded and used to create a sculpture by the artist. Without Tiegs' consent, Simeonov later modified the alginate impression of Tiegs to create a plaster casting of her head resting on a pillow. Some time later, at the request of Tiegs' husband, the plaster cast was taken to their apartment so that he could view the plaster casting of his wife. While at the apartment, the plaster cast was accidentally damaged. Simeonov had intended to exhibit the sculpture and create a limited edition of 10 bronze copies to be sold for $20,000 each. Simeonov filed suit against Tiegs and others to recover damages for the loss of the plaster cast. Tiegs raised the New York privacy statute as a defense, arguing that because Simeonov's intended actions allegedly would violate the New York privacy statute, Simeonov would not be able to legally sell copies of the sculpture and, therefore, could not recover his lost profits. The New York court rejected Tiegs' defense. In its holding, the court noted that artwork such as Simeonov's sculpture was creative expression protected by the First Amendment. In the court's view, the fact that Simeonov intended to sell a "limited number" of copies did not transform the activity into one for the "purposes of trade." "It is the content that counts," the court remarked, and thus, Simeonov had a right to disseminate his speech, including selling a limited number of copies.

The *Simeonov* case stands for the proposition that the artistic rendering of a recognizable person is protected by the First Amendment, under certain circumstances (at least in New York). Following the reasoning of that case, a museum exhibiting works of fine art would likely be similarly protected from publicity claims to the extent that the exhibition serves primarily an educational ("non-commercial") purpose. Here again, the degree to which such activities will be protected is largely a function of the law of each state, which may vary. For instance, the California publicity statute recognizes First Amendment concerns to a limited extent through its statutory exemption for "single and original works of fine art" (i.e., not reproductions, or multiple editions). However, the exemption only applies to the publicity rights of deceased persons. As such, it would appear that California courts applying the California statute might not have come to the same conclusion as the New York court in *Simeonov*.

It is critical to remember that all uses by a museum of works featuring the name or likeness of a recognizable individual may not be protected. For instance, use of reproductions of such works on items for sale in the museum store may not be defensible on First Amendment grounds. Museums are well advised, therefore, to seek appropriate permission before using a work in connection with activities that arguably may be characterized as principally "commercial," notwithstanding the fact that an educational objective may also be motivating the use.

Right of publicity issues may arise in other areas of museum activity. Consider, for instance, a candid photograph of a student interacting with a museum docent. Use of such a photograph to publicize or promote the benefits of the institution's educational and outreach programs may be considered advertising (albeit for noncommercial purposes) and fall outside the scope of permissible use. Moreover, as a general matter, great care should be taken when considering the use of images of children, as courts are highly protective of children's privacy rights.

The combination of the ambiguity of the term "commercial use" and courts' seeming inability to clarify which uses are definitely immunized by the First Amendment results in a certain degree of unpredictability for museums encountering right of publicity and right of privacy issues. However, being sensitive to these issues and following the general guidelines offered here will help a museum avoid the most obvious pitfalls.

Practical Tips

Because the rights of privacy and publicity vary greatly from state to state, broad principles applicable to every institution are difficult to formulate. Thus, when confronted with a situation or circumstance that potentially implicates the rights of publicity and privacy, museums must take immediate steps to determine the precise contours of the law in the relevant jurisdictions. As a precautionary measure, to avoid unknowingly impinging on individuals' rights of privacy or publicity, museum administrators should be guided by the following general principles:

- Never assume that a visual artist, filmmaker, or photographer has obtained the necessary releases from the subjects of his or her work. Strongly consider including an indemnification provision in purchase and loan agreements involving works featuring representations and depictions of real individuals.

- Consider whether the subject of the representation or portrayal would find the use of his or her image or identity unflattering (for example, nudes or critical or embarrassing portrayals). The more unflattering or embarrassing a representation or portrayal is, the greater the potential exposure to privacy liability.

- Consider whether the subject of the representation is famous. If so, and if the subject has not been dead for a long time (i.e., less than 50

years), exercise particular caution before making any use of his or her image that may arguably be characterized "commercial" or "for purposes of trade" (i.e., in connection with merchandise). Right of publicity claimants (or their heirs) may receive the profits that they otherwise would have received under a license.

- Consider whether the use can be characterized as "commercial" or whether there is an arguable public interest in the use (i.e., scholarship, reporting, or commentary). Certain uses of the name, image, or likeness of an individual may be "mixed," in that they involve both commercial and noncommercial objectives. In such instances, the greater the public interest in the content, and the less commercial the character of the use, the more defensible the use will be from publicity claims.

- Obtain written consent whenever possible from each person whose name, likeness, or identity is to be referenced in materials that in any way promote or "advertise" the institution and its programs. Written consent is important because some state statues provide that consent is not valid unless in writing. Also, unless the consent is in writing, a dispute may arise in the future about whether such consent was actually given and/or the scope of the grant.

- Assuming that other rights are not being violated (such as copyright), the use of the name or a representation of an individual is permitted in some circumstances. For instance, use of photographs, film, or video of public settings where individuals are not readily recognizable or where the use is merely incidental and isolated do not violate the rights of privacy or publicity. Similarly, photographs, film, and video taken of participants and spectators in connection with a newsworthy event (for example, an exhibition opening, museum fund raiser, lecture, or symposium) may be used in newspaper reports, photo essays, and documentaries of the event, even if the individual portrayed is clearly identifiable.

Appendix F
ADVISORY COMMITTEES

Museum Advisory Committee

Stephen D. Busack
Director, Research and Collections
North Carolina Museum of Natural Sciences

Thomas Costello
Deputy Director
The Baltimore Zoo

Conrad Froehlich
Director
Martin and Osa Johnson Safari Museum

Douglas Greenberg
CEO and President
Chicago Historical Society

Catherine Howett-Smith
Associate Director/Director of Academic Services
Michael C. Carlos Museum, Emory University

Kent Lydecker
Associate Director of Education
The Metropolitan Museum of Art

Jack Nokes
Executive Director
Texas Association of Museums

Susan Stein
Curator
Monticello

Rowena Stewart
Executive Director
Museums at 18th and Vine, Kansas City

Stephen Weil
Senior Scholar Emeritus
Smithsonian Institution

Legal Advisory Committee

Stephen W. Clark
Associate General Counsel
The Museum of Modern Art

Elizabeth Croog
Deputy Secretary and Deputy General Counsel
National Gallery of Art

Jeffrey P. Cunard
Debevoise and Plimpton

Cristina Del Valle
Associate Counsel
The Metropolitan Museum of Art

Ildiko P. DeAngelis
Director
Museum Studies Program
The George Washington University

Lauryn Guttenplan Grant
Assistant General Counsel
Smithsonian Institution

Deborah L. Kanter
Vice President and General Counsel
Los Angeles County Museum of Art

Mary Berghaus Levering
Associate Registrar for National
   Copyright Programs
U.S. Copyright Office

Patty Lipshutz
Secretary and General Counsel
The Museum of Modern Art

Melissa Smith Levine
Legal Advisor
National Digital Library Project
Library of Congress

Maria A. Pallante
Assistant General Counsel
Solomon R. Guggenheim Museum

Thaddeus J. Stauber
Eckhart, McSwain, Silliman and Sears

Beverly M. Wolff
Special Advisor
Solomon R. Guggenheim Museum

Notes

Introduction

1. U.S. International Trade Commission definitions, quoted in Anthony D'Amato and Doris Estelle Long, eds., *International Intellectual Property Anthology* (Cincinnati: Anderson Publishing Co., 1996), 5–7.
2. "Fair Use." U.S. Copyright Office Factsheet (FL 102). Available on the Copyright Office Web site at: lcweb.loc.gov/copyright/fls/fl102.htm.

Chapter 1

Copyright

1. U.S. Const., art. 1, §8, cl. 8.
2. *Twentieth Century Music Corp. v. Aiken*, 422 U.S. 151, 156 (1975).
3. Copyright Act of 1976, 17 U.S.C. § 102(a) (1998).
4. *Community for Creative Non-Violence v. Reid*, 490 U.S. 730, 737 (1989).
5. *Bleistein v. Donaldson Lithographing Co.*, 188 U.S. 239, 250 (1903).
6. *Feist Publications, Inc. v. Rural Telephone Service Co.*, 499 U.S. 340, 345 (1991).
7. *Bleistein*, 188 U.S. at 251.
8. *Id.* at 252.
9. *Bridgeman Art Library, Ltd. v. Corel Corp.*, 25 F. Supp. 2d 421 (S.D.N.Y. 1998), *on reconsideration*, 36 F. Supp. 2d 191 (S.D.N.Y. 1999).
10. *Id.* at 427.
11. *Id.*
12. *Id.*
13. *Bridgeman*, 36 F. Supp. 2d at 196–97.
14. *Id.* at 197.
15. 17 U.S.C. § 102(a).
16. H. R. Rep. No. 94–1476, at 52 (1976).
17. *Id.*
18. 17 U.S.C. § 101 (defining "fixed").
19. *Id.* (defining "copies").
20. *Id.* (defining "fixed").
21. *See MAI Sys. Corp. v. Peak Computer, Inc.*, 991 F.2d 511, 518 (9th Cir. 1993), *cert. dismissed*, 510 U.S. 1033 (1994).
22. 17 U.S.C. § 101 (defining "literary works").
23. *See id.; see also* H. R. Rep. No. 94–1476, at 54.
24. H. R. Rep. No. 94–1476, at 54.
25. 17 U.S.C. § 101 (defining "pictorial, graphic, and sculptural works").
26. *See Mazer v. Stein*, 347 U.S. 201 (1954).
27. 17 U.S.C. § 101 (defining "pictorial, graphic, and sculptural works").
28. *Id.* (defining "useful article").
29. *See Burrow-Giles Lithographic Co. v. Sarony*, 111 U.S. 53 (1884).

30. *See, e. g., Kisch v. Ammirati & Puris, Inc.,* 657 F. Supp. 380, 382 (S.D.N.Y. 1987).

31. See "Originality," earlier in this chapter. *Bridgeman,* 25 F. Supp. 2d at 427.

32. 17 U.S.C. § 101 (defining "audiovisual works").

33. *Id.* (defining "motion pictures").

34. *Id.* (defining "architectural works").

35. *Id.*

36. *Id.,* § 120.

37. For a discussion of a case involving The Rock and Roll Hall of Fame and Museum, see chapter 4.

38. 17 U.S.C. § 101 (defining "derivative work").

39. *Id.* (defining "compilation").

40. *See id.*

41. *See id.* (defining "collective work").

42. *See id.* § 103(b).

43. *Id.* § 103(a).

44. *L. Batlin & Son, Inc. v. Snyder,* 536 F.2d 486, 491 (2d Cir. 1976), *cert. denied,* 429 U.S. 857 (1976).

45. *See Lee v. A. R. T. Co.,* 125 F.3d 580 (7th Cir. 1997).

46. *Id.* at 581.

47. *See Munoz v. Albuquerque A. R. T. Co.,* 829 F. Supp. 309 (D. Alaska 1993), *aff'd,* 38 F.3d 1218 (9th Cir. 1994); *Mirage Editions, Inc. v. Albuquerque A. R. T. Co.,* 856 F.2d 1341 (9th Cir. 1988), *cert. denied,* 489 U.S. 1018 (1989).

48. *See Greenwich Workshop, Inc. v. Timber Creations, Inc.,* 932 F. Supp. 1210 (C.D. Cal. 1996).

49. *See Feist Publications, Inc. v. Rural Telephone Service Co.,* 499 U.S. 340 (1991).

50. *See id.* at 364.

51. *See Lipton v. The Nature Co.,* 71 F.3d 464 (2d Cir. 1995).

52. 17 U.S.C. § 102(b).

53. 37 C.F.R. § 202.1(a).

54. 17 U.S.C. § 102(b).

55. *Publications Int'l., Ltd. v. Meredith Corp.,* 88 F.3d 473, 481 (7th Cir. 1996).

56. *Wainright Sec., Inc. v. Wall Street Transcript Corp.,* 558 F.2d 91, 95–96 (2d Cir. 1977), *cert. denied,* 434 U.S. 1014 (1978).

57. See *Kregos v. Associated Press,* 937 F.2d 700 (2d Cir. 1991).

58. The leading case on the merger doctrine is *Baker v. Seldon,* 101 U.S. 99 (1879), which denied copyright protection for blank forms contained in a book describing a bookkeeping system.

59. *See Hart v. Dan Chase Taxidermy Supply Co.,* 86 F.3d 320 (2d Cir. 1996).

60. *Id.* at 322.

61. *See* 17 U.S.C. § 105.

62. *See id.* § 101 (definition of a "work of the United States government").

63. *See id.* § 105.

64. Under the current regulations of the National Endowment for the Arts and the National Endowment for the Humanities, for example, copyright generally is vested in the grantee.

65. H. R. Rep. No. 94–1476, at 59 (1976).

66. *See* 1909 Copyright Act, 17 U.S.C. § 21 (repealed 1976). Copyright notice warns unauthorized users and deprives alleged infringers of the "innocent infringement defense."

67. *See* Berne Convention Implementation Act, Pub. L. No. 100–568, 102 Stat. 2854 (codified as amended in scattered sections of 17 U.S.C.).

68. 17 U.S.C. §§ 401(b), 402(b).

69. 1909 Copyright Act, 17 U.S.C. § 26 (repealed 1976).

70. 17 U.S.C. § 101 (defining "publication").

71. The great significance for museums of publication under the 1909 Copyright Act is discussed more fully in "Works Created and Published Before January 1, 1978," later in this chapter.

72. *See* 17 U.S.C. § 411(a).

73. *See id.* § 410(c).

74. *See id.* § 412.

75. *See id.* §§ 409, 407(a); 37 C.F.R. § 202.3.

76. *See* 17 U.S.C. § 407.

77. *See id.* § 106. To a much more limited extent, U.S. copyright law protects certain noneconomic rights of creators, which are discussed more fully in "Moral Rights," later in this chapter.

78. *See* Digital Performance Right in Sound Recordings Act of 1995, Pub. L. No. 104–39, 109 Stat. 336 (codified as amended at 17 U.S.C. §§ 106, 114, 115).

79. *See* 17 U.S.C. §§ 107–21.

80. *Id.* § 101 (defining "copies").

81. *See id.* §§ 101, 106(2).

82. *See id.* § 106(3).

83. Licensing agreements are discussed in detail in chapter 4.

84. 17 U.S.C. § 109(a).

85. *See* California Resale Royalties Act, Cal. Civ. Code § 986.

86. 17 U.S.C. § 101 (defining "perform" and to "perform . . . publicly"). The public performance right applies only to literary, musical, dramatic, choreographic, pantomimes, motion pictures, and other audiovisual works. *See id.* § 106(4).

87. *See id.* § 101 (defining "perform . . . publicly").

88. *Id.*

89. *Id.* (defining "transmit").

90. *See* Digital Performance Right in Sound Recording Act of 1995, Pub. L. No. 104–39, 109 Stat. 336 (codified as amended at 17 U.S.C. § 106(6)).

91. 17 U.S.C. § 101 (defining "display").

92. *See id.* §§ 110(1)–(2).

93. *Id.* § 109(c).

94. *See id.* § 106A.

95. *See id.* § 301(f).

96. The definition expressly excludes books, databases, electronic information services, electronic publications, maps, motion pictures, magazines, and newspapers, and works made for hire. *See* 17 U.S.C. § 101 (defining "work of visual art").

97. H. R. Rep. No. 101–514 (1990).

98. *See* 17 U.S.C. §106A(a).

99. *See id.* § 106A(a)(3).

100. *See id.* § 106A(c).

101. *See* Sonny Bono Copyright Term Extension Act, Pub. L. No. 105–298, 112 Stat. 2827 (1998) (hereinafter 1998 Term Extension Act).

102. *See* 17 U.S.C. § 302(a).

103. *See id.* § 302(b).

104. *See id.* § 302(c).

105. *See id.* §§ 302, 303, 305.

106. *See* Copyright Amendments Act of 1992, Pub. L. No. 102–307, 106 Stat. 264 (1992).

107. *See id.*

108. *See* 1998 Term Extension Act at § 102(d)(1)(A) (codified as amended at 17 U.S.C. § 304(a)).

109. L. Ray Patterson and Stanley W. Lindberg, *The Nature of Copyright: A Law of Users' Rights* (Athens: University of Georgia Press, 1991), 50.

110. *See* 17 U.S.C. § 105.

111. *See id.* § 102(b).

112. The U.S. Copyright Office Web site can be found at lcweb. loc.gov/copyright/.

113. *See* 17 U.S.C. § 102(a).

114. *See id.* § 101 (defining "joint work").

115. *See id.* § 201(a).

116. Museums should be aware, however, that the copyright laws of many foreign countries require that all joint owners consent to the grant of a license.

117. *See* 17 U.S.C. § 101 (defining "work made for hire").

118. Under certain circumstances, the museum also should consider taking an assignment, a concept discussed more fully later in this chapter.

119. *See Community for Creative Non-Violence v. Reid,* 490 U.S. 730, 751–52 (1989).

120. *See id.*

121. *See* 17 U.S.C. § 101 (defining a "work made for hire").

122. *See id.*

123. *See id.* § 101 (defining "collective work").

124. *See* 17 U.S.C. § 201(d)(1) (stating that copyright ownership "may be transferred in whole or in part by any means of conveyance or by operation of law, and may be bequeathed by will or passed as personal property by the applicable laws of intestate succession").

125. *See id.* § 203.

126. *See id.* § 202.

127. *Id.*

128. *See id.* §101 (defining "transfer of copyright ownership" and "copyright owner"); *id.* § 201(d).

129. *See* 17 U.S.C. § 501(b).

130. *See* 17 U.S.C. § 204(a). Licensing is discussed in detail in chapter 4.

131. *See id.* § 205.

132. *See id.* § 203.

133. *Id.* § 501(a).

134. *See id.* § 411(a).

135. *See id.* § 412.

136. *Id.* § 502(a).

137. *See, e. g., Publications Int'l., Ltd. v. Meredith Corp.,* 88 F.3d at 478.

138. *See Ty, Inc. v. GMA Accessories, Inc.*, 132 F.3d 1170–71 (7th Cir. 1997).

139. *Peter Pan Fabrics, Inc. v. Martin Weiner Corp.*, 274 F.2d 487, 489 (2d Cir. 1960).

140. *See* 17 U.S.C. § 504(c).

141. *See id.* § 505.

142. *Sony Corp. of Am. v. Universal City Studios, Inc.*, 464 U.S. 417, 487 (1984) (quoting *Gershwin Publ'g Corp. v. Columbia Artists Management, Inc.* 443 F.2d 1159, 1162 (2d Cir. 1971)).

143. *See Shapiro, Bernstein & Co. v. H. L. Green Co.*, 316 F.2d 304, 307 (2d Cir. 1963).

144. *See Rosemont Enter., Inc. v. Random House, Inc.*, 366 F.2d 303 (2d Cir. 1966), *cert. denied*, 385 U.S. 1009 (1967).

145. *Campbell v. Acuff-Rose Music, Inc.*, 510 U.S. 569, 575 (1994) (quoting *Emerson v. Davies*, 8 F. Cas. 615, 619 (C.C.D. Mass. 1845).

146. *See* 17 U.S.C. § 107.

147. *Id.* § 107(1).

148. *Hustler Magazine, Inc. v. Moral Majority, Inc.*, 796 F.2d 1148, 1153 (9th Cir. 1986) (quoting *MCA, Inc. v. Wilson*, 677 F.2d 180, 182 (2d Cir. 1981)).

149. Pierre N. Leval, "Toward a Fair Use Standard," *Harvard Law Review* 103 (1990): 1105, 1111.

150. *Campbell*, 510 U.S. at 586.

151. 17 U.S.C. § 107(3)C.

152. *Maxtone-Graham v. Burtchaell*, 803 F.2d 1253, 1263 (2d Cir. 1986), *cert. denied*, 481 U.S. 1059 (1987).

153. *See Harper & Row, Publishers, Inc. v. Nation Enter.*, 471 U.S. 539, 564–65 (1985).

154. *Ringgold v. Black Entertainment Television, Inc.*, 126 F.3d 70, 80 (2d Cir. 1997).

155. *Rogers v. Koons*, 960 F.2d 301, 311 (2d Cir. 1992).

156. *Campbell*, 510 U.S. at 586–87.

157. *Id.* at 590.

158. *See Sony Corp.*, 464 U.S. at 450–51.

159. *Campbell*, 510 U.S. at 578.

160. *Id.* at 590.

161. *American Geophysical Union v. Texaco, Inc.*, 802 F. Supp. 1, 25 (S.D.N.Y. 1992), aff'd, 37 F.3d 881 (2d Cir. 1994), *cert. dismissed*, 516 U.S. 1005 (1995).

162. *See* 17 U.S.C. § 108.

163. *See id.* § 108(i).

164. *See id.* § 108(a)(2).

165. *See id.* § 108(e).

166. *See id.* § 108(c)(1).

167. *See id.* § 108(i).

168. *See* Digital Millennium Copyright Act of 1998, Pub. L. No. 105–304, 112 Stat. 2860 (1998).

169. 17 U.S.C. § 108(c).

170. S. Rpt. 105–190 (1998).

171. *See* 17 U.S.C. § 110(1).

172. *Id.*

173. *Id.* § 110(2)(A).

174. *See* H. R. Rep. No. 94–1476 at 81 (1976).

175. *See* 17 U.S.C. § 110(4).

Chapter 2

Trademark

1. *See* Lanham Trademark Act of 1946, 15 U.S.C. § 1127 (the Lanham Act) (defining "trademark"). Colors, musical notes, and sounds, as well as smells, may also be protectable as trademarks. *See, e. g., Qualitex Co. v. Jacobson Products Co.*, 514 U.S. 159 (1995) (color held to be protectable as trademark); *In re General Electric Broad. Co.*, 199 U.S.P.Q. 560 (T.T.A.B. 1978) (combination of notes "G, E and C" originally registered by the General Electric Co. registrable as federal trademark by NBC); *In re Clarke*, 17 U.S.P.Q. 2d. 1238 (T.T.A.B. 1990) (fragrance used to identify sewing thread registrable as trademark).

2. *See* "Establishment of Trademark Rights and Bases for Protection," later in this chapter, for a discussion of what constitutes "use."

3. *See* 15 U.S.C. § 1057(c).

4. *See id.* § 1114.

5. *See id.* §§ 1058(a), 1059(a).

6. *See id.* §§ 1057(b), 1115(a).

7. *See id.* § 1117.

8. *See id.* § 1051 *et. seq.*

9. *See id.* § 1117(a).

10. *See Abercrombie & Fitch Co. v. Hunting World, Inc.*, 537 F.2d 4, 9–11 (2d Cir. 1976) (describing the types of marks that fall along the spectrum of distinctiveness).

11. *See* 15 U.S.C. § 1052(e) (prohibiting the registration of "merely descriptive" marks).

12. *See* U.S. Federal Trademark Registration No. 1,646,826.

13. *See* U.S. Federal Trademark Registration No. 2,095,414.

14. *See* U.S. Federal Trademark Registration No. 1,986,961.

15. *See* U.S. Federal Trademark Registration No. 1,190,678.

16. *See* U.S. Federal Trademark Registration No. 1,114,894.

17. *See* U.S. Federal Trademark Registration No. 2,017,582.

18. *See* U.S. Federal Trademark Registration No. 2,162,729.

19. *In re Gyulay*, 820 F.2d 1216, 1217 (Fed. Cir. 1987); see appendix A for a discussion of the effect of descriptiveness finding in the PTO registration context.

20. *See Carter-Wallace, Inc. v. Procter & Gamble Co.*, 434 F.2d 794, 802 (9th Cir. 1970) (discussing "secondary meaning"); 15 U.S.C. § 1052; see appendix A for a discussion of what evidence is sufficient to show secondary meaning.

21. *See* U.S. Federal Trademark Registration No. 2,161,352.

22. *See* U.S. Federal Trademark Registration No. 2,161,264. Under the doctrine of "foreign equivalents," words in common, modern foreign languages are translated into English in order to determine the strength of the mark (*i.e.*, generic, descriptive, suggestive,l or arbitrary/fanciful) and to ascertain whether a mark is confusingly similar to another English word mark for registration and/or infringement purposes. *See In re Hag Aktiengesellschaft*, 155 U.S.P.Q. 598 (T.T.A.B. 1967). The test is whether a domestic consumer familiar with the foreign language would consider the foreign language and English terms to be equivalent in meaning. The doctrine of foreign equivalents does not necessarily apply to words from dead or obscure languages.

23. *See* U.S. Federal Trademark Registration No. 1,989,718.

24. *See* U.S. Federal Trademark Registration No. 736,933.

25. *See* 15 U.S.C. §§ 1052(e)–(f).

26. *See* "Proper Names as Trademarks," later in this chapter, for additional considerations with respect to use of personal names as trademarks.

27. *See* 15 U.S.C. § 1052(e).

28. *See id.* § 1127 (defining "certification mark").

29. *See id.* § 1127 (defining "collective mark").

30. *See In re Letica Corp.*, 226 U.S.P.Q. 276, 277 (T.T.A.B. 1985).

31. *See* 15 U.S.C. § 1052(c).

32. *See id.* § 1052(e)–(f).

33. *See* 15 U.S.C. § 1115(b)(4).

34. *See In re Wood*, 217 U.S.P.Q. 1345 (T.T.A.B. 1983) (holding that an artist's name on an original work of art is a "trademark" with the definition of that term in the Lanham Act).

35. Under VARA, however, an artist may prevent the use of his or her name as the author of a work that has been distorted, mutilated, or otherwise modified in a manner that would be prejudicial to his or her honor or reputation. *See* chapter 1, "Exclusive Rights and Their Limitations: Moral Rights."

36. *See* chapter 1, "Subject Matter of Copyright," for a discussion of the distinction between trademark and copyright protection for architectural works.

37. *See* U.S. Federal Trademark Registration No. 1,126,888.

38. *See* U.S. Federal Trademark Registration No. 1,761,655.

39. *See* U.S. Federal Trademark Registration No. 2,060,633.

40. *See* U.S. Federal Trademark Registration No. 995,497.

45. *See* "The Federal Registration Process," later in this chapter.

46. *See* "Permitted Uses and Defenses to Trademark Infringement: Fair Use," later in this chapter.

47. *See* 37 C.F.R. § 202.1(a).

48. *See In re Hal Leonard Publ'g Corp.*, 15 U.S.P.Q. 2d 1574 (T.T.A.B. 1990); see "Descriptive Marks," earlier in this chapter, for a discussion of secondary meaning/acquired distinctiveness.

49. *See* U.S. Federal Trademark Registration No. 2,126,853.

50. *See* U.S. Federal Trademark Application Ser. No. 75/097,342.

51. *See* U.S. Federal Trademark Registration No. 1,947,967.

52. *See* 15 U.S.C. §§ 1051, 1052, 1127; see also *In re Morton-Norwich Prods., Inc.*, 671 F.2d 332 (C.C.P.A. 1982).

53. *See Romm Art Creations, Ltd. v. Simcha Int'l, Inc.*, 786 F. Supp. 1126 (E.D.N.Y. 1992) (applying trade dress concepts to commercial reproductions of works of art and granting preliminary injunction against producer of posters based on "inherently distinctive" style of works of Israeli artist Itzachak Tarkay); *but see Galerie Furstenberg v. Coffaro*, 697 F. Supp. 1282, 1289–91 (S.D.N.Y. 1988) (unique artistic style of Salvador Dali held not to be a trademark, but protectable through copyright law); see also Winnie Hu, "Store Wars: When a Mobile is Not a Calder," *New York Times*, August 6, 1998, p. E1 (reporting that the Whitney Museum of American Art in New York and the Phillips Collection in Washington, D.C., ceased selling mobiles in their museum shops during the Alexander Calder retrospective exhibition out of deference to the Calder estate's concern that the public would not differentiate the mass-merchandised objects from actual Calder works).

54. *See* "Descriptive Marks," earlier in this chapter, for a discussion of descriptiveness; *see* appendix A for a discussion of evidence needed to show secondary meaning.

55. *See Bridgeman Art Library, Ltd. v. Corel Corp.*, 25 F. Supp. 2d 421, 427 (S.D.N.Y. 1998), *on reconsideration*, 36 F. Supp. 2d 191 (S.D.N.Y. 1999) (rejecting Lanham Act claim based solely on plaintiff's argument that, because the public may associate works of art with particular institutions, subsequent use of reproductions of these works by third parties necessarily implies sponsorship by or association with plaintiff and/or the institution that owns the underlying work).

56. *See Hughes v. Design Look, Inc.*, 693 F. Supp. 1500 (S.D.N.Y. 1988).

57. *See Harlequin Enters., Ltd. v. Gulf & W. Corp.*, 644 F.2d 946 (2d Cir. 1981) (reproductions of drawings adorning the covers of novels found to be protected by trademark law); *Hartford House, Ltd. v. Hallmark Cards, Inc.*, 647 F. Supp. 1533, 1540 (D. Colo. 1986) (reproductions of paintings on greeting cards found to be protected by trademark law), *aff'd*, 846 F.2d 1268 (10th Cir. 1988), *cert. denied*, 488 U.S. 908 (1988).

58. *See* 15 U.S.C. § 1125.

59. *See* "The Federal Registration Process," earlier in this chapter, for a discussion of the role of legal counsel in clearance, registration, and enforcement.

60. *See* "Scope of Trademark Protection," earlier in this chapter.

61. Readers should note that effective October 30, 1999, the PTO is anticipated to implement changes in the procedures and requirements governing federal trademark applications and registration maintenance and renewal, as well as in its fee structure. Many of the changes are a result of the Trademark Law Treaty which has been adopted by 51 countries, including the United States. *See* Trademark Law Treaty, *adopted* at Geneva Oct. 27, 1994, entered into force Aug. 1, 1996, in WIPO, Industrial Property and Copyright, Industrial Property Laws and Treaties, Multilateral Treaties, Jan. 1995, at 1–12 (hereinafter Trademark Law Treaty). The Trademark Law Treaty is designed to achieve global harmonization and simplification of national trademark registration standards. Although the Lanham Act has already been amended to add some of the treaty's features into U.S. trademark law, its full implementation in this country requires that additional adjustments be made to PTO regulations with respect to registration maintenance and renewal requirements, revival of abandoned applications, and recordation of assignments, among other subjects. *See* Trademark Treaty Implementation Act of 1998, Pub. L. No. 105–330, 112 Stat. 3064 (codified as amended in scattered sections of 15 U.S.C.).

62. *See* 15 U.S.C. § 1051(a)–(b). The federal trademark statute provides an additional basis for applying for federal trademark registration, which likely has limited applicability for the vast majority of U.S. institutions. Applicants who have previously registered marks or who have filed applications (not more than six months old) for trademark registration in countries that have entered into certain international agreements with the United States have special rights in the United States. *See id.* § 1126. Such registrants or applicants may obtain a U.S. registration based upon a bona fide intent to use the foreign mark in the United States. The registration will be retroactive to the date on which the foreign application was filed, if the U.S. application is filed during the six-month period following the filing date of the foreign application. Under these provisions, for instance, a foreign museum that holds a trademark registration in its home country may file an application with the PTO and obtain a federal trademark registration (even without use of the mark in the U.S.). A federal trademark infringement suit cannot, however, be brought by that foreign museum before actual use of the mark commences in the U.S. (*See* chapter 5 for further discussion of international trademark issues.)

63. *See id.* § 1057(c).

64. *See id.* § 1052.

65. *See id.*

66. *See id.* § 1127 (defining "use in commerce").

67. *See id.* §§ 1052(d)–(e), 1062(a).

68. *See id.* § 1063(b).

69. *See id.* § 1063(b)(2).

70. *See* 37 C.F.R. § 2.89. If the applicant commences use of a mark early in the registration process, the applicant may establish such use in the form of an "Amendment to Allege Use," which can be filed any time after the application is filed and before the mark is approved for publication. If an Amendment to Allege Use is submitted and accepted, the application will proceed to registration as if it had been filed as a use-based application. *See* 37 C.F.R. § 2.76(f).

71. *See* 15 U.S.C. § 1091.

72. *See* chapter 5 for a discussion of international trademark protection.

73. *See id.* § 1058.

74. *See id.* § 1065.

75. *See* 37 C.F.R. § 2.168.

76. *See* 15 U.S.C. §§ 1065, 1115.

77. *See id.* § 1059. For trademark registrations issued prior to November 16, 1989, the term of registration is 20 years. Renewals for such registration that come due subsequent to that date are for 10-year periods.

78. *See* "Distinguishing Trade Names from Trademarks," earlier in this chapter.

79. *See Copeland's Enter., Inc. v. CNV, Inc.,* 945 F.2d 1563 (Fed. Cir. 1991).

80. *See* 15 U.S.C. §1127 (defining when a mark will be deemed "abandoned").

81. *See* chapter 4, "Trademark Licenses: Formal Requirements."

82. *See* "Permitted Uses and Defenses to Trademark Infringement," earlier in this chapter.

83. *See* 15 U.S.C. §§ 1114(1), 1125(a).

84. *See Beer Nuts, Inc. v. Clover Club Foods Co.,* 805 F.2d 920, 925 (10th Cir. 1986); *Specialty Brands, Inc. v. Coffee Bean Distribs., Inc.,* 748 F.2d 669, 671–76 (Fed. Cir. 1984); *In re E. 1. du Pont de Nemours & Co.,* 476 F.2d 1357, 1361 (C.C.P.A. 1973); *Polaroid Corp. v. Polarad Elec. Corp.,* 287 F.2d 492 (2d Cir. 1961), *cert. denied,* 368 U.S. 820 (1961).

85. *See* 15 U.S.C. § 1127 (defining when a mark will be deemed "abandoned").

86. Commercial search firms that offer watching services include Thomson & Thomson (www.thomson-thomson.com), Corsearch (www.corsearch.com), and MarkWatch (www.markwatch.com).

87. *See* "Maintaining and Renewing Federal Registration," earlier in this chapter.

88. *See* appendix A for further discussion of the use of private investigations in the clearance context.

89. *See* "Settlement of Trademark Disputes," later in this chapter.

90. *See* "Proper Trademark Usage," earlier in this chapter, for a discussion of trademark monitoring strategies.

91. *See* 15 U.S.C. §§ 1114, 1125.

92. *See id.* § 1116.

93. *See id.* § 1117.

94. *See id.* § 1125(c).

95. *See id.* § 1125(a).

96. *See* Trademark Counterfeiting Act of 1984, Pub. L. No. 98–473, 98 Stat. 2178 (1984) (codified at 18 U.S.C. § 2320).

97. *See* 15 U.S.C. § 1114(1).

98. *See id.* §§ 1116(d), 1117(c).

99. *See id.* § 1125.

100. *See id.* § 1063; 37 C.F.R. § 2.101.

101. *See* 15 U.S.C. § 1064; 37 C.F.R. § 2.111.

102. *See* 37 C.F.R. § 2.104.

103. *See* 15 U.S.C. § 1063; 37 C.F.R. § 2.101(c).

104. *See* 37 C.F.R. §§ 2.111–2.112.

105. *See* 15 U.S.C. § 1071.

106. *See, e. g., Polo Fashions, Inc. v. Samuel Schlesinger, Inc.,* 224 U.S.P.Q. 886 (D.N.J. 1984) (holding defendant distributor liable for infringement in the absence of knowledge that goods were infringing).

107. *See, e. g., Hard Rock Cafe Licensing Corp. v. Concession Serv., Inc.,* 955 F.2d 1143, 1148–50 (7th Cir. 1992). However, the Supreme Court has stated that secondary liability should be more narrowly drawn in the trademark context than in the copyright context. *See Sony Corp. of Am. v. Universal City Studios, Inc.,* 464 U.S. 417, 439 n. 19 (1984), *reh'g denied,* 465 U.S. 1112 (1984).

108. *See American Tel. & Tel. Co. v. Winback and Conserve Program, Inc.*, 42 F.3d 1421, 1430–31 (3d Cir. 1994) (holding that defendant could be liable for the acts of its independent sales representatives), *cert. denied*, 514 U.S. 1103 (1995).

109. *See Sealy, Inc. v. Easy Living, Inc.*, 743 F.2d 1378, 1382 (9th Cir. 1984) (affirming the district court's holding that the defendant foresaw and intended that its mattress foundations would be passed off as plaintiff's product by distributors).

110. *See Hard Rock Cafe*, 955 F.2d at 1149 (stating that the reason-to-know standard "does not impose any duty to seek out and prevent violations").

111. *See* "Joint Ownership and Transfer of Trademark Rights," earlier in this chapter.

112. *See* chapter 4 for discussion of trademark licensing.

113. *See* 15 U.S.C. § 1115(b)(4).

114. *See, e. g., Seaboard Seed Co. v. Bemis Co., Inc.*, 632 F. Supp. 1133, 1138 (N.D. Ill. 1986) (applying the statutory fair use factors of 15 U.S.C. § 1115(b)(4)).

115. *See, e. g., New Kids on the Block v. New America Publ'g, Inc.*, 971 F.2d 302, 305–09 (9th Cir. 1992) (holding that defendant's use of plaintiff's mark NEW KIDS ON THE BLOCK was fair use when used to describe the plaintiff's product (*i.e.*, a rock band)).

116. *See id.* at 308–309.

117. *See New York Racing Ass'n, Inc. v. Perlmutter Publ'g., Inc.*, No. 95–CV–994, 1996 U.S. Dist. LEXIS 11764, at *20–21 (N.D.N.Y. July 19, 1996) (holding that an artist's use of registered words and logos in a painting that depicts a scene in which the marks actually exist is protected because such use serves the "artistically relevant purpose of accurately depicting that scene." However, with respect to the artist's inclusion of other protected marks that did not actually exist in the depicted scene, the court found this use to be of "minimal . . . artistic relevance" and, therefore, unprotected), *reconsideration denied*, 959 F. Supp. 578 (N.D.N.Y. 1997).

118. *Dr. Seuss Enter., L.P. v. Penguin Books USA, Inc.*, 109 F.3d 1394, 1405 (9th Cir. 1997) (quoting J. Thomas McCarthy, *McCarthy on Trademarks and Unfair Competition*, 4th ed. (Eagan, MN: West Group, 1999), sec. 31.38[1], pp. 31–216) *cert. dismissed*, 118 S. Ct. 27 (1997).

119. *See Dr. Seuss*, 109 F.3d at 1403, 1405–06 (holding that a book that satirically commented on the O. J. Simpson case by using the style of Dr. Seuss could be enjoined as copyright and trademark infringement because the book used the substance and style of Dr. Seuss books to comment on a matter other than to parody the books themselves).

120. *See* 15 U.S.C. § 1115(b)(1), (2), (8).

121. *See* chapter 4 for a discussion of trademark licensing.

122. *See* 15 U.S.C. § 1060.

123. *See* "Federal Registration Requirements and Procedures" for a discussion of ITU applications generally.

Chapter 3

Museums and the Web

1. *See* Steven Henry Madoff, "Where the Venues Are Virtually Infinite," New York Times, January 10, 1999, sec. 2, p. 41.

2. Maxwell Anderson, introduction to *The Wired Museum: Emerging Technology and Changing Paradigms* (Washington, D.C. : American Association of Museums, 1997), p. 20.

3. *See* Digital Millennium Copyright Act, Pub. L. No. 105–304, 112 Stat. 2860 (1998) (codified as amended in scattered sections of 17 U.S.C.).

4. World Intellectual Property Organization Copyright Treaty (adopted by the Diplomatic Conference, December 20, 1996); Performances and Phonograms Treaty (adopted by the Diplomatic Conference, December 20, 1996).

5. *See* 17 U.S.C. § 106(1).

6. *See MAI Sys. Corp. v. Peak Computer, Inc.*, 991 F.2d 511, 517–18 (9th Cir. 1993), *cert. dismissed*, 510 U.S. 1033 (1994); *Vault Corp. v. Quaid Software Ltd.*, 847 F.2d 255, 260 (5th Cir. 1988).

7. *See Playboy Enters., Inc. v. Frena*, 839 F. Supp. 1552, 1554–56 (M.D. Fla. 1993).

8. *See Marobie-FL, Inc. v. National Ass'n. of Fire Equip. Distrib.*, 983 F. Supp. 1167, 1173 (N.D. Ill. 1997).

9. *See Sega Enters. Ltd. v. MAPHIA*, 948 F. Supp. 923, 932–33 (N.D. Cal. 1996).

10. *See Religious Tech. Ctr. v. Netcom On-Line Communication Servs.*, 907 F. Supp. 1361, 1378, n. 25 (N.D. Cal. 1995).

11. *See* 17 U.S.C. § 106(2). The derivative work right is also discussed in chapter 1, "Exclusive Rights and Their Limitations."

12. *See, e. g., Bridgeman Art Library, Ltd. v. Corel Corp.*, 25 F. Supp. 2d 421 (S.D.N.Y. 1998), on reconsideration, 36 F. Supp. 2d 191 (S.D.N.Y. 1999). The *Bridgeman* case is discussed in chapter 1, "Subject Matter of Copyright: Criteria for Protection."

13. *See Leibovitz v. Paramount Pictures Corp.*, 137 F.3d 109 (2d Cir. 1998) (finding no infringement due to fair use defense).

14. *See* 17 U.S.C. § 106(3). For a discussion of distribution rights, see chapter 1, "Exclusive Rights and Their Limitations."

15. *See Frena*, 839 F. Supp. at 1556 (public distribution right implicated by downloading of copyrighted photography from bulletin board service); *Netcom*, 907 F. Supp. at 1372 (public distribution right not violated by service provider that merely served as conduit for remote Internet servers).

16. *See* 17 U.S.C. § 106(4). The public performance right applies only to literary, musical, dramatic, pantomimes, motion pictures, and other audiovisual works. For a discussion of the public performance right, see chapter 1, "Exclusive Rights and Their Limitations."

17. *See id.* § 101 (defining to perform "publicly").

18. *See id.* § 101 (defining to "transmit" to mean "to communicate it by any device or process whereby images or sounds are received beyond the place from which they are sent").

19. *See id.* § 106(5). For a discussion of the public display right, see chapter 1, "Exclusive Rights and Their Limitations."

20. *Frena*, 839 F. Supp. at 1557 (noting that the "display right precludes unauthorized transmission of the display from one place to another, for example, by a computer system").

21. *See Playboy Enters., Inc. v. Russ Hardenburgh, Inc.*, 982 F. Supp. 503 (N.D. Ohio 1997).

22. *See, e. g., Frena*, 839 F. Supp. at 1556.

23. *See, e. g., Netcom*, 907 F. Supp. at 1372.

24. The implications under the Digital Millennium Copyright Act of the museum's response to this letter are discussed later in this chapter.

25. 17 U.S.C. § 501(a).

26. *See Feist Publications, Inc. v. Rural Tel. Serv. Co., Inc.*, 499 U.S. 340, 361 (1991).

27. *See, e. g., Russ Hardenburgh, Inc.*, 982 F. Supp. at 512–14.

28. *See* Digital Millennium Copyright Act, Pub. L. No. 105–304, § 202, 112 Stat. 2860 (1998) (codified as amended at 17 U.S.C. § 512).

29. *Gershwin Publ'g. Corp. v. Columbia Artists Management, Inc.*, 443 F.2d 1159, 1162 (2d Cir. 1971).

30. *See Shapiro, Bernstein & Co. v. H. L. Green Co.*, 316 F.2d 304, 307–08 (2d Cir. 1963).

31. *See Marobie-FL, Inc.*, 983 F. Supp. at 1178.

32. 17 U.S.C. § 107(1)–(4).

33. *See Twin Peaks Prods., Inc. v. Publications Int'l, Ltd.*, 996 F.2d 1366, 1374–76 (2d Cir. 1993).

34. *See id.* at 1374–75.

35. *Harper & Row, Publishers, Inc. v. Nation Enters.*, 471 U.S. 539, 562 (1985).

36. *Campbell v. Acuff-Rose Music, Inc.*, 510 U.S. 569, 579 (1994), *on remand*, 25 F.3d 297 (6th Cir. 1994).

37. *Sheldon v. Metro-Goldwyn Pictures Corp.*, 81 F.2d 49, 56 (2d Cir. 1936), *aff'd*, 309 U.S. 390 (1940).

38. *Campbell*, 510 U.S. at 586.

39. *See Twin Peak*s, 996 F.2d at 1376.

40. *Harper & Row Publishers, Inc.*, 471 U.S. at 565.

41. *See Castle Rock Entertainment v. Carol Publ'g Group, Inc.*, 955 F. Supp. 260, 269 (S.D.N.Y. 1997), *aff'd*, 150 F.3d 132 (2d Cir. 1998).

42. *Sega Enters. Ltd.*, 857 F. Supp. at 688.

43. *Campbell*, 510 U.S. at 590–91.

44. *See* Digital Millennium Copyright Act, Pub. L. No. 105–304, 112 Stat. 2860 (1998) (codified as amended in scattered sections of 17 U.S.C.).

45. *See* 17 U.S.C. § 512(c)(2).

46. *See id.* § 512(c)(3).

47. *See id.* § 512(g). On November 3, 1998, the Copyright Office issued interim regulations governing these requirements, which may be found on the Copyright Office Web site at lcweb. loc.gov/copyright/onlinesp/. *See also* Library of Congress, Copyright Office, Designation of Agent to Receive Notification of Claimed Infringement, 63 Fed. Reg. 59,233 (1998).

48. *See* 17 U.S.C. § 512(g).

49. *See id.* § 512(b).

50. *See id.* § 512(c).

51. *See id.* § 512(c)(1).

52. *Id.* § 512(c)(1)(B).

53. *See id.* § 512(d).

54. *See* H. R. Rep. No. 105–551(II), at 53–54 (1998).

55. *See id.*

56. World Intellectual Property Organization Copyright Treaty (adopted by the Diplomatic Conference, December 20, 1996); the Performances and Phonograms Treaty (adopted by the Diplomatic Conference, December 20, 1996).

57. *See* 17 U.S.C. § 1201(a)(1)(A).

58. H. R. Rep. No. 105–551(I), at 17 (1998).

59. *See* 17 U.S.C. § 1201(a).

60. *See id.*

61. *See id.* § 1201(d).

62. *See id.* §1202.

63. *See id.* § 1202(c).

64. *See id.* § 1202(a)–(b).

65. *See id.* § 1202(c).

66. *See id.* § 1202(b)(3).

67. *See id.* § 1203(c)(3)(B).

68. *See id.* § 1203(c)(5)(B).

69. "Whois" searches of other registries may be conducted at the following sites: www.ripe.net/db/whois.html (European IP address allocations); www.apnic.net (Asia Pacific IP address allocations); nic.mil (U.S. military); nic.gov (U.S. government).

70. *See* chapter 2 and appendix A for a discussion of commercial search firms.

71. The RIPE NCC Web site is located at www.ripe. net.

72. The APNIC Web site is located at www.apnic. net.

73. NSI offers international domain name registration services at www.idnames.com. Detailed information regarding domain registration in particular countries can also be found at the IANA Web site (www.iana.org/cctld.html).

74. *See* U.S. PTO guidance on the registration of domain names as trademarks at www.uspto.gov/web/offices/tac.

75. *See, e. g., Comp. Examiner Agency, Inc. v. Juris, Inc.*, No. 96-0213-WMB, 1996 U.S. Dist. LEXIS 2059 (C.D. Cal. Apr. 26, 1996); *Playboy Enters., Inc. v. Chuckleberry Publ'g, Inc.*, 939 F. Supp. 1032, 1038 (S.D.N.Y. 1996).

76. *See* U.S. PTO policy statement at www.uspto.gov/web/offices/tac/domain/domcl.html.

77. *See* NSI Domain Name Dispute Resolution Policy (Rev. 03) (effective Feb. 25, 1998), available at www. netsol.com/rs/dispute-policyb.html.

78. *See* chapter 2 for a discussion of trademark monitoring strategies.

79. The Final Report of the WIPO Internet Domain Name Process, dated April 30, 1999, is available at wipo2.wipo. int.

80. *See* chapter 2, "Trademark Availability Searches," and appendix A.

81. *See* 15 U.S.C. §§ 1114, 1125(a); see chapter 2.

82. *See, e. g., Brookfield Communications, Inc. v. West Coast Entertainment Corp.*, 1999 U.S. App. LEXIS 7779 (April 22, 1999); see chapter 2.

83. *See, e. g., Comp. Examiner Agency*, 1996 U.S. Dist. LEXIS 20259; *Actmedia, Inc. v. Active Media Int'l, Inc.*, No. 96C 3448, 1996 U.S. Dist. LEXIS 20814.

84. *See Interstellar Starship Servs., Ltd. v. Epix, Inc.*, 983 F. Supp. 1331, 1334–35 (D.Or. 1997); *but cf. Planned Parenthood Fed'n of Am., Inc. v. Bucci*, 42 U.S.P.Q. 2d 1430, 1437–39 (S.D.N.Y. 1997) (employing traditional likelihood of confusion analysis), *aff'd*, 152 F.3d 920 (2d Cir. 1998), *cert. denied*, 119 S. Ct. 90 (1998).

85. *See, e. g., Toys "R" Us, Inc. v. Akkaoui*, 40 U.S.P.Q. 2d 1836, 1838–39 (N.D. Cal. 1996).

86. *See* 15 U.S.C. § 1125(c); see chapter 2.

87. *See* 141 Cong. Rec. 319,321 (daily ed. Dec. 29, 1995) (statement of Sen. Leahy).

88. *But see I. P. Lund Trading ApS v. Kohler Co.*, 163 F.3d 27, 45–47 (1st Cir. 1998) (holding that marks must go far beyond the "distinctiveness" required by the Lanham Act for trademark infringement protection before they qualify for protection against dilution, and imposing a rigorous standard in evaluating whether a mark is "famous" for dilution purposes).

89. *See Panavision Int'l, L. P. v. Toeppen*, 141 F.3d 1316 (9th Cir. 1998); *Intermatic Inc. v. Toeppen*, 947 F. Supp. 1227 (N.D. Ill. 1996).

90. *See Paine Webber, Inc. v. wwwpainewebber.com*, 1:99cv0056 (E.D.V.A. filed April 2, 1999). A preliminary injunction was granted prohibiting a pornographic Web site proprietor's use of "wwwpainewebber.com," reasoning that Paine Webber is a famous mark that will be diluted by being linked with pornography. *See also* Ianthe Jeanne Dugan, "Judge Strips Look-Alike Web Name," *Washington Post*, April 16, 1999, E-1. Courts have been strongly influenced by equity in deciding both the merits of cybersquatting cases and disputes over personal jurisdiction associated with them. Online jurisdiction is discussed later in this chapter.

91. *See Prince Plc v. Prince Sports Group, Inc.*, No. CH 1997 P 2355 (High Ct., Ch. Div., Jul. 31, 1997).

92. *See Juno Online Serv., L. P. v. Juno Lighting, Inc.*, 979 F. Supp. 684, 690 (N.D. Ill. 997) (rejecting an allegation of trademark misuse where plaintiff produced no facts to support its contention that the defendant attempted to use its trademark rights to drive plaintiff out of business).

93. *See Playboy Enters., Inc. v. Calvin Designer Label*, 985 F. Supp. 1220 (N.D. Cal. 1997).

94. *See Niton Corp. v. Radiation Monitoring Devices, Inc.*, 27 F. Supp. 2d 102 (D. Mass. 1998).

95. *See Playboy Enters., Inc. v. Welles*, 7 F. Supp. 2d 1098 (S.D. Cal. 1998), *aff'd*, 162 F.3d 1169 (9th Cir. 1998).

96. *See* chapter 2.

97. *See Brookfield Communications*, 1999 U.S. App. LEXIS 7779 (finding use of federally registered trademark as a metatag to be actionable under the Lanham Act reasoning that such use is "much like posting a sign with another's trademark in front of one's store," but acknowledging that descriptive terms may legitimately be used as metatags without liability).

98. *See Ticketmaster Corp. v. Microsoft Corp.*, 97–3055 (C.D. Cal. filed Apr. 28, 1997).

99. Web linking agreements are discussed more fully in chapter 3, "Linking and Framing on the Internet."

100. *Washington Post Co. v. Total News, Inc.*, 97 Civ. 90 (S.D.N.Y. filed Feb. 2, 1997).

101. *See* Robin Bierstedt, *Plaintiff's Complaint in The Washington Post Co. v. Total News, Inc. et al.*, 480 PLI/Pat 235 (1997).

102. The Stipulation and Order of Settlement and Dismissal can be viewed at legal.web.aol.com/decisions/dlip/washorde.html.

103. Cease and desist letters are discussed more fully in chapter 1 (copyright context) and chapter 2 (trademark context).

104. 17 U.S.C. § 101 (defining "derivative work").

105. Unlike the reproduction right, the derivative work right may be violated even where the underlying work is not fixed. *See* H. R. Rep. No. 94–1476, at 62 (1976).

106. *See Futuredontics, Inc. v. Applied Anagramics, Inc.*, 45 U.S.P.Q. 2d 2005, 2010 (C.D. Cal. 1998), *aff'd*, 152 F.3d 925 (9th Cir. 1998).

107. *Hanson v. Denckla*, 357 U.S. 235, 253 (1958).

108. *See International Shoe Co. v. Washington*, 326 U.S. 316 (1945).

109. *See Bensusan Restaurant Corp. v. King*, 937 F. Supp. 295 (S.D.N.Y. 1996), aff'd, 126 F.3d 25 (2d Cir. 1997).

110. *Id.* at 301. *See also Hearst Corp. v. Goldberger*, No. 96 Civ. 3620, 1997 U.S. Dist. LEXIS 2065 (S.D.N.Y. Feb. 26, 1997) (refusing to exercise jurisdiction over the defendant merely because his Web site was accessible to, and had been electronically "visited" by, computers in New York).

111. *See Inset Sys., Inc. v. Instruction Set, Inc.*, 937 F. Supp. 161 (D. Conn. 1996); see also *Liu v. DeFelice*, 6 F. Supp. 2d 106 (D. Mass. 1998) (holding that e-mail alone may be enough to subject a defendant to state jurisdiction).

112. *See Maritz, Inc. v. Cybergold, Inc.*, 947 F. Supp. 1328, 1333 (E.D. Mo. 1996), *reconsideration denied*, 947 F. Supp. 1338 (E.D. Mo. 1996).

113. *See Zippo Mfg. v. Zippo Dot Com, Inc.*, 952 F. Supp. 1119 (W.D. Pa. 1997).

114. *See Bunn-O-Matic Corp. v. Bunn Coffee Serv., Inc.*, 46 U.S.P.Q. 2d 1375 (C.D. Ill. 1998).

115. *See Playboy Enters., Inc. v. Chuckleberry Publ'g, Inc.*, 939 F. Supp. 1032 (S.D.N.Y. 1996).

Chapter 4

Licensing

1. *See Rey v. Lafferty*, 990 F.2d 1379 (1st Cir. 1993), *cert. denied*, 510 U.S. 828 (1993).

2. *See Cohen v. Paramount Pictures Corp.*, 845 F.2d 851 (9th Cir. 1988).

3. *Bartsch v. Metro-Goldwyn-Mayer, Inc.*, 391 F.2d 150, 155 (2d Cir. 1968), cert. denied, 393 U.S. 826 (1968).

4. *Boosey & Hawkes Music Publishers, Ltd. v. Walt Disney Co.*, 145 F.3d 481, 487 (2d Cir. 1998).

5. *Bloom v. Hearst Entertainment, Inc.*, 33 F.3d 518, 521 (5th Cir. 1994).

6. *See Cohen*, 845 F.2d at 854.

7. 17 U.S.C. § 201(c).

8. *See Ryan v. Carl Corp.*, 23 F. Supp. 2d 1146 (N.D. Cal. 1998) (holding that the "revision" privilege of section 201 of the Copyright Act does not permit the simple reproduction of a single article of a collective work (*i.e.*, an article from a periodical or magazine).

9. *See Tasini v. New York Times Co.*, 972 F. Supp. 804 (S.D.N.Y. 1997), *reconsideration denied*, 981 F. Supp. 841 (S.D.N.Y. 1997).

10. *See* 17 U.S.C. § 201(d).

11. The Digital Millennium Copyright Act of 1998 makes it unlawful to tamper with or remove copyright management information. *See* 17 U.S.C. § 1202; see chapter 1.

12. *See* 17 U.S.C. § 204(a).

13. *See Lulirama Ltd. v. Axcess Broadcast Serv., Inc.*, 128 F.3d 872, 879–82 (5th Cir. 1997); *Effects Assoc., Inc. v. Cohen*, 908 F.2d 555, 556–59 (9th Cir. 1990), *cert. denied sub nom. Danforth v. Cohen*, 498 U.S. 1103 (1991).

14. *See MacLean Assoc., Inc. v. Wm. M. Mercer-Meidinger-Hansen, Inc.*, 952 F.2d 769, 778–79 (3d Cir. 1991).

15. *See* 17 U.S.C. § 202.

16. *See Marshall v. Music Hall Ctr. for the Performing Arts, Inc.*, No. 95-CV-709910, 1995 U.S. Dist. LEXIS 17904 (E.D. Mich. Nov. 2, 1995).

17. *See* Christie Stephenson and Patricia McClung, eds., *Delivering Digital Images: Cultural Heritage Resources in Education* (Los Angeles: The J. Paul Getty Trust, 1998); Patricia McClung and Christie Stephenson, eds., *Images Online: Perspectives on the Museum Educational Site Licensing Project* (Los Angeles: The J. Paul Getty Trust, 1998).

18. For more information on the MDLC project, visit its Web site at www.digitalmuseums.org/index.html.

19. For more information on AMICO, visit its Web site at www.amn.net/AMICO.

20. Harry Fox Agency, Inc., 711 Third Ave., New York, NY 10017; (212) 370-5330; www.nmpa.org/hfa.html.

21. ASCAP, One Lincoln Plaza, New York, NY 10023; 212-621-6000; www.ascap.com. BMI, 320 W. 57 St., New York, NY 10019; (2120 586-2000; www.bmi.com; SESAC, 55 Music Square East, Nashville, TN 37203; (8000 826-9996; www.sesac.com.

22. *See ProCD, Inc. v. Zeidenberg*, 86 F.3d 1447 (7th Cir. 1996).

23. *See* Uniform Computer Transactions Act, Part 1, § 112 (Draft April 26, 1999).

24. *See Hotmail Corp. v. Van$ Money Pie, Inc.*, 47 U.S.P.Q. 2d 1020 (N.D. Cal. 1998).

Chapter 5

International Protection

1. The term "market" is used broadly throughout this chapter to refer to both the nonprofit and commercial activities of museums overseas.

2. *See* 3 Melville B. Nimmer and David Nimmer, *Nimmer on Copyright* 12.04[A][3][b], at 12–85 (1998).

3. *Vanity Fair Mills, Inc. v. V. T. Eaton Co.*, 234 F.2d 633, 643 (2d Cir. 1956), *cert. denied*, 352 U.S. 871 (1956), *reh'g denied*, 352 U.S. 913 (1956).

4. *See* 4 *Nimmer on Copyright*, § 17.02, at 17–19 to 17–20.

5. *See Vanity Fair Mills, Inc.*, 234 F.2d at 642.

6. *E.E.O.C. v. Arabian Am. Oil Co.*, 499 U.S. 244 (1991).

7. *Id.* at 248 (quoting *Foley Bros., Inc. v. Filardo*, 336 U.S. 281, 285 (1949)).

8. *Id.* (quoting *Benz v. Compania Naviera Hidalgo, S.A.*, 353 U.S. 138, 147 (1957)).

9. *Subafilms, Ltd v. MGM-Pathe Communications Co.*, 24 F.3d 1088 (9th Cir. 1994), cert. denied, 513 U.S. 1001 (1994).

10. *See Curb v. MCA Records, Inc.*, 898 F. Supp. 586, 593–95 (M.D. Tenn. 1995).

11. *Id.* at 595.

12. *See* Paris Convention for the Protection of Industrial Property, *opened for signature* Mar. 20, 1883, as amended at Stockholm, July 14, 1967, 21 U.S.T. 1749, 828 U.N.T.S. 3 (hereinafter Paris Convention).

13. *See* Berne Convention for the Protection of Literary and Artistic Works of Sept. 9, 1886, in force July 14, 1967, 331 U.N.T.S. 217 (hereinafter Berne Convention).

14. *See* Universal Copyright Convention, *opened for signature* Sept. 6, 1952, 6 U.S.T. 2732, 216 U.N.T.S. 132, revised July 24, 1971, 25 U.S.T. 1341, 943 U.N.T.S. 194 (hereinafter UCC).

15. *See* WIPO Copyright Treaty, *signed* Dec. 20, 1996, WIPO Doc. CRNR/DC/94 (hereinafter WIPO Copyright Treaty).

16. *See* 1961 International Convention for the Protection of Performers, Producers of Phonograms and Broadcasting Organizations, *done* at Rome, Oct. 26, 1961, 496 U.N.T.S. 43 (hereinafter Rome Convention).

17. *See* Convention for the Protection of Producers of Phonograms Against Unauthorized Duplication of Their Phonograms, *signed* Oct. 29, 1971, 25 U.S.T. 309, 88 U.N.T.S. 67 (hereinafter Geneva Convention).

18. *See* Trademark Law Treaty, as discussed in chapter 1, note 61.

19. *See* Protocol Relating to the Madrid Agreement Concerning the International Registration of Marks, *adopted* June 28, 1989, WIPO Pub. No. 204(E) (hereinafter Madrid Protocol).

20. *See* Marrakesh Agreement Establishing the World Trade Organization, *signed* Apr. 15, 1994, Agreement on Trade-Related Aspects of Intellectual Property Rights, Annex 1C, 33 I.L.M. 1197 (1994) (hereinafter Marrakesh Agreement).

21. *See* Agreement on Trade-Related Aspects of Intellectual Property Rights, Including Trade in Counterfeit Goods, GATT Doc. MTN/FA I–A1C (hereinafter TRIPs).

22. Under U.S. law, the Office of the United States Trade Representative (USTR) is authorized to investigate and initiate dispute settlement proceedings on its own initiative and on behalf of U.S. citizens.

23. *See* Uruguay Round Agreements Act of 1994, Pub. L. No. 103-465, 108 Stat. 4809 (codified as amended at 17 U.S.C. § 104A).

24. *See* Treaty Establishing the European Economic Community, Mar. 25, 1957, 298 U.N.T.S. 11 (hereinafter Treaty of Rome).

25. *See* Canada-Mexico-United States: North American Free Trade Agreement, *entered into force* Jan. 1, 1994, 32 I.L.M. 289 (hereinafter NAFTA).

26. *See* Berne Convention Implementation Act of 1988, Pub. L. No. 100-568, 102 Stat. 2853 (codified as amended in scattered sections of 17 U.S.C.).

27. *See* Digital Millenium Copyright Act of 1998, Pub. L. No. 105-304, 112 Stat. 2860 (codified as amended in scattered sections of 17 U.S.C.).

28. WIPO's Web site is located at www.wipo.org.

29. UNESCO's Web site is located at www.unesco.org.

30. The WTO's Web site is located at www.wto.org.

31. Barbara Ringer, *The Role of the United States in International Copyright: Past, Present, and Future*, 56 Geo. L.J. 1050, 1051 (1968).

32. U.S. Copyright Office Circular 38a, *International Copyright Relations of the United States*, contains a convenient list of countries with which the United States has copyright relations (available at www.loc.gov/copyright/circs).

33. For many years prior to joining the Berne Convention, the United States took advantage of such "simultaneous" publication to gain protection for U.S.-origin works in the Berne Union. For example, simultaneous publication in Canada, the nearest Berne member, provided so-called "backdoor" protection for the works of U.S. authors.

34. *See* 17 U.S.C. § 104(a).

35. *See id.* § 104(b).

36. Berne Convention, Art. 2.

37. *See* 17 U.S.C. § 405.

38. Berne Convention, Art. 2(1).

39. *See id.*

40. *Id.* Art. 2(8).

41. *Guide to the Berne Convention for the Protection of Literacy and Artistic Works* (World Intellectual Property Organization, 1978).

42. *See* WIPO Copyright Treaty, Art. 8.

43. Berne Convention, Art. 6bis.

44. French Copyright Statute, Art. 6, Law No. 57–298 of Mar. 11, 1957, J.O. Mar. 14, 1957, p. 273, *as amended* July 3, 1985, translated in United Nations Educational Scientific and Cultural Organization, *Copyright Laws and Treaties of the World*, France section, Item 1 (1990).

45. *See* Final Report of the Ad Hoc Working Group on U.S. Adherence to the Berne Convention, *reprinted* in 10 Colum.-VLA J. Law & Arts 513 (1986).

46. *See* Visual Artists Rights Act of 1990, Pub. L. No. 101-650, 104 Stat. 5128 (codified in scattered sections of 17 U.S.C.).

47. *See* French Copyright Statute, Art. 6.

48. *See* U.S. Copyright Office, Waiver of Moral Rights in Visual Artworks: Final Report of the Register of Copyrights (March 1, 1996).

49. Berne Convention, Art. 9(2).

50. *See* Directive 96/9/EC of European Parliament and of the Council of 11 March 1996 on the Legal Protection of Databases, 1996 O.J. L77 (1996).

51. *See Feist Publications, Inc. v. Rural Tel. Serv. Co.,* 499 U.S. 340 (1991).

52. *See* Collections of Information Antipiracy Act, H.R. 354, 106th Cong. (1999).

53. *Fuji Photo Film Co. v. Shinohara Shoji Kabushiki Kaisha,* 754 F.2d 591, 599 (5th Cir. 1985), *reh'g denied,* 761 F.2d 695 (5th Cir. 1985).

54. For a useful summary of the trademark laws of particular countries, including the treaties to which the particular nation is a member as well as information regarding the registration process and requirements, refer to *T&T's International Guide to Trademarks*, available at www.thomson-thomson.com. Comprehensive treatment of national trademark laws can be found in Jeanine M. Politi, *Trademarks Throughout the World*, 4th ed. (Eagan, MN: West Group, 1998).

55. *See* Trademark Law Treaty, Art. 16.

56. *See id.* Art. 3(5).

57. A listing of Paris Convention signatory nations can be found on the WIPO Web site, www.wipo.org/eng/ratific/d-paris.htm.

58. *See* chapter 2 for a discussion of subject matter that is not registrable with the U.S. PTO.

59. *See* chapter 2, "The Federal Registration Process: Initial Considerations—Selection of Marks and Classification of Goods and Services."

60. *See* Council Regulation EC No. 40/94 of 20 Dec. 1993 on the Community Trademark, 1994 O.J. L11.

61. Current members of the Madrid Protocol are China, Cuba, Denmark, Finland, Germany, Norway, Spain, Sweden, and the United Kingdom. Although many interested groups in the U.S. favor adherence to the Madrid Protocol, the Clinton administration disfavors U.S. membership. *See* Capitol Hill Hearing Testimony, Prepared Statement of Shaun Donnelly, Deputy Assistant Secretary of State, before the House Committee on the Judiciary Subcom. on Intellectual Property and Judicial Administration, May 22, 1997.

62. *See* Madrid Protocol, Art. 2(1).

63. Ironically, the fact that trademark rights under U.S. law are established by use rather than registration provides foreign trademark owners a distinct advantage in the U.S. that is not available to U.S. trademark owners in other countries. Consider the foreign trademark owner who, despite maintaining a business abroad and entering U.S. commerce wholly through Internet-based acts, is capable of using its mark in U.S. commerce, thereby satisfying the requirements for federal registration solely as the result of the Internet's global reach.

64. *See* chapter 2, "Trademark Enforcement: Strategies for Policing and Monitoring Marks."

65. Article 6bis of the Paris Convention states: "countries of the Union undertake . . . to refuse or to cancel the registration, and to prohibit the use, of a trademark which constitutes a reproduction, an imitation, or a translation, liable to create confusion, of a mark considered by the competent authority of the country of registration or use to be well known in that country . . . and used for identical or similar goods." Paris Convention, Art. 6bis.

66. After the commencement of the GATT, representatives of Canada, the U.S. and Mexico held talks aimed at the elimination of trade barriers between countries. These talks resulted in the North American Free Trade Agreement (NAFTA). NAFTA also addressed minimum standards for intellectual property protection (including trademarks) and parallels TRIPS in many respects, particularly with regard to expanded protection of well-known marks.

67. Under the language of TRIPS, this broadened protection, however, is only available to registered marks.

68. *See* General Inter-American Convention for Trade-Mark and Commercial Protection, Feb. 20, 1929, 46 Stat. 2907, 124 L.N.T.S. 357.

Appendices

1. *See* 37 C.F.R. § 2.32.

2. *See id.* §§ 2.51–2, 52.

3. *See id.* § 2.56.

4. *See id.* § 2.33(a)(1)(vii).

5. *See id.* § 2.6(a)(1).

6. *See id.* § 2.33(b)(2).

7. *See id.* § 2.21(a)(4).

8. *See id.* § 6.1.

9. *See id.* § 2.71(b).

10. *See* U.S. Federal Trademark Registration No. 1,981,093.

11. *See* U.S. Federal Trademark Registration No. 1,694,273.

12. *See* U.S. Federal Trademark Registration No. 1,661,733.

13. *See* U.S. Federal Trademark Registration No. 1,731,260.

14. *See* U.S. Federal Trademark Registration No. 2,091,399.

15. *See* U.S. Federal Trademark Registration No. 1,975,411.

16. *See* U.S. Federal Trademark Registration No. 1,962,821.

17. *See* U.S. Federal Trademark Registration No. 1,994,590.

18. *See* 37 C.F.R. § 2.52.

19. The date of first use "in commerce" is the date on which the goods were first sold or transported, or the services first rendered, under the mark in commerce that may be regulated by Congress. *See* 15 U.S.C. § 1127 (defining "use in commerce"). The most common example of such commerce is trade that crosses state lines. Only use in commerce gives rise to federal trademark rights. The date of first use "anywhere" need not be connected with any particular flow of goods. For instance, it may reflect the date the mark was first used within the institution itself or in local advertising.

20. *See* 15 U.S.C. § 1127.

21. *See id.* § 2.51.

22. *See id.* § 2.56.

23. *See id.* § 2.57.

24. *See id.* § 2.58.

25. *See In Re Pierce*, 164 U.S.P.Q. 369 (T.T.A.B. 1970).

26. *See* chapter 2 for a discussion of the Supplemental Register.

27. *See* 37 C.F.R. § 2.61.

28. *See* chapter 2 for a discussion of factors considered in a "likelihood of confusion" analysis.

29. *See* 15 U.S.C. § 1052(d); 37 C.F.R. § 2.83.

30. *See* chapter 2 for a discussion of what characterizes a "descriptive mark."

31. *See* 15 U.S.C. § 1052(e).

32. *See id.* § 1052(f).

33. *See* 37 C.F.R. § 2.41.

34. *See* 15 U.S.C. § 1056(a).

35. For example, federal trademark registrations for the following marks each include a disclaimer of certain descriptive words: ROCK AND ROLL HALL OF FAME AND MUSEUM for museum services (Reg. No. 1,989,718) ("hall of fame" and "museum" disclaimed); GREAT LAKES SCIENCE CENTER PLUS DESIGN for science museum services (Reg. No. 2,123,257) ("science center" disclaimed); THE MOMA DESIGN STORE for retail store services (Reg. No. 1,623,051) ("store" disclaimed).

36. *See* 15 U.S.C. § 1052.

37. *See* 37 C.F.R. § 2.65(a).

38. *See* chapter 2 for a discussion of the role of counsel in the trademark registration process.

39. It is important to distinguish between the right of privacy as recognized under state statue and/or common law, and a different but related body of law arising out of concerns for privacy and the integrity of personal information in the digital and online environments. This latter species of privacy—namely "information privacy"—has been the subject of increasing debate and recent legislative activity. *See, e.g.,* Children's Online Privacy Protection Act of 1998, Pub. L. No. 105–277, 112 Stat. 2681–728 (1998); Online Privacy Protection Act of 1999, S. 809, 106th Cong. (1999); Electronic Rights for the 21st Century Act., S. 854, 106th Cong. (1999).

40. *See Restatement (Second) of Torts* § 652a (1976).

41. However, according to the Restatement, the appropriation of name or likeness prong of the right of privacy may survive death. *See id.* § 652I. As discussed earlier in this appendix, the appropriation prong has considerable overlap with the right of publicity.

42. As a species of trespass requiring physical intrusion upon an individual's solitude or into his or her private affairs (*i.e.,* eavesdropping, opening another's mail), the first type of invasion of privacy has limited applicability to the museum context. The second type of invasion of privacy, invasion by "false light," involves a publication of a false statement, representation, or imputation about the individual. This violation is similar to the tort of defamation. For more detailed handling of privacy rights, refer to J. Thomas McCarthy, *The Rights of Publicity and Privacy* (Eagan, MN: West Group, 1999).

43. *Campbell v. Seabury Press*, 614 F.2d 395, 397 (5th Cir. 1980).

44. *See, e. g.,* Tenn. Code Ann. § 47–25–1103(b), 1104(a) (publicity right descendible, permitting a maximum of 10 years after death for the estate to exercise or capitalize on right before it enters public domain).

45. *See, e. g.,* Cal. Civ. Code § 990(g) (50 years); Fla. Stat. Ann. § 540.08(4) (40 years); Ind. Code Ann. § 32–13–1–8 (100 years); Ky. Rev. Stat. Ann. § 391.170(2) (50 years); Nev. Rev. Stat. § 597.790(1) (50 years); Okla. Stat. Ann. tit. 12, § 1448(g) (100 years); Tenn. Code Ann. § 47-25-1104(a) (10 years); Tex. Prop. Code Ann. § 26. 012(d) (50 years); Va. Code Ann. § 8. 01–40(b) (20 years).

46. *Compare Lugosi v. Universal Pictures,* 25 Cal. 3d 813, 603 P. 2d 425 (1979) (under California law, the right of publicity terminates if not exploited during lifetime), *with Martin Luther King, Jr. Ctr. for Social Change, Inc. v. American Heritage Prods., Inc.,* 250 Ga. 135, 296 S. E. 2d 697 (1982) (recognizing under Georgia law a post-mortem right of publicity where exploitation of pecuniary value of name and likeness commenced after death).

47. *See Allen v. National Video, Inc.,* 610 F. Supp. 612 (S.D.N.Y. 1985) (refusing to hold that unauthorized use of photo of Woody Allen look-alike in advertisement violated New York privacy law, but finding Lanham Act Section 43(a) applicable).

48. *See Stephano v. News Group Publications, Inc.,* 485 N.Y.S. 2d 220, 474 N.E. 2d 580 (Ct. App. 1984) (denying existence of independent common law right of publicity and maintaining that all remedies must be sought under statutory right of privacy).

49. N.Y. Civ. Rights Law §§ 50, 51.

50. Cal. Civ. Code § 990(a).

51. *See Simeonov v. Tiegs,* 602 N.Y.S. 2d 1014 (1993).

Resources

Legal Treatises and References

Crews, Kenneth D. *Copyright, Fair Use, and the Challenge for Universities: Promoting the Progress of Higher Education.* Chicago: University of Chicago Press, 1993.

Fletcher, Anthony L., and David J. Kera (vol. 1), Theodore C. Max and Reese Taylor (vol. 2). *1998 Trademark Law Handbook.* New York: International Trademark Association, 1998.

Goldstein, Paul. *Copyright.* 2nd ed. Boston: Little, Brown, 1996.

McCarthy, J. Thomas. *McCarthy on Trademarks and Unfair Competition.* 4th ed. Eagan, MN: West Group, 1999.

————. *The Rights of Publicity and Privacy.* Eagan, MN: West Group, 1999.

Nimmer, Melville B., and David Nimmer. *Nimmer on Copyright.* New York: Matthew Bender & Co., 1998.

Patry, William F. *The Fair Use Privilege in Copyright Law.* 2nd ed. Washington, DC: Bureau of National Affairs Books, 1995.

Stuckey, Kent, ed. *Internet and Online Law.* New York: Law Journal Seminars-Press, 1998.

Museum-Specific Publications

Baron, Robert, ed. "The Great Image Debate." *Visual Resources* 22, nos. 3–4 (1997). Special issue on copyright and fair use.

Buck, Rebecca A., and Jean Allman Gilmore, eds. *The New Museum Registration Methods.* 4th ed. Washington, DC: American Association of Museums, 1998.

College Art Association Committee on Intellectual Property, ed. *The College Art Association Guide to Copyright and Fair Use for Art Historians and Artists in Academia.* New York: College Art Association, 1999 (forthcoming).

Gasaway, Laura N., and Sarah K. Wiant. *Libraries and Copyright: A Guide to Copyright Law in the 1990s.* Washington, DC: Special Libraries Association, 1994.

Harris, Lesley Ellen. *Digital Property: Currency of the 21st Century.* Toronto: McGraw-Hill Ryerson Ltd., 1997.

Jones-Garmil, Katherine. *The Wired Museum.* Washington, DC: American Association of Museums, 1997.

McClung, Patricia, and Christie Stephenson, eds. *Images Online: Perspectives on the Museum Education Site Licensing Project.* Los Angeles: The J. Paul Getty Trust, 1998.

Malaro, Marie C. *A Legal Primer on Managing Museum Collections*. 2nd ed. Washington, D.C.: Smithsonian Institution Press, 1998.

"Museums and Fair Use." *Museum News* 76, no. 5 (September/October 1997). Special issue with articles by Christine Steiner, Michael S. Shapiro, and Stephen E. Weil.

National Park Service. *Museums Collections Use*. Pt. 3 of *1998 Museum Handbook*. Washington, DC: National Park Service Museum Management Program, 1998. See ch. 1, "Evaluating and Documenting Museum Collections Use"; ch. 2, "Legal Issues"; ch. 4, "2-D Reproductions."

Samuels, Geoffrey, ed. *Sample CD-ROM Licensing Agreements for Museums*. Washington, D.C.: American Association of Museums, 1996.

Stephenson, Christie, and Patricia McClung, eds. *Delivering Digital Images: Cultural Heritage Resources for Education*. Los Angeles: The J. Paul Getty Trust, 1998.

Zorich, Diane M. *Introduction to Managing Digital Assets: Options for Cultural and Educational Organizations*. Los Angeles: The J. Paul Getty Trust, 1999.

Selected Web Sites

American Association of Museums
> www.aam-us.org/

American Law Institute–American Bar Association
> www.ali-aba.org

Association of Science-Technology Centers. Proposed Ethical Guidelines on Intellectual Property
> www.astc.org/newsltr/property.htm

Basic Intellectual Property Primers. Berkman Center for Internet and Society, Harvard Law School
> cyber.law.harvard.edu/property/library/primerlib.html

Basic Principles for Managing Intellectual Property in the Digital Environment. National Humanities Alliance, March 24, 1997
> www.ninch.org/#issues

Coalition for Networked Information (CNI). CNI-Copyright Forum
> www.cni.orq/Hforums/cni-copyright

Conference on Fair Use (CONFU)
> www.uspto.gov/web/offices/dcom/olia/confu/

Copyright Crash Course. University of Texas
> www.utsystem.edu/ogc/intellectualproperty/cprtindx.htm

Copyright and Fair Use. Stanford University Libraries
> fairuse.stanford.edu/

Copyright, Intellectual Property Rights, and Licensing Issues. Berkeley Digital Library SunSITE
> sunsite.berkeley.edu/Copyright/

Copyright Law of the United States of America. Copyright Office, Library of Congress
lcweb.loc.gov/copyright/title17/#top

International Trademark Association
www.inta.org/

LibLicense: Licensing Digital Information. Yale University Library
www.library.yale.edu/~llicense/index.shtml

National Initiative for a Networked Cultural Heritage (NINCH)
www.ninch.org/

Rights and Reproduction Information Network (RARIN). AAM Registrars Committee
www.panix.com/~squigle/rarin/01rcsite.html

THOMAS: Legislative Information on the Internet
thomas.loc.gov/

Trademark Resources on the Internet: A Bibliography. Edited by Minde C. Browning
www.iulaw.indy.indiana.edu/library/TMRbibliography.htm

U.S. Copyright Office
lcweb.loc.gov/copyright/

U.S. Patent and Trademark Office
www.uspto.gov/

U.S. House of Representatives Internet Law Library
law.house.gov/

Visual Resources Association: Copyright, Intellectual Property Rights, Fair Use
www.oberlin.edu/~art/vra/copyright.html

Volunteer Lawyers for the Arts
www.artlaw.org

World Intellectual Property Organization
www.wipo.org/

Government Resources

Intellectual Property and the National Information Infrastructure: Report of the Working Group on Intellectual Property Rights. U.S. Information Infrastructure Task Force, Working Group on Intellectual Property Rights, Bruce A. Lehman, Chair. Washington, DC: U.S. Patent and Trademark Office, 1995.

Basic Facts about Registering a Trademark. Available online at www.uspto.gov/web/offices/tac/doc/basic/

Copyright Office Information Circulars and Form Letters. Available online at www.loc.gov/copyright/circs/

Contributors

Michael S. Shapiro, formerly general counsel of the National Endowment for the Humanities, is in private law practice and serves as a consultant to museums and cultural organizations in the United States and around the world. Mr. Shapiro also serves as general counsel of the International Intellectual Property Institute and of the Art Museum Image Consortium (AMICO). As a member of the adjunct faculty of George Mason University, he teaches "Global Intellectual Property Rights and International Trade" and "Culture and International Transactions" within the International Commerce and Policy program.

The first full-time director of the Museum Studies Program at George Washington University, Mr. Shapiro has written extensively and lectured widely on a broad range of legal and cultural topics. He is the editor and contributing author of *The Museum: A Reference Guide* (1990), and contributing author to *International Intellectual Property: The European Community and Eastern Europe* (1992). Mr. Shapiro earned a Ph.D. in American civilization from Brown University and a J.D. from the George Washington University Law School.

Brett I. Miller is an associate in the Intellectual Property Practice Group of Morgan, Lewis & Bockius LLP in Washington, D.C. Mr. Miller's practice focuses on domestic and international copyright and trademark issues. He also has in-depth experience in museum and art-related intellectual property issues, and currently serves as outside intellectual property counsel to the Philadelphia Museum of Art, among others.

Mr. Miller received his bachelor's degree in art history in 1985 from Emory University and his law degree in 1995 from the University of Virginia. He did graduate work in art history at New York University's Institute of Fine Arts and Columbia University and served as the associate curator of collections of the Norton Museum of Art in West Palm Beach, Florida, prior to attending law school. Mr. Miller also served as a postgraduate law clerk in the General Counsel's Office of the Museum of Modern Art in 1995.

Christine Steiner is in private law practice in Los Angeles, California, specializing in art law and intellectual property. She teaches visual arts law as a member of the adjunct faculty of Loyola Law School and is a frequent lecturer on education, museums, and the arts. Ms. Steiner was secretary and general counsel of the J. Paul Getty Trust, and prior to her position with the Getty, she was assistant general counsel of the Smithsonian Institution. She earlier served in the Office of the Attorney General of Maryland, representing the state's colleges, universities, and educational governing boards. She received her undergraduate degree from Johns Hopkins University and her law degree from the University of Maryland.

An active participant in the field of intellectual property in the new technologies, Ms. Steiner has addressed these issues at numerous national and international conferences. She was a member of the national Conference on Fair Use (CONFU), presently chairs the Museums, Libraries, and Collections Section of the National Association of College and University Attorneys (NACUA), and participates in numerous arts-related bar activities.

Index

S